Andy Hayman, CBE, QPM, joined the police service as a constable straight from school in 1978, quickly rising through the ranks with the Essex Police and then the Metropolitan Police in London. He worked part-time to obtain a degree in police studies from Exeter University and a post-graduate diploma in applied criminology from Cambridge University. He was promoted to chief constable of Norfolk before returning to the Met in 2005 to take up the post of assistant commissioner, Special Operations. Based in New Scotland Yard, he was in overall charge of the Counter-Terrorism Command and Special Branch and was the UK's national counter-terrorism co-ordinator. He is now a writer and security consultant.

Margaret Gilmore is a writer and broadcaster. She was the BBC's Home Affairs correspondent and reported many of the incidents covered in this book. She is a senior research fellow at the Royal United Services Institute, specializing in home-land security.

GW00702956

THE TERRORIST HUNTERS

ANDY HAYMAN with MARGARET GILMORE

BANTAM PRESS

LONDON · TORONTO · SYDNEY · AUCKLAND · JOHANNESBURG

TRANSWORLD PUBLISHERS
61–63 Uxbridge Road, London W5 5SA
A Random House Group Company
www.rbooks.co.uk

First published in Great Britain
in 2009 by Bantam Press
an imprint of Transworld Publishers

This book is a work of non-fiction based on the experiences and
recollections of Andy Hayman. The authors have stated to the
publishers that the contents of this book are true.

A CIP catalogue record for this book
is available from the British Library.

ISBNs 9780593063354 (cased)
9780593063347 (tpb)

Addresses for Random House Group Ltd companies outside the UK
can be found at: www.randomhouse.co.uk
The Random House Group Ltd Reg. No. 954009

The Random House Group Limited supports The Forest Stewardship
Council (FSC), the leading international forest-certification organization.
All our titles that are printed on Greenpeace-approved FSC-certified
paper carry the FSC logo.
Our paper procurement policy can be found at
www.rbooks.co.uk/environment

Typeset in 11.5/15pt Sabon by
Falcon Oast Graphic Art Ltd.
Printed and bound in Great Britain by
CPI Mackays, Chatham, ME5 8TD

2 4 6 8 10 9 7 5 3 1

Mixed Sources
Product group from well-managed
forests and other controlled sources
www.fsc.org Cert no. TT-COC-2139
© 1996 Forest Stewardship Council
FSC

The purpose of writing this book was to provide an inside account and commentary which illustrates the outstanding work of the police and the security and intelligence agencies in fighting terrorism. Such accounts are sometimes dodged for security reasons and we miss an opportunity to show how difficult a job these men and women are doing to keep us safe. They are unsung heroes.

During my time at the helm, I saw firsthand how their hard work and dedication prevented a repeat of the 7 July atrocities. We didn't always get it right but I think on balance a good job was done by all.

It is these efforts which this book celebrates.

Acknowledgements

Many colleagues and friends have contributed to this book. Rather than name them all, they know who they are, so thank you.

The assistance of Catherine Crawford, chief executive of the Metropolitan Police Authority, along with officers at the Security Service MI5, has been invaluable. Their time and meticulous vetting of the content ensured responsible reporting.

Thank you also to our agent Andrew Gordon, without whom this book would never have been written. He gave such pertinent guidance and advice. Also, the team at Transworld Publishers has been so helpful in supervising the book.

Finally, our thanks to Simon Thorogood, our editor at Transworld, for his patience, dedication and belief in the book.

Contents

Prologue

IT WAS 24 JULY 2005, SEVENTEEN DAYS AFTER THE LONDON bomb attacks. For the first time I was to meet the families of the fifty-two people who had died, and some of nearly seven hundred people who were injured. I was nervous as I drove across London, the city quiet and subdued because it was a Sunday morning. Beyond the door I was about to open, in the Royal Horticultural Halls in Vincent Square, dozens of people were waiting for me: they had been traumatized by the sudden and horrific way their loved ones had lost their lives, or by what they themselves had been through. Most of those killed and injured were young people on their way to work. They came from all walks of life and all religions.

For a senior police officer who has handled some of the toughest crimes of the past thirty years, I was unusually anxious. I wanted to help. If we didn't fill the vacuum of information, those who were distressed might fill the gaps themselves – inaccurately. There was incorrect speculation on the number of people killed and hurt. It was important, and I believed it might be cathartic, to tell those in the room as much as we knew of the truth about what had happened and what we were doing to gather information about the terrorists who had carried out the atrocities.

The first hour of the meeting went well. My deputy, who was head of the Anti-Terrorist Branch, the coroner and I had all said our bit and we were taking questions. There were family-liaison officers in the audience – police trained in trauma and grief counselling – who had been individually allocated to families who wanted them to act as a point of contact day or night with the police, and as gatekeepers to other agencies.

Suddenly a man to my left stood up. He looked worn out, dark bags under his eyes, his head sunk into his heavy shoulders. He spoke very slowly so that every carefully chosen word fell with impact on the silent room. 'Mr Hayman, I know you can't answer this question but I need to know the answer. My son was going to a job interview. He doesn't know London that well and he'd already visited the city once to work out his route. On the morning of 7 July, because of the first blasts, his underground train was diverted through two stations. When he eventually came up overground, he was completely disoriented. Mr Hayman, what I need to know is this. Why is it that the first bus he got on to he lost his life?'

There was a long pause. People started quietly to weep. And then, like a Mexican wave across the room, others stood up and gave their testimonies. An Asian woman stood up in traditional dress – I wondered if she was Muslim. I thought, How doubly tragic if you're from the Muslim community and this turns out to have been Islamic extremism. Not only will you have to cope with your family loss, but you'll also have to deal with knowing it was done in the name of your religion. How hard it would be for anyone to settle that in their minds.

As I listened I worried that the meeting, which should have

been a positive experience, was now on a negative down-ward spiral – people would leave feeling worse than they had when they'd arrived. Yet I had to let it run: no one could interrupt these devastating personal testimonies. Nothing could have reminded me more powerfully that our job was to stop such an atrocity happening again.

When it was over, we left the room in silence, stunned. I wanted never to repeat an experience like that – not because it was distressing and difficult but because it would mean that terrorists had succeeded again.

I have covered some horrendous assignments in my time. I have dealt with bereavement and grief. I consider myself a tough operator. But when I left that room on that Sunday morning, I dismissed my driver and took a walk. In acute frustration that those attacks had happened, in my seething determination to bring to justice those who'd helped the bombers, in my sadness and grief for the families – I wept.

1. Target: London

IT STARTED LIKE ANY ROUTINE WORKING DAY. THERE WAS nothing to indicate when I woke that, by the end of it, my life and hundreds of thousands of others would have changed irrevocably. I was up at the crack of dawn. By 6.30 a.m. I was in the gym in the basement of London's Metropolitan Police Headquarters at New Scotland Yard for my usual four miles on the running machine. I nodded at the other two who were always there early – a muscular male body-builder pumping iron and a dark, athletic woman cycling. At times this was so boring. But it was also a great chance to be alone. It was my private thinking time – an opportunity to plan the day ahead. I'd rehearse what I'd be saying in meetings later or mull over problems and dilemmas.

In that respect, though, this particular morning was different: London had won the 2012 Olympics. I found myself reminiscing about my younger days, running hard against opponents and the clock. Suddenly I wasn't in the gym any longer but on the home straight in the finals, heading for Olympic glory, urged on by roaring crowds. I vividly remember this because the success of winning the Olympic vote meant that as assistant commissioner in charge of Specialist Operations it would be my job to oversee security planning for the Games and to brief the police commissioner and government ministers. I was excited at the prospect but I also thought, How scary. It's one thing to be pitching for the Games to come to London, hoping that your planning will gain the support of the International Olympic Committee but something else when you realize you have to put your money where your mouth is and deliver.

The Olympic dream is not just for those who stand to win medals. It's a dream for the rest of us too, for avid spectators and budding athletes. The glee with which the veteran athletes met the announcement about 2012 reverberated across the UK. At the Yard the night before there'd been a mix of 'What a nightmare challenge' and 'This is a real chance to showcase British policing'. Given my overall responsibility for security at national events, I wondered what role I would play, and reflected on how far I'd come in my career.

I'd left school at sixteen and worked my way up through Essex Police, training early as a detective. I loved my job and gave it all the hours I could. When I decided I wanted a more responsible role and rank, I realized I needed more qualifications. This would be a distraction from the work, but I knew it was important to develop myself so I worked part-time while I took A levels, a part-time degree in police studies at Exeter University (MA) and a postgraduate diploma in applied criminology at Cambridge University. The investment in education paid off: I rose to the rank of chief superintendent, then left for the Metropolitan Police in London. I was promoted to director of Professional Standards, then became chief constable of Norfolk. I never shied away from the toughest jobs – in fact I relished them.

In July 2005, I was back at the Met – this time among those at the very top, on the Management Board of senior officers, as assistant commissioner in charge of Specialist Operations, from counter-terrorism to Special Branch to protecting VIPs. What a brilliant job – and I was up for it.

As I shared in the country's excitement over the Olympics, I knew it was my responsibility to turn into reality the security plan we'd submitted with the UK application for the Games. In the great scheme of things, seven years is not a long time when you have to make the site secure to build on, before the buildings have been designed, let alone constructed. I remembered how the bomb at the Grand Hotel in Brighton in 1984 had been planted behind a bath panel on a timer nearly a month before it exploded, killing and maiming Conservative cabinet ministers, their colleagues and families. The bomb found by police in the Rubens Hotel in London in 1985 had also been planted weeks before.

In this far more technologically advanced age we have to ensure that nothing like that can happen. I knew we would need to put a blanket of security over the entire Olympic park before building began, checking everyone going in and out, from construction worker to VIP. We had to make it a sterile area, free of any flaws that might have the potential for terrorists to mount an attack. Workers had to operate there and, come the day, the public must know it was safe. Would the politicians understand what was needed?

I felt security needs in the UK application had been underestimated. The security costs were woefully short of the mark – it might have been a political tactic to underestimate, to avoid scaring the taxpayer. But the cost was already way beyond what was budgeted for. At some point the inadequate security budget would have to be exposed or the police would be carrying all the operational risk and be penniless. Not good. For example, the document didn't reflect how many VIPs would need guarding, in particular from the USA, which regards the UK as one of Al Qaeda's top targets. It's not as if the Olympics haven't been targeted before. At the 1972 Games terrorists murdered eleven members of the Israeli team, along with a German police officer. A bomb was detonated at the Atlanta Olympics, killing two people and injuring more than a hundred.

My boss, the Metropolitan Police commissioner Sir Ian Blair, and my colleagues on the Met's Management Board would want briefing on Olympic security – as would the prime minister. I pulled myself back to reality: I'll have to get some meetings off the ground and work out what this really means for us, I thought.

I had other things on my mind too. In Scotland leaders of the top eight great world economies were meeting for a G8 summit. Were security arrangements there good enough? My colleague Steve House was leading the day-to-day security operation on the ground, which was complicated by big anti-globalization protests, and the fact that the US President had brought along 250 of his own bodyguards – just like something out of the Clint Eastwood movie *In the Line of Fire*. It never crossed my mind that the very next day there'd be a security breach in the form of a road-traffic accident: President Bush, while out exercising, cycled full speed into one of the police officers and fell off his bike. Imagine the scene – the indignity. Luckily there were only minor injuries or we might have had a full-scale diplomatic incident on our hands, but it ended in smiles and pats on the back.

Showered, fired up after the workout, the adrenalin pumping overtime, I was in buoyant mood. I swung into my office on the fifth floor of Scotland Yard at a quarter to eight, just in time to catch Martin, my driver, putting my breakfast on the desk. It was always the same – two slices of white toast with a banana and a cup of tea. I flicked on Sky News and pulled out the three volumes of files containing the UK's Olympic bid, turning quickly to the chapter on security. I looked at it and jotted notes to crystallize my thoughts on what we needed to do next. Had we really said we could do all this? It had seemed like a good idea at the time. Now I brought into the equation the fact that the Yard was already at full stretch – how would we train enough officers for 2012, and what would we do with them afterwards when they were no longer needed? This was an ongoing problem for me: whenever there was a major incident I needed another three hundred or so trained men and women – but I couldn't justify them when things were quiet.

At about eight minutes to nine one of my two deputies, Suzanna Becks, knocked on the door and popped in without waiting for an answer. 'Andy, there's a fire on the Underground – it's causing a commotion in the City.'

She wasn't her normal happy-go-lucky, bouncy self – I sensed she was worried. 'Where?' I asked.

'Looks like Liverpool Street or Aldgate. Circle Line.'

Suzanna was a very experienced colleague and friend – she had been chief of staff to the former commissioner and frequently handled high-stress situations. On my appointment I was amazed that Commissioner Sir Ian Blair wanted to move her to a different post. This would leave the senior command in Specialist Operations – which deals with the most high-risk areas of policing, including terrorism – with a brand-new boss and a new deputy, possibly with no experience in the department. Before I had even settled into the job I found myself challenging the commissioner. He was then both my boss and my friend, and this was one of the first things that would set me at odds with him.

To this day I fail to understand why he wanted to move Suzanna aside – she was a person with a proven record, who should one day become a chief constable. The tall, striking mother of two had become well versed in the terrorist threat as she worked alongside former commissioner Lord Stevens. Maybe Ian felt uneasy with a strong ally of John Stevens in an influential post. Who knows? John had trusted, respected and valued her highly. As the new boy in town I needed her. Luckily my predecessor, Sir David Veness, agreed, and Suzanna stayed, but only for the meantime. Ian would eventually get his way.

Suzanna knew how to keep a grip on my frenetic timetable. She knew how to juggle the meetings, how to deal with the politicians and players in government and the Metropolitan Police Authority, which oversees the work of the Met. Her route map around Whitehall was second to none. The way she handled her behind-the-scenes role in dealing with the 7 July attacks was exemplary and I remain bewildered as to why she was, as far as I can tell, the only one of the few people at the top directly involved not decorated for it. That was seen by many as an unnecessary snub.

The second I heard her words and sensed her anxiety, the alarm bells rang and I was filled with dread. 'Thanks – get the response team organized. When you know more come back.' City of London police would be dealing with this but if there was anything untoward about the fire our counter-terrorism detectives might be needed. I turned up the sound on the television: Sky was reporting that the fire had apparently been caused by a 'power surge'.

I glanced at my computer to establish who was in today. I checked the diary to see where I was supposed to be – I saw

I was due to meet my colleague Tarique Ghaffur for a routine 'catch-up'. Like me he was an assistant commissioner at the Met, his brief to lead the Specialist Crime Directorate. Because he dealt with serious and organized crime there was often crossover with our anti-terrorist investigations. I knew he would understand if I cancelled and, in any case, he would be involved if this turned out to be a major emergency.

Minutes later Suzanna was back. 'Seems like two dead. Could be more,' she said. 'Rendezvous point for response teams, City Road.' Now every phone on my desk was ringing.

At five past nine, thirteen minutes after she'd told me of the first fire, Suzanna was back again: 'Two more fires – Circle Line at Edgware Road and Piccadilly Line near King's Cross.'

Martin Brunt, Sky TV's excellent crime correspondent, had the news too. He was being interviewed and was suggesting all three fires were probably the result of 'power surges'.

Hang on a second, I thought. This isn't right. This is absolutely not right. We had often rehearsed the scenario of terrorist attacks on the Underground. I realized we could now be in the middle of a wave of assaults. My initial reaction, though, was not necessarily what people would expect.

I sat down with Suzanna, looked into her eyes, and said, 'Well, Suzanna. What do we do now?'

We sat quietly for several minutes, thinking hard about the series of commands and actions we would need to take. Then I mobilized my private office staff. We needed to alert Special Branch and counter-terrorism officers – fast. I knew there would be a massive emergency response already from police, fire and ambulance. It was still rush-hour and the

Underground would be teeming with commuters. If these were terrorist attacks our job would be to investigate who'd carried them out – the sooner we started, the more likely we were to find them. We had to make sure that, as far as possible, the scenes of the attacks were left untouched once victims had been rescued so that we could search for evidence. I had to stand back, stay calm and think strategically.

It was now seven minutes past nine and my other deputy, Peter Clarke, was in my office. Deputy Assistant Commissioner Clarke was specifically head of the Anti-Terrorist Branch, then known as SO13 (Specialist Operations Department 13, now combined with Special Branch and called Counter-Terrorism Command). Peter told us uniformed officers from the Met, British Transport Police and the City of London were already at the three scenes, sealing off the areas, helping fire and ambulance officers get survivors out. He had detectives and forensics teams ready to assess the situation. He had already arranged for our major investigation team to gather at Aldgate bus garage in the City of London. Later, if needed, they would go in to search for evidence. He had other officers checking the status of current surveillance operations to ensure there was nothing linked with the movements of known suspects. This included studying the regular overnight intelligence reports we received from MI5 and other sources. They revealed nothing. This was a complete bolt from nowhere, our worst-case scenario – an attack from left field.

At 9.10 a.m. – just under fifteen minutes after the three incidents had been reported – I could see from the emails on the internal police system that the fires were now being described internally as explosions. On the television, eyewitness accounts were running live, via mobile phone. They were talking about smoke from trains in front of them, about darkness and chaos.

'Let's bring in people who are off-duty or on leave,' I said to Suzanna, and to Peter: 'Do we need to evacuate the whole Underground or would that be an overreaction?'

We were thinking the same thing – praying this was not a concerted attack but knowing there was every sign that it was. We phoned Andy Trotter, then deputy chief constable of British Transport Police, now promoted to chief constable – a man who would take no prisoners. Andy had a killer instinct – you wouldn't want to cross him. We told him that the assessment from our Anti-Terrorist Branch was that these could be terrorist attacks and there might be more. We contacted MI5, responsible for intelligence-gathering on national security, and GCHQ, the government's communications centre where they monitor suspects and spies here and abroad.

These calls were made on my 'Brent' phone – an apparently secure phone issued to a small number of senior officers. Whenever it rang my heart beat faster. I never ceased to be surprised when it wasn't MI5, the commissioner or the prime minister at the other end, but some call centre trying to sell insurance. I couldn't be sure how secure those phones really were.

At 9.15 a.m. things were escalating. An emergency was declared across the entire London Underground network and a major evacuation operation began. The decision had ultimately been taken at the London Underground Network Operations Centre round the corner from New Scotland Yard, just behind St James's Park Underground station, where they were still co-ordinating the emergency response. That was about to change.

Peter and Suzanna returned to their posts, Suzanna to set up a series of meetings. We'd agreed she would ensure contacts were maintained within Scotland Yard, and established with other forces, government departments and the intelligence agencies. Peter took charge of operational deployments on the counter-terrorism side.

My job was to adopt overall command in establishing our game plan and making sure it was stuck to. I would also liaise with other strategic leaders to ensure we were all supporting each other. Colleagues elsewhere in the Met were also deploying to maintain public order, deal with injuries and investigate the fires. I knew it would not be long before I would have to leave my team to it and go to Downing Street to brief ministers. I felt a sense of apprehension and trepidation.

The atmosphere in New Scotland Yard began to bubble like a volcano. From the basement to the highest floors people were preparing to fly into action. We needed more officers at the scene and at control centres to manage the situation. The explosion at Edgware Road meant that the emergency was no longer limited to the City of London police area. We needed to set up a Casualty Bureau for the injured: it would keep a record of who was hurt, and where they were being treated so that we could pass on relevant information and provide a point of contact for their families.

I didn't want to miss anything in my response. I worked my way mentally up the floors of the building. Second floor: all major event/public-order people – despatched. Fifth floor: Suzanna and me – strategists pulling the strings. Eighth floor: the commissioner – must see him in person. Thirteenth floor: media – need to get accurate information to the public through them. Fourteenth and fifteenth floors: Anti-Terrorist Branch – working out what to do right now to prevent further attacks today in London. Sixteenth to eighteenth floors: Special Branch – they'd be critical in amassing intelligence to aid the investigation I thought was now inevitable. The higher up the building I went, the more complex and critical the roles would be.

At 9.30 a.m. I phoned Chris Fox, who ran the Association of Chief Police Officers (ACPO). I first met Chris, a calm pragmatist, twenty years ago when he was chief constable of Northamptonshire. I told him it was possible we'd need help from other forces – people with almost all types of skills. I told him he must warn them there might be attacks outside London too – we didn't know where this would end. They must plan and prepare. Predictably, he was already on the case.

And all this time there was huge frustration – we still didn't know exactly what we were up against. Like everyone else, we were frantic for information and clarity. The temptation is to react as we do when we're on the beach and a child loses a tiny toy. We frantically search the sand for it. The more we scramble and move the sand, the more we hide it, when in fact the best thing is to sit and look – then make a move once you have devised the best plan.

Yet without a certain degree of detail, if you're working at half pitch, you can't deploy accurately – the worst outcome is that you send resources where they're not needed, or make terrible assumptions about fatalities which, if they leaked out, would cause unnecessary distress to worried families.

My training kicked in – I had to be incredibly self-disciplined: forcing emotion into the background, constantly checking information as it came in by email, phone and even television. Was it fact or speculation? It's like putting yourself outside your body: you've got to hold back until you know for sure or the response will be inadequate. I remember the awful tension, being desperate for facts but in the middle of complete mayhem, knowing we'd never get the information at that early stage. You can't be over-inhibited or too cautious because you've got to do something – but you can't overreact because that would be irresponsible. We were in a fog, a real pea-souper, trying desperately to get the balance right.

At 9.40 a.m. bloodied, smoke-blackened faces began to appear from the tunnels. I could see this on television. Peter Clarke was now telling me he'd heard there were heavy casualties. He had to get his men kitted out to deal with the dark and the heat when the time came for them to go underground. I remember thinking what an awful job faced the forensics teams. Any fire, let alone a bomb scene, is difficult enough, but to operate underground for long periods after such fatalities would be ghastly.

It was nearly an hour since the explosions. Until then we'd kept an open mind – we still couldn't say for sure that this was the work of terrorists, but we had to be up to the challenge.

Then came the explosion on the number 30 bus at 9.47 a.m. in Tavistock Square.

Now we pushed the terrorism button hard. I knew from past bomb attacks by Irish terrorists that the more we got in the immediate aftermath the quicker we'd find the bombers. And it appeared we had at least four so far. Were they suicide bombers like those who had committed the 11 September 2001 attacks in America? Critically, we were clearly witnessing a wave – how many more would there be? What could we do to prevent them, if more were planned? How could we disrupt the terrorists without causing further panic among the public? Would they try to snare the emergency services by pulling them into a further bomb attack like the IRA used to do? We had trained for this – but were we up to par? Why hadn't we had an inkling that this was imminent? My mind was racing.

Firearms units were called in, the intelligence agencies asked to search back through intelligence reports to see if they'd missed anything, forensics teams despatched, hospitals warned to prepare for the worst.

At 9.50 a.m., three minutes after the bus bomb – an hour after the three Underground explosions, there was a call from Downing Street. Suzanna took it and popped her head round my door: 'Ten minutes to COBRA, home sec's chairing – PM's still up north at G8. I've put Martin [the driver] on standby downstairs.'

COBRA is the government's crisis committee. It meets at times of emergency in a secure cellar below the great government institutions in Whitehall, somewhere between the Houses of Parliament and Trafalgar Square. It's linked by corridor to Downing Street, the Foreign and Commonwealth Office and the Cabinet Office. Its dramatic name is an acronym for the room it's held in: Cabinet Office Briefing Room A. The committee itself is a forum for the big decision-makers: politicians (who take the lead and usually chair it), the police and intelligence agencies, the army, and any other major department involved in the particular emergency. It was likely that I would have to brief the home secretary face to face and I would have to admit I didn't know exactly what was happening.

For the next ten minutes I was flying around Scotland Yard like a whirlwind. I spoke again with my deputy, Peter Clarke. He had to deal with at least four crime scenes and would have to despatch his teams accordingly to manage the marathon task of sifting through the debris, collecting every tiny piece of evidence that could potentially be vital in identifying the bombers. He also had to make contingencies for further possible attacks – one early concern was the gap between the Underground attacks and the bus attack. We didn't know then why there had been nearly an hour between the first three bombs and the explosion on the bus. We had to assume there'd be more and that they could take place anywhere in the country. We put ports and airports on standby to check who was leaving. Later we'd check who'd recently come in.

Peter sent officers to talk with colleagues at MI5, to start working backwards, looking at past intelligence as well as evidence we began gathering now, to find out who was responsible. There were thousands, if not millions, of hours of CCTV footage to get hold of from across London and elsewhere. There must surely be pictures of the killers just before the bombs were detonated. Off-duty detectives were called in.

Peter is a man of great composure and integrity. Publicly he is well spoken and courteous, but he doesn't suffer fools gladly. That morning he tackled the situation with extra-ordinary calm, a clear sense of direction and steely professionalism. Later that day he let slip that he, like thousands of other worried parents that morning, hadn't known for several hours whether his own son, who'd been travelling on the Underground through the site of one of the attacks, had survived. This harrowing situation was made worse when Peter learnt of the bus bomb. To attempt to stop his son using the Underground he'd advised him to get on a bus. Had he been on that bus? Peter couldn't contact him as the mobile phones weren't working properly.

We had to find office space to set up computers for what would be a mass-murder investigation. We had to pull enough staff from other tasks to run what was already an operation way bigger than any I'd seen in my life. The Casualty Bureau was still not up and running and we were inundated with calls from the public – families searching for loved ones they hadn't been able to track down since the bomb attacks and others who thought they might have information. At its peak that morning the Bureau received 43,000 attempted calls within an hour – 7823 people would be reported missing. It was a real problem. Once a person is reported missing they remain on the missing list until either they are found at one of the scenes or the person looking for them rings back to update us. In normal circumstances the database can handle the 'unresolved' status but in the days to come the sheer number of people on it threatened to freeze the entire process. The nightmare was that a critical piece of information might be lost in the stockpile of leads we needed to follow up from those calls: later that day, for example, one of the bombers was reported missing by a family member. How could we have spotted that that call was different from the thousands of others?

There were moments on the morning of 7 July 2005 when I felt I was not truly in charge. People were asking, 'What you got, then?' and I couldn't answer because I didn't know – I couldn't speculate and yet it was my job to know. Imagine what it's like to tell the commissioner or the secretary of state, as I would have to, 'I don't know what's going on.' It makes you feel inept. But you've got to stick to it: if you don't know, you've got to say you don't know, and the skilled leader or politician should admire you for that honesty.

Within minutes of the bus explosion I had to give the commissioner, my boss Sir Ian Blair, the heads-up on what was happening. It was 9.52 a.m. – five minutes after the bus bomb. I left my office with no idea of what I would say. By the time I'd walked through to an adjoining building and up several flights of stairs I was focused. It was never a journey I rushed: it calmed me, gave me time to gather my thoughts and work out how I was going to position the briefing. That day, as I made my way through the gallery joining the two buildings that make up Scotland Yard, I was acutely aware of the portraits of past commissioners and, in particular, that of Lord Stevens, his eyes boring into me as if to say, 'This is history in the making: conduct yourself fittingly.'

I knew that whatever I and my colleagues did on that day and however we responded we would be following the plans worked out by Lord Stevens and Sir David Veness in the years since 9/11. They had put in place outstanding contingency proposals for any potential international terrorist attack. Those plans came into their own that day.

'I'm sorry but I have bad news, Ian,' I said, as I reached his large office with its views over Westminster. 'I think we're in the middle of a wave of terrorist attacks – and they're co-ordinated. I can't confirm this but I do think the bus bomb implies it. It looks as if it's the type of scenario we've been preparing for. I can't tell you exact locations apart from the bus. I can't tell you what's caused the explosions. I can't tell you anything about the bombers. But I want you to start thinking we're hosting a sustained terrorist attack.'

We stared at each other across his desk. Only yesterday we had had a lengthy meeting of the Met's Management Board, in a conference room in Carlton Terrace by the river Thames, to thrash out how we were to make cutbacks. It had begun at 8.30 a.m. and did not end until 5.30 p.m., although we had taken a lunch break. At that point I had rushed back to the Yard to tell my team that the board didn't believe the current structures we had in place were good enough to handle a major terrorist event.

On 6 July 2005, I wanted to gauge the views of those in my team who would be affected by plans to merge the two largest sections of my department – Special Branch (SO12) and the Anti-Terrorist Branch (SO13). Many in Special Branch opposed the merger – they were a tight-knit unit with a proud history. They viewed themselves solely as intelligence-gatherers whereas detectives in the Anti-Terrorist Branch took a broader, more flexible approach and saw themselves as evidence-gatherers, too. I believed the two had to go hand in hand in the modern world because of the need to produce sound evidence from the intelligence in order to prosecute criminals. On 7 July 2005 Sir Ian was due to have a question-and-answer session with officers on the ground. Of course it was cancelled – and however much he and I believed our structures were no longer fit for purpose, we had to operate within them to the very best of our abilities.

Ian's style was 'need to know'. He wanted the overview but, I believe, in the first instance, not necessarily the detail. I remember how shocked he was. He made the link with the announcement on the Olympics the day before and said how dreadful it was. He was concerned about what we should say to the public. We agreed I would go to COBRA and brief the government in person while he would go on television with a prepared statement. I was determined to see he kept what he said short – we didn't want to step into the realms of speculation – but I agreed that, as commissioner, he should say something: it would be expected of him. By eleven o'clock he had declared London temporarily shut. Emergency signs were flashed up on the motorways into the city warning 'London Closed' and there were traffic jams as people began to leave the city.

Ian told me he'd appointed Assistant Commissioner Alan Brown, one of our senior officers, as Gold commander. The police convey rank and seniority in investigations by describing officers as Gold, Silver or Bronze. The fire and ambulance services do the same. Gold is the top person who looks after strategy; Silver is the deputy who implements the plans and policies; and Bronze normally delivers tactics on the ground. You're more likely to see Gold and Silver in the command suite than Bronze – and there may be more than one of each depending on what's needed.

I took a minute to contact Alan. His job was to co-ordinate the multi-agency response minute by minute. Operating out of New Scotland Yard, he was already setting up a committee with senior people from all the services involved. The key players were the Fire Brigade, the Ambulance Service, London Transport, the Met, the City of London Police, the British Transport Police, the Home Office and the army. He told me he'd convened a meeting at the Yard for 10 a.m. – the same time as the planned COBRA meeting. As the scale of events became clearer, and while no one knew whether there would be further attacks in London, he said that the Gold Co-ordinating Group would move away from the centre to Hendon in the north, as part of a pre-plan for such emergencies – though that proved difficult as traffic prevented key players getting there for several hours. Gold was soon back at the Yard.

Alan is a fast-thinking career detective who doesn't waste time on small talk. He had to secure the horrendous scenes of crime and ensure the rescue operation was as fast and as smooth as possible, before our detectives could go in and search for evidence. He also had to provide the resources to put in place the counter-terrorist strategy I had devised to prevent further attacks, and help reassure the public. I said that a ring of steel must be put round Scotland Yard and all other buildings used by the Met centrally, more armed officers there and around Underground and bus stations. We needed to check and possibly restrict the movements of key figures, like the prime minister and the Queen. We had to find out what the London boroughs could offer in terms of manpower and resources, and we'd need extra officers from elsewhere in the country.

In the brief time we had we also discussed communications – finding out what was happening underground was clearly a major issue. Unbelievably, our radio system and the Ambulance Service's weren't compatible with the one used by London Transport and City of London Police. (It would be nearly four years before we had an accessible system.) Mobiles were hopeless as the system was overloaded, so we had to rely on London Transport's special antennas, known as 'leaky feeders', which boost reception underground and continued to work – they had to relay what was happening to almost everyone else.

But at this point it was confused. We didn't even have precise locations and we didn't have enough emergency vehicles in the right places. We saw on television that some buses had been commandeered – by visionary police and emergency workers – to transport the walking wounded to hospital.

Alan wanted mobile-phone access around Aldgate to be limited to emergency workers, many of whom were relying on mobiles to deal with those trapped underground. It was a specific request and could not be denied. The mobile-phone networks have a voluntary network management scheme called ACCOLC (ACCess OverLoad Control). Officers from City of London Police spoke to managers at one company only, O2 plc, who agreed to invoke ACCOLC, limiting calls around Aldgate station for four hours to emergency workers with a special sim card, plus 999 calls. I certainly didn't have one of those cards, although the BBC did as part of its public-service remit to keep people informed, as did other broadcasters.

We decided not to shut down the entire mobile-phone system but many people thought it had been closed because it was so busy. The networks can deal with a 20 per cent increase in calls but it was way beyond that. They did, however, introduce a calming measure, known as 'call gapping', to reduce voice quality, allowing more calls to be made at the same time. It's a technique they often use at New Year to deal with the vast number of calls made just after midnight.

For me now, as head of Specialist Operations, the important thing was to define people's roles and responsibilities. In the last few seconds before I left the building that morning I spoke again briefly to my immediate team. I was in overall command. Peter Clarke was in charge of the investigation. I told him my role would be to create an environment that best allowed him to do that job without being sidetracked. I would initially take on all critical briefings and strategic work, keeping ministers and other police departments in the loop. I would put an umbrella over Peter and his team so that the investigation could develop without distraction or interruption. Suzanna would liaise with other parts of the Metropolitan Police and Whitehall, and be responsible for security in London. She would also help keep me up to date with the necessary strategic information so that I could deliver it professionally when I dealt with the Police Authority, the commissioner, my other colleagues on the Met's Management Board, and at COBRA. We were in for the long haul on this one. We had to ensure there was adequate living accommodation and that there were enough officers. We needed to set in place structures to deal with staff we would second from other forces to help with the investigation. Critically, we had to create what we call a 'preventive deterrent', a hostile environment that makes it really hard for a terrorist to carry out further attacks. And we had to do all of this without further alarming the public. A heavy-handed police approach would scare, but too light a presence might encourage the terrorists.

By now it was almost ten and I was due at the emergency meeting of COBRA. This first meeting had been convened in response to the underground fires, and since the initial gathering is usually held within the first hour and a half of an incident, it was decided to go ahead, even though news of the bus explosion was only just coming in.

Martin was waiting for me outside the Yard in the customary green Range Rover. Because of the security risk that came with my job I was allocated an unmarked vehicle although inside it had emergency sirens, anti-blast mechanisms and radio contact with the Yard. I asked him to drive me to the Cabinet Office in Whitehall, but it quickly became clear that it was going to take time because central London was gridlocked. We only had a mile to travel but it seemed to take a lifetime as the area was so snarled up. I considered getting out and running, but I had plenty to do as I jotted down my plans and if I arrived with a sweaty brow I might give the impression I was panicking. Anyway, there'd be enough sweat once I got into COBRA.

Furious motorists beeped their horns, bus drivers cursed, passengers jumped impatiently out of cabs and buses to walk. It was hot, it was jammed and no one knew why. People must have been speculating that it was an accident or that a bendy bus had jack-knifed. This was road rage to the nth degree. Later the aggression turned to real concern – no one would care two hoots about how long it took.

As we crept along I realized I wouldn't be able to do my job with this vehicle. I asked Martin to change it later for a marked police car so that people could see us and we could speed through more easily if we needed to. In the end he went for it through the jam, driving like a madman, albeit very skilfully. I get travel sick at the best of times but on this occasion I was feeling lousy within half a mile. I held firm to the FM internal-grip handles – they're known as FM handles because when you're a passenger and driving fast in an emergency with blue flashing lights on, you invariably think, F**k me.

Some time after 10 a.m., fifteen or twenty minutes after the bus explosion, I walked into the Cabinet Office. Normally I'd have had a bit of banter with the security staff, who knew me from previous meetings. I had been there on security discussions ahead of the G8 meeting in Edinburgh and to discuss kidnap incidents abroad. Today there was no chat. I handed over my mobile phone and was ushered through a series of doors and down a flight of stairs into the basement. In the corridor there are dedicated back rooms – one for intelligence, one for the Home Office, one for the armed services, one for us and so on. They are connected to the main COBRA room by laptops so that if you need to communicate with your back-room team to get inform-ation or clarification you can make email contact without disrupting the meeting. It's high-tech but nothing like the kind of set-up you see on TV dramas. When you're practising procedures in mock-up incidents it can get dull and you end up email-chatting with your team – 'Have you seen the minister's dodgy tie?'

It was just over an hour since the first attacks and I hope I don't cause offence when I describe what was happening in there as like the first day of the Harrods sale – everyone flying everywhere trying to get into different rooms to set things up, bumping into each other, carrying boxes of paper and equipment, trying to have the rooms ready to go before the key players arrived.

We knew that first meeting was going to be a bit clunky. It was a Thursday, which was the day the cabinet normally met. Tony Blair and the foreign secretary were away at the G8 meeting at Gleneagles in Scotland but the other senior members of the government were meeting at Number 10, so they just had to walk down to COBRA. Quite conveniently that first meeting had a full attendance. It was chaired by the home secretary, Charles Clarke, and nearly all the secretaries of state were there, plus Eliza Manningham-Buller, head of MI5, and John Scarlett, head of MI6, the Secret Intelligence Service responsible for spying in the UK's interests abroad. I represented the Met.

The last time we had all met it was in very different circumstances. It was at MI5's annual summer drinks party for the great and the good of the intelligence world, a business party, and for me a good chance to network and catch up with contacts. The relaxed atmosphere then was replaced now with sombre formality. I nodded to the intelligence-agency chiefs and we got straight down to the job in hand. There were to be many meetings post-7/7 and we eventually became good friends.

I sat down and remember thinking, This is for real – we're hosting a series of terrorist attacks and we've now got the cabinet coming in to do what the public expects of them – to give clarity on a very serious event. I was pleased that Charles Clarke was chairing the meeting: I knew him because he was the local MP when I'd been chief constable of Norfolk. I respected him and had a good relationship with him. We both loved football and I used to go and watch Norwich play and seek him out to catch up on things informally. I think our relationship helped in the early days of the attacks – I had a home secretary who knew me and I knew him, and the police were very much left to carry out an operational response and get things back to normal.

As Charles walked through the door that morning it was absolutely clear he was determined to get a grip on this. Normally he'd be jovial, larger than life. Today, no smile, just a clinical focus. He asked for a factual overview of the current situation from the intelligence people, then turned to me. At that first COBRA I couldn't deal in fact: I could only tell him what I thought was the case.

'There's a lot of confusion,' I said. 'We can't be one hundred per cent sure how many fatalities there are. All our responders are there, and once everyone's out my team will focus on preserving the evidence.' Like many in the room, the last place we really wanted to be was in that meeting because it stopped us being at our posts.

People kept saying it was just like the desktop exercise we'd carried out three months earlier with the Americans, called Exercise Atlantic Blue. It had been a five-day non-stop operation and the first ever transatlantic one. It was based on two catastrophic explosions, in London and in the USA, and included a possible radiological, chemical, biological or nuclear attack. In London two thousand people took part from the Met, City of London and British Transport Police, the Ministry of Defence, fourteen government departments and agencies, two London borough councils, the Fire Brigade, and the Ambulance and National Health Services. At the same time a full-scale scenario was run in the USA, involving eight thousand people. Today in COBRA it made us think we'd got the potential scenario right, albeit not on the Underground. At least we'd practised our response.

In the event it was a relatively short meeting. It was agreed the home secretary would speak with the prime minister by secure phone, then go to Downing Street to issue a statement to the press, confirming there'd been a major incident with extensive casualties and explaining that the entire public-transport system in London had been closed down.

From then the COBRA offices operated round the clock for the next eight days, eventually shutting down on 15 July. We were soon in the swing of coming back for further meetings – almost hourly at times. At that first COBRA session I remember I was sitting three people away from Patricia Hewitt, the health secretary: her mobile phone went off even though we weren't supposed to have them in there.

In a meeting later on the morning of 7 July I had a tense and frank exchange of views with her. Charles Clarke was anxious to establish how many scenes we had – was there one, five or ten? 'How many?' he kept asking. By this time I *knew* there were four: Aldgate, Edgware Road, King's Cross and Tavistock Square.

'We have four scenes,' I piped up, and began to describe each one.

Imagine my surprise when Patricia Hewitt interrupted and challenged this. 'I'm sorry, Home Secretary, I don't think that's an accurate report. I am being told . . .' maybe she was getting it live from her backroom team via her laptop '. . . there are at least six or even seven or eight scenes.'

It really mattered that we got this right. If we sent emergency rescuers to eight places we'd be spreading our resources a lot more thinly than we should have done – and any future debrief, any public inquiry, would be scandalized by the mistake and the way it would divert resources away from those who needed them. I was absolutely sure there were only four, and I sat there thinking, How am I going to tell the secretary of state she's completely wrong, without making her feel awkward or silly, and without me appearing arrogant, egotistical or inappropriate?

But I had to do it. 'Sorry, I disagree with you. I believe

there are only four.' It was like a tennis match. The challenges ping-ponged between us, everyone looking at me, then at her. It wasn't exactly a row: it was conducted in a courteous and professional manner, with the home secretary as umpire as we played out a rally that neither of us was prepared to lose.

I guessed why she was getting it wrong: it was partly because the media were confused by the way we were resourcing the attacks – we were sealing off various different parts of London. The Ambulance Service, for example, had different rendezvous points from the police, which made it look as if there were two incidents when there was only one. In the case of King's Cross, emergency workers were accessing the scene from both King's Cross and Russell Square stations so some people assumed there'd been two explosions underground.

'You're secretary of state for health,' I ventured. 'These are likely to be rendezvous points for your emergency people where the injured or people who've passed away are being taken.'

Neither of us gave way and Charles Clarke was getting frustrated. He called deuce: 'We need clarification on this,' he said, and sent us packing to get it.

As the COBRA meetings continued in the coming days and weeks I became frustrated and disappointed with them, and came to question their fundamental efficacy. I wondered if politicians should be making these key decisions about terrorism – or, at other times, about floods and kidnappings abroad. There was so much jockeying for position and attention. Politics was always close to the surface. Put another way, would you want the chief executive of a hospital to operate on you, or the surgeon?

Take Alistair Darling: one minute he's in a cabinet meeting

discussing transport rules or Terminal 5 at Heathrow, the
next he's in COBRA making decisions about protecting us
from terrorism. He was secretary of state for transport and
on my case all the time, telling me the Underground needed
to be opened. And I kept asking him, 'Do you want me to
secure the scenes and get the evidence to prosecute the
terrorists, or do you want me to get the traffic moving?'

At 10.45 a.m. on 7 July I was back at my desk. It was now
almost an hour since the bus attack. I wondered if the
bombers had blown themselves up – or had they dumped a
bag and cynically walked off? Were more devices about to
detonate? Were terrorists even now going into some
shopping mall or railway station holding bags loaded with
explosives? As if we weren't moving fast enough already, we
needed to step up a gear – but where to start? How soon
before Peter's teams could get hold of the critical CCTV
tapes that might help to tell the story?

Suzanna was back in my office. She had called an
emergency meeting of the Security Review Committee.
Officers representing every Operational Command Unit –
from the Diplomatic Protection Unit to Traffic Patrols – all
the London boroughs, and the City of London and British
Transport Police were on their way to Scotland Yard to
attend. It was a group of about fifty policemen and policewomen, which I usually chaired every Friday morning to
review what security measures were in place in London and
around the VIPs we protect. This morning we decided that
Suzanna, as deputy assistant commissioner, Specialist
Operations (DACSO), would chair it. She would seek their
help to put the ring of steel round the building we were sitting in and other key offices of the Metropolitan Police
Estate. This included our VIP branch down the road in

St James's, Firearms' base in East London, our training centre in Hendon and numerous other police offices. She would ask the meeting for immediate help in providing extra armed officers. She would advise those attending to put into action well-rehearsed plans to reassure the public that we were on top of the job. This meant high-visibility policing, with as many officers in fluorescent jackets on the streets as possible. Community officers would need to contact Muslim leaders and explain any action we might take that would involve their communities – searches and arrests, for example – and we would need to ensure there was no backlash against them. We had to cover all eventualities at this early stage. We didn't yet know for sure that this was an attack from terrorists hiding within the Muslim community – but it was a strong possibility.

I also authorized Suzanna to begin 'Operation Griffin' at this meeting. At that time, Griffin was a system operating in the City of London for alerting financial and other institutions of immediate changes in the security situation. We have a security co-ordinator in the Square Mile who is rung with the alert message. He in turn would call or email security officers in other businesses, and they would cascade the message across the City. We agreed it should be absolutely clear: London was under attack and they must increase their security measures to the highest levels; further attacks might be imminent. Their primary concern would be to secure their businesses to minimize the impact on the stock market.

Finally Suzanna would organize the check on the official movements of VIPs. For the time being any diary engagements that might make them vulnerable – if they were travelling by train for example – had to be cancelled. The same Security Review Committee would meet again at

6 p.m. that evening to review the situation. This was an exceptional day – and exceptional measures were needed. I knew all these actions would create an environment that would make it much more difficult for any other terrorists to operate.

Suzanna told me the Gold committee, which had met while I was at COBRA, had agreed to this strategy. She had collated the latest information – hundreds were injured; the injuries bore the hallmarks of bomb attacks; many were still trapped underground. There was no sign that the bombs had had chemical or radiological components; there had been no warnings.

At 11 a.m., as we finished our briefing, Ian Blair was appearing on television. Like me, he'd only been in his current position for five months – and his longevity in the job might hang on his handling of the bombings. He brought to the public a measured message that combined reality and reassurance. 'The situation has been very confused but is now coming under control,' he said.

I wished I shared his confidence. The truth was, we had no idea whether or not it was over. Way below us the rescue operation was under way and it was possible people in desperate need of medical attention were still underground. It was more than two hours since the first attacks.

At 11.15 I received confirmation from specialist officers at the scene that the bus explosion had been a bomb attack. I did a quick assessment of where we were on resources. Peter Clarke had despatched anti-terrorist officers from SO13 to the four bomb scenes. The Casualty Bureau had still not been established. This was not good enough. There were technical difficulties in the rooms allocated to us. If this went on much longer we would start losing the confidence of emergency-response partners and the public. Complaints were starting to mount up: no one could make contact because none of the lines were connected. People wanted to find out if their loved ones had been identified – and we couldn't do anything about it.

We alerted every London borough and advised they put officers urgently on 'public-reassurance duty', out and about and manning local phone lines to show that we were on top of the job. Our shift workers were coming in early, and those who should have been going home stayed on. I gleaned from email messages and from Suzanna that the London Fire Brigade now had 240 fire-fighters and around fifty fire appliances working, while the Ambulance Service had two hundred vehicles and double the number of staff ferrying the injured to hospital or treating them on site. It took about three hours to treat or evacuate all those who were injured.

London hospitals had been put on full alert – more than a thousand beds were quickly freed up – Accident and Emergency departments expanded to deal with hundreds of casualties.

I was concentrating on the bigger picture, the strategy, and Suzanna was as ever on top of practicalities. It may seem trivial but someone had to make sure there was somewhere for us to sleep – no one would be going home for the foreseeable future. When I got back to Scotland Yard after the COBRA meeting on the morning of 7 July, I was told there was hardly a hotel room left in London. The world's media, commuters unable to get home and the emergency services were booking them. We decided to block-book whatever we could get.

It was a wise move. At noon the Met's travel department reported there were no rooms left in London.

Suzanna went into her meeting and I into a series of briefings with other senior managers at the Yard – in particular

with Peter Clarke. We checked that we had invoked everything on our official counter-terrorist list of tactical options
– it's known as the 'Rainbow List' because every action is
colour-coded for convenience. Throughout the crisis
Rainbow would be used as a template by which to measure
our response. Red stood for Highways, and covered the
action we needed to take to deal with any critical attack on
the transport infrastructure. On the roads all our number-
plate recognition teams were out – if accomplices to the
attacks were trying to escape we wanted to make it difficult
for them to do so. We had checkpoints across London with
armed officers supporting them, and armed mobile patrols
and mobile response vehicles that could be sent anywhere at
the drop of a hat.

Orange was the bomb-threat responder: the Bomb Squad
was out dealing with suspect packages people were reporting. Maroon meant covert policing: I saw we already had
officers monitoring live CCTV cameras in control rooms in
police stations, council control rooms, private car parks and
offices. MI5 and counter-terrorism police officers were
posted strategically at observation posts where we thought
there might be activity linked to the attacks.

Light Blue, Purple and Green covered aviation, maritime
and railways. I checked that adequate undercover officers
were conducting counter-surveillance operations, watching for suspicious activity, and that ports and airports had
more armed officers, armed checkpoints and increased undercover activity. Should we close the Gatwick or Heathrow
Express or the Channel Tunnel? For now we decided not
to – it would cause panic. But we increased security
massively. On the railways, British Transport Police were
doing minute trackside searches – we had the previous
year's Madrid bombings in mind – and would need

armed and unarmed support at all major railway stations.

I looked further down the Rainbow List: Dark Blue – searches. A massive operation was under way. Armed officers were searching sites from which mortar bombs or surface-to-air missiles could potentially be launched. They were checking rented lock-up garages. Self-storage warehouses were being searched, and specially trained officers were combing car parks for suspicious vehicles. And now CCTV footage was coming into the Yard. Video and digital viewing machines were in place – we had teams looking through every frame that came in.

Light Green marked the section protecting VIPs and the military. I knew Suzanna had put in motion the procedures for VIPs, and Ministry of Defence Police would be dealing with areas in their remit that needed extra vigilance.

Finally, there was Yellow: high-visibility policing. We were doing what we could to calm and reassure the public, and we needed them to know we were doing our best. As well as the high-visibility foot and vehicle patrols, every armed officer we could lay our hands on was on duty. If there were terrorists still out there, we wanted them to see we were armed and ready to take them on. We wanted to intimidate them – I had never been more determined. I sat in my office, fired up, vowing I would leave no stone unturned in our mission to seek and punish those people who sought so ruthlessly to destroy our society. I was on tenterhooks, my mind working furiously to make certain I hadn't forgotten anything. Whoever was responsible had indiscriminately attacked innocent people: they would be found, if they were still alive, and prosecuted. If they were dead by a suicide attack, they would not be martyrs: they were murderers.

Closer to home, the parts of Westminster that house the main government and security buildings, including Scotland

Yard, MI5 headquarters, Buckingham Palace, Downing Street, Parliament and various government departments, are known as the Government Security Zone and security within this area was put at an unprecedentedly high level.

At 11.30 radio and phone calls from officers at the scenes further confirmed mass fatalities and casualties. I jotted in my notebook as the news came in: '200 casualties at Russell Square, smoke billowing from Underground, people fleeing, confused; all four incidents confirmed as explosions'. Now we had a call from our investigators in Tavistock Square, telling us that there was every sign, from the positioning of the bodies and the way the blast had blown up the bus, that a device had been detonated by a suicide bomber – he had blown himself up too.

At twelve noon the prime minister, Tony Blair, gave a live televised statement from the G8 summit at Gleneagles in Scotland. He carried himself with real authority. 'It is reasonably clear there has been a series of terrorist attacks in London,' he began. Then he and other world leaders led the global condemnation of the attacks. It was the first of a series of political statements aimed at reassuring the public that we were on top of things.

I went back to COBRA, where we agreed the tactics my department had set in motion and I updated Charles Clarke before he spoke to Parliament. At 12.55 he told the House of Commons there'd been four explosions on the London transport network. 'As yet we do not know who or which organization is responsible for those criminal and appalling acts,' he said. Other politicians followed with condemnation of the attacks and sympathy for those bereaved and injured.

By lunchtime most people in the UK must have known London had been attacked. For a moment I felt anxious – I have a lot of friends in the City of London, we were talking about mass casualties, and I kept thinking, I hope they're OK.

We had a system for receiving protected emails and I now noticed one from JTAC, the Joint Terrorism Analysis Centre. In 2003 a new system for measuring the threat level to the UK had been introduced, and now it had been raised to its highest state of alert: 'Critical'. This meant that intelligence analysts believed there was a very strong chance that more attacks were imminent. JTAC is based at MI5's headquarters and is staffed by intelligence experts from sixteen different government agencies and departments, including the police. Their job is to analyse all the intelligence that comes to every UK intelligence agency. At the time of the bombings in July 2005 this information was classified, available only to security executives within government and in key business organizations outside.

It crossed my mind that JTAC had lowered the threat level just five weeks ago for the first time in eighteen months, indicating that while the terrorists had the will, and indeed might mount an attack, nothing specific was imminent. It appeared that they had not anticipated this attack. Right now, addressing that was not a priority.

I was becoming increasingly uneasy that there might be more attacks. My instinct drew me towards the Friday-morning rush-hour: was another terrorist cell planning to carry out a second wave of attacks twenty-four hours after the first? What more could we do to stop it happening?

It was now early afternoon on 7 July and, amazingly, on this extraordinary and awful day, some of the buses were running: London was slowly beginning to move again. By four o'clock most of the buses were back, overground rail-ways were operating and London Transport was indicating that parts of the Underground network would be in action next morning. Right now thousands of Londoners were walking home. No complaints, no riots, just quiet stoicism.

At 3 p.m. I had briefed Ian Blair on the latest developments ahead of a private meeting he held with the prime minister – who had flown down from the G8 meeting in Scotland – and the home secretary. At four, just over seven hours after the first attacks, I was summoned to another COBRA meeting, this time chaired by Tony Blair.

Charles Clarke had been good, but the prime minister was outstanding. He walked in, grave-faced, energetic, charismatic. The room fell silent. He set us all in one strategic direction, rallying his secretaries of state and the others in the room, setting out priorities. It felt like the half-time chat in the dressing room of a football match, although we knew we were nowhere near half-time. He wanted to know what messages we should be giving the public. To his right he had the security chiefs – the heads of MI5, MI6, GCHQ, and officers from Military Defence and JTAC. To his left his secretaries of state and the police – myself, Ian Johnston, the chief constable of British Transport Police, and Chris Fox, president of the Association of Chief Police Officers (ACPO), representing forces in the rest of England, Wales and Northern Ireland. Behind us sat our immediate back-up staff and just outside there were many others. We were constantly messaging on the laptops in front of us, updating the prime minister instantly as information came up.

First he took a situation report from the intelligence chiefs. In truth they had little to say. They said honestly that they were aware of no intelligence that had predicted today's events. But they were working frantically, acting on every piece of information coming from the bombsites. Perhaps it was a small relief for them to know that I could take the pressure off them in the first twenty-four hours by focusing on the police response and the details that were emerging about casualties and the type of bombs that had been detonated. It gave them breathing space to develop intelligence links.

I told the prime minister that early forensic analysis suggested that, from the positioning of the bodies in the carriages and near the bus scene, this was the work of suicide bombers, but I was adamant we should keep an open mind and think laterally so that we didn't miss anything. It may sound insensitive and callous, but as the bodies of the dead were removed, our forensics teams paid most attention at first to those we suspected might have been the bombers. We needed to identify them fast in order to track any accomplices and check links to any other potential terrorists.

The meeting agreed a forward deployment for the military at RAF Northolt, just to the west of London. In other words, the Ministry of Defence would convene a little standby army presence in case we needed extra help. It would have the capacity to deal with a chemical, nuclear, radiological or biological (CBRN) attack or to help with any major evacuations.

Tony Blair told us he wanted to reassure the public about the type of professional operational actions we were now taking to find the bombers. He spurred us on to reach new heights in our efforts to get on top of this – just as we might have begun to flag. He devised a statement that he delivered publicly, promising the 'most intense police and Security Service action to make sure we bring those responsible to justice'. Then he returned to the G8 summit in Scotland.

As he travelled north, the United Nations Security Council was meeting in New York to discuss the bombings. Within an hour it would condemn the attacks without reservation. Once more, I realized how big this situation was.

We didn't see the prime minister again until Friday night. He remained at the G8 summit: he would not let the terrorists interfere with what he saw as 'business as usual'. That doesn't mean he wasn't all over what was happening. He must have made dozens of phone calls to the home secretary, and held video conferences with him and other key players.

At this point another problem slipped into the equation and compounded the tasks we already faced. Because we still didn't know if there'd be more attacks, we needed people to be on the look-out. Sir Ian Blair and the government warned everyone to be vigilant. Many were frightened, and it was inevitable they would err on the side of caution and report almost everything. It turned into a bit of a nightmare: we were inundated with what turned out to be false alarms. While we were pushing to get things back to normal, the public were pulling us every which way to deal with what were ultimately unfounded fears. It was, of course, perfectly understandable. People would worry about something, wonder whether to make a call or whether they'd be wasting police time, and make the call anyway. We knew the score and we wanted the calls – even though they made our job tougher. We couldn't ignore them in case one was authentic.

On top of that we didn't want to confuse people. But we were now aware of the necessity to publish two emergency phone numbers. One was for the Casualty Bureau, which was at last functioning smoothly. The second was for the Anti-Terrorist Hotline to report suspicious packages and other information that might help the investigation. Our message had to be simple. If you're concerned about a loved one, ring the Casualty Bureau; if you see something suspicious ring the Anti-Terrorist Hotline.

At 6 p.m. I was again briefing colleagues and the commissioner. Like many people I wondered what would have happened if these attacks had come the day before the announcement of the decision to hold the 2012 Olympics in London. Would the International Olympic Committee have given 2012 to Paris instead?

Suzanna chaired another meeting of the Security Review Committee. Officers agreed resources over the coming days and made sure everyone understood clear lines of command and communication. They went through the Rainbow options and discussed the latest intelligence from JTAC.

Afterwards we got together to send an emergency message to police services across the UK. We outlined what we knew of the four attacks and discussed the implications for policing. We again asked what manpower other forces could offer. In particular we needed counter-terrorist officers – and warned they could be in for the long haul. We didn't know how long we'd need to keep them, and had no real idea who'd pay for this. We outlined the strategy for ports and airports, for dealing with the media and community reassurance. And we highlighted the fact that the terrorist threat level was now Critical – there might be more attacks.

Peter's team in the Anti-Terrorist Branch were now making real progress. Where we knew them, we were looking at the names of those who had died close to where it seemed the bombs had gone off, sifting through thousands more names that the Casualty Bureau had now received. At 22.19 the family of one Hasib Hussain reported him missing. An hour and a half later a police exhibits officer, who was putting together documents and possessions found near the bombs, phoned the Anti-Terrorist Branch with a number of names identified on cards and personal items. Among them were gym membership cards that bore the names Sidique

Khan and Mr S. Tanweer. The proximity of these cards to the rucksacks that we believed had contained the bombs meant we immediately suspected they were those of the bombers. The breakthrough swept across the Anti-Terrorist Branch like a breeze in sweltering sun, driving them through the night to formally identify the killers.

To our disappointment, though, we discovered that the CCTV camera on the bus had been out of order since 15 June so would not be bringing us any clues.

At 6.30 p.m. I was back in COBRA. This time Sir John Gieve, the permanent secretary and thus the most senior civil servant at the Home Office, chaired the meeting. We discussed the lack of warning of the attacks and that no intelligence linked them to current suspects whom we and MI5 had under surveillance (of which there were hundreds). We agreed this had all the hallmarks of an attack sponsored by Al Qaeda. We also agreed further measures to visit and engage with the Muslim community.

I received an update on conditions in the tunnel between Russell Square and King's Cross Underground stations. The explosion had happened about five hundred yards from Russell Square – a considerable distance when it came to rescuing and removing casualties. Although there was the most awful carnage, the tunnel had not collapsed. But it was hot and conditions were very difficult to work in. Further description I cannot give you – it is too grim. What I learnt served only to fire my anger with and abhorrence of the killers who had perpetrated the atrocity.

I looked at the updated list of casualties. Hundreds of injured had been treated and gone home. Ninety-nine people remained in hospital; eight were, sadly, not expected to live and thirty-seven had been confirmed dead. Fourteen trains remained stuck in tunnels.

I can't tell you everything that went on that day – we don't want the terrorists to know operational secrets about how we do things. But on reflection I'm convinced we did what we could – and I remain proud of and grateful to the thousands of police officers and civilian staff who went that extra mile, way beyond their duty, spurred on by outrage. I remember sitting at my desk – high above most Londoners – aware of the terrible tragedy that was still unfolding with every new discovery made below ground. And as I sifted through the intelligence documents that appeared on my desk, I wondered how I would keep everyone focused and buoyant through the coming days and months. One thing I did know was that motivation would not be a concern for the team or me.

2. Aftermath

ON 7 JULY I WAS PUT UP IN THE GRANGE HOTEL AT TOWER HILL.
I thought it would be for a couple of nights, but Room 918,
with its panoramic view over the rooftops to the Tower of
London and the river Thames beyond, would become my
home for the next six months. The hotel typified much of the
City of London – a modern building, juxtaposed against
the City's two-thousand-year-old Roman walls and, behind
it, visible above those walls, the thundering trains of
Fenchurch Street station.

If my stretch was tough, it was even harder for some of my
team. Within a few days I was sending them north to West
Yorkshire, where we suspected some of the bombers had
come from. It would be two years before they were based
back in London and many more before the trials that would
emanate from their work had taken place and they could
move on. It would be eighteen months before I would meet
the entire team up there – and in the meantime other horrific
and increasingly sophisticated plots would come to light.

As I went to bed in the early hours of 8 July, I realized that
in the white heat of the day's horrendous events I had stifled
my own reaction to them. Now, in the darkness, graphic

images of the bombings caught by the public on mobile phones kept running through my mind. I was filled with an overwhelming mix of despair and sympathy – despair that such atrocities had occurred on my watch, and sympathy for the dead, their families and friends, and the injured. My despondency was compounded by the knowledge that some were celebrating the bombings. I was sickened by public support, in small far-off corners of the globe, that the attacks had attracted.

I wondered whether the public here understood just how shocking, how unprecedented, this was for the country. We had had four almost simultaneous suicide attacks, carried out, we would soon learn, by British citizens; unknown to us, there would be more, which would stretch us way beyond anything we had faced before. A new threshold for terror attacks had been reached. We had suffered many atrocities at the hands of the IRA, but most of us had only read about suicide bombs and seen the images on television. Now the rest of the world was viewing the UK as the victim of such attacks.

I was worried about how we would equip the public to understand the heightened threat. Although we'd often warned there would be such attacks, I would have been condemned as alarmist and even irresponsible if I'd suggested that, in the summer of 2005, fifty-two people would be killed and more than seven hundred injured by UK citizens.

The next morning I was back at Scotland Yard by twenty past seven, knowing that some of my team would not have left the building all night. Special Branch and the Anti-Terrorist Branch had taken over extra floors at the Yard and in other police buildings, and as I walked the floor to encourage the team, passing through offices we'd just set up, some cops had dozed off at their desks. Others, who'd been working underground and at the bus scene, had lain down on the floor and fallen asleep, while a few, red-eyed, were still searching every tiny frame of CCTV footage for evidence of the perpetrators. These men and women were mentally and physically exhausted, but they worked with fierce determination – and they were already getting results.

As I reached my office and sifted through papers that Suzanna had left on my desk my heart lifted. Patterns were developing – not a definitive breakthrough yet but some clear leads. I saw that the working theory that these had been Al Qaeda-inspired suicide bombings was gaining momentum. It was less than twenty-four hours since the attacks but we had a list of possible suspects among those who had died, based on where their bodies were found in relation to the bombs, on possessions found nearby and on the fact that two of them had not even been reported missing. Three names already stood out: Hussain, Khan and Tanweer.

Something else had entered the equation too, in the overnight intelligence reports. They never came by email but were always delivered by hand for security reasons. That morning some were wackier than normal – and they made me jumpy. Several suggested further attacks on the transport network. Was this our intelligence sources or the analysts getting nervous? The messages were coming from all directions, to our police Anti-Terrorist Hotline, and via intelligence analysts at the different agencies.

I was already convinced there'd be another attack and I thought it would quite likely come twenty-four hours after the 7 July bombs. I had no firm grounds on which to base that opinion, just intuition. As we got close to 9 a.m. I grew increasingly nervous. I kept thinking it would be at the airports, or an iconic tourist site – imagine the irony if it was the Tower of London, the site I'd virtually been sleeping over. It would have been so easy to spiral downwards mentally, trying to anticipate and solve something that hadn't even happened. Instead we had to force ourselves to deal with the task in hand.

Suzanna Becks and Peter Clarke came up to my office. We sat around the conference table drinking tea. Our success or otherwise in discovering who had carried out the attacks would rest in the main on the strategies we would set in place over the next twenty-four hours, and we owed it to the families of those who had died, and to the injured, to get it right. Peter updated me on the investigation: members of his team were working with MI5 counter-terrorism officers to follow up the identities. We needed to find a link between suspects at the different bombsites in order to work out exactly who the members of the deadly cell were. In future plots, terrorists would try to outwit us by doing all their planning on the Internet – never meeting their co-conspirators in person – but that was not the case this time.

All three of us had grasped the gravity of the task. We were now in the middle of the biggest criminal investigation ever undertaken in the UK and I was in charge. I had to ensure that Peter and his team could operate to the best of their ability. I knew it would not be long before things would begin to move even faster than they already were. Once the bombers were identified I had no doubt we would be raiding addresses across the UK and possibly abroad. The CCTV footage would bring major breakthroughs – it nearly always does. Our scientists would work out the make-up of the explosives and this would help lead us to the 'bomb factory' – where the home-made devices had been put together – which could be anywhere in the country. Now, crucially, we had to build strong relationships with the intelligence agencies, with outside forces like the FBI, with government and the press.

One of the messages we had been sending out via the media was 'Don't come to work in London if you don't need to.' It resembled the advice given at the time of a severe weather warning. Although we were seeking the same public response, the scenario could not have been more different. We didn't want to scare people but we needed time and space to get on top of the current investigation, take every precaution against further attacks and to make sure that, if they came, we could cope.

The City didn't like our message of caution. The big financial institutions had to maintain confidence in London as one of the half-dozen or so biggest financial centres in the world. The stock market had dipped immediately after the bombings but quickly recovered – 'a metaphor for the City as a whole', according to the *Guardian*. We decided Suzanna would give a factual briefing to around eight of the big City banks later in the day in the hope that if they had a better understanding of what we were doing it would calm their anxieties. We could also help them estimate how long it would be before all parts of the City were functioning normally.

Suzanna said Buckingham Palace had been in touch: the Queen, Prince Charles and the Duchess of Cornwall planned to visit the injured in hospital; there'd also been strong statements of condemnation from the Palace. Suzanna would get the Protection Unit to contact me about security during the visits. She reminded me that my driver was waiting downstairs. I was about to embark on a round of meetings and the first COBRA session of the day was due to begin, chaired by the home secretary.

The drive to Whitehall was in stark contrast to the day before. It was the height of the rush-hour and we were in a marked police car but there were no traffic jams. London felt empty. As we drove I felt a growing unease. The COBRA sessions were already causing me concern. We were at the very early stages of an incredibly difficult, finely balanced investigation. It was difficult to decide how much information to make public. Too much might help any terrorists who were still alive but had aided the bombers to escape. If we were too secretive, though, we would not be exploiting the eyes and ears of the public who could lead us to them more quickly – and we risked fuelling public anxiety. We needed people to know we were making progress to reassure them.

I was worried, and so were colleagues in the intelligence agencies, that information discussed at COBRA might not be secure. It is very difficult to point the finger at anyone specifically, and I never knew exactly who was responsible – whether it was politicians, civil servants or others – but we couldn't escape the fact that, as time went on, details of discussions were briefed outside the COBRA membership and in some cases appeared in the press. I only briefed the press on details that were not confidential or sensitive – and what I gave was, more often than not, guidance to nip wild stories in the bud. Of course people should talk to the press – as long as the briefing is legitimate and enlightening – but details were being shared that threatened to undermine the investigation and our intelligence sources, and compound my growing dissatisfaction with the whole COBRA system – a theme to which I would return in my role as police UK lead for counter-terrorism.

Somehow a workable solution was needed. If I couldn't trust that what I said at that table wouldn't be leaked to the press I would hold back – which meant that other people round the table were probably doing the same. How much could I safely brief COBRA colleagues from other departments without being compromised?

Perhaps Charles Clarke had similar fears. When I arrived the home secretary called for a short pre-meeting attended only by the security chiefs – MI5, MI6, GCHQ, the Cabinet Office, the Home Office and the police. I was very much happier with this arrangement and glad that it became routine.

The COBRA meetings at this stage had two key priorities: to get reliable intelligence flowing and to ensure media messages were consistent between government and law-enforcement agencies. Intelligence was the biggest nightmare. Bearing in mind there had been nothing on the bombings ahead of the event, the likelihood of getting anything immediately afterwards was slim. But MI5, MI6 and GCHQ pulled out all the stops: they called in all their 'human resources' – the agents who infiltrate communities and spy on them. The home secretary and the prime minister wanted to know if there was any whispering going on, anyone credibly claiming responsibility: had any group contacted the Arab television station Al Jazeera, as Al Qaeda sometimes did when there'd been bombings? What sort of celebrations were going on along the Pakistan/Afghanistan border that would suggest links to Osama bin Laden and his supporters?

We discussed how to restore public confidence in the Underground. Passengers were significantly down (by 20 per cent during the first week after the bombs, Transport for London confirmed later). Inevitably some tube passengers acted illogically, getting out of a carriage if they saw someone with a rucksack and moving into the next, which wouldn't have been much safer if a bomb had been hidden in the rucksack.

While I was at the COBRA meeting, senior police officers from across the UK were converging on Scotland Yard for a meeting of the Advisory Group. The forty-three police forces in England and Wales are divided into regions. Each region elects representatives to sit on various committees run by the Association of Chief Police Officers (ACPO). The terrorism committee is called 'Terrorism and Allied Matters' or TAM. In the main this group develops terrorist policy and strategy for ACPO. The tactical deployment is delegated to the sub-committee known as the Advisory Group. It's an old-fashioned title but it's apt. Every chief constable is operationally independent. None can be told or instructed what to do – crazy, perhaps, and a recurring point of concern for me: the group can only 'advise' them on the tactics to deploy. This could mean forty-three different ways of doing things.

Usually we met four times a year. But on 8 July, for the first time I can remember, we'd called an extraordinary meeting to deal with the exceptional events of the preceding twenty-four hours. At one o'clock I walked in to chair the meeting. There were assistant chief constables or their equivalent from the geographical regions in England and Wales, along with representatives from Scotland and the head of Special Branch in Northern Ireland. MI5 had sent someone, as had the other intelligence agencies, and there were people from the military. I knew the group well enough to deduce that the meeting would not be easy. I needed them to agree on a unified message to the media and the public. I needed their co-operation in upping security nationwide. And I desperately needed extra manpower from them. The irony was lost on nobody in that room: how were they supposed to increase security in their own regions to unprecedented levels and send us the backup we needed, especially in terms of firearms specialists and counter-terrorism officers? Not unreasonably, my request was challenged.

My team and I quickly gave the operational nuts and bolts on what had happened, as did the intelligence agencies. Our message was clear: this was not a London problem; other attacks might be planned elsewhere. It was less than ten years since the devastating IRA bomb attack on the centre of Manchester, for example – the entire country had to be aware and prepared.

We moved on to the thorny and controversial issue of Section 44, the Terrorism Act, 2000, which gives the police special stop-and-search powers. In my view it's an essential tool in intelligence-gathering, and fighting and preventing terrorism. Normal stop-and-search powers can only be used if there are reasonable grounds to suspect an offence has been committed. Section 44 gives police the power to search any person or vehicle within a defined geographical area *without* having a particular reason for doing so. This power can only be used if authorization is in place defining the area and the length of time Section 44 will be in operation. It has to be approved by the home secretary. I knew Charles Clarke would be on board, given the current circumstances – but would the chief constables up and down the country agree to apply for it? We in the Met wanted pan-London authorization to use it. You may well argue there is only a slim chance of catching a terrorist in this way, but I believe it also acts as a deterrent: if a terrorist knows he or she may be stopped they will think twice about being at large, let alone walking around with a bomb. It's part of creating an environment hostile to them. However, some chief constables believe it can have an adverse effect on community relations if specific groups feel they are being disproportionately targeted.

We had to have unity on this. There was no point in using Section 44 in the Met if a would-be terrorist knew he could just nip across the border to the next county where he couldn't be stopped. We had a healthy discussion and in the end most approved. But that brought a second problem. The Home Office was slow at the best of times in processing Section 44 applications. Each force had to apply separately: how would we get immediate approval with such a huge influx of paperwork? I agreed to take this to COBRA, and by the end of the day we had negotiated a fast-track process to get the authorities signed.

Next at the meeting we needed to be sure we had adequate security around the UK's Critical National Infrastructure, or CNI – the places and things that are critical to keeping life and the economy running normally. We needed to check security plans and, in many instances, invoke worst-case procedures at places like ports and airports, for the transport infrastructure, water and electricity plants, around nuclear, military, government, economic and commercial establishments. In reality this meant more armed police and more high-visibility policing up and down the country, which would also help as a deterrent and go hand in hand with a national plan for community reassurance. Already Muslim leaders were anxious that their communities could be scapegoated unfairly if, as we all expected, the killers turned out to be Islamic extremists. Footprints already suggested the bombers might have come from outside London and in particular the North of England – though we still weren't absolutely sure of all their identities. Would we be overreacting if we upped the ante outside London and, if so, to what extent?

It was my request for extra resources, though, that caused the greatest tension. Peter Clarke had told me we were getting close to exhausting our forensics capability in London and were already sending some of the evidence to other cities because we had to get critical exhibits from the scene analysed fast – those gym passes, for example. Officers at the meeting kept telling me we couldn't rob Peter to pay Paul. 'How can you expect us to help London and at the same time look after our own backyard? We don't have staff sitting around waiting for things like this to happen.' We agreed a balance, a 'proportionate' amount of help would be given to the Met, and 'AG (Advisory Group) Message 27/05' was sent out to all forces setting the boundaries we'd established.

It also confirmed the messages we wanted to put out to the public: 'Be alert but not alarmed.' We wanted to reassure but we also needed the public's help. They are more powerful than we can ever be: we have access to some 150,000 cops; in mobilizing the public we massively increase that number.

The meeting raised another fundamental flaw in the systems we have for covering terrorism: that while the discussion was important, we, as chief police officers, spent a considerable amount of time debating issues that, given the circumstances, should have been the responsibility of one person.

So, although I was the UK police lead for counter-terrorism, no one was actually in overall charge of operational strategy: I could not order these officers to hand over extra support. Neither I nor the ACPO president had any leverage over individual chief constables: I had to persuade them to agree to our strategy. Similarly, we had no leverage over the politicians. I had to answer to COBRA, the

Met's Management Board and the Metropolitan Police Authority – our watchdog – as well as ACPO. Also, the City of London, British Transport and Military Police have their own autonomous forces. We needed someone to take overall responsibility for bringing together the police response to such tragedies. The 7 July attacks exposed the problem and, to a degree, I simply took on the mantle – I'm sure I sometimes did things in an unconventional way but I don't regret it. It was at least a year later that I managed to establish the idea of a national co-ordinator who would ultimately be in charge. Sadly, three years on, it still remained an idea.

By the time the Advisory Group disbanded I was exhausted. I needed to check the state of the investigation and do some forward thinking to make sure we were covering all bases. I went straight into a meeting of the Met's Management Board. Then it was back to my office and a session round my conference table with my own close-knit team, the key people running Specialist Operations, Peter Clarke, Suzanna Becks, Commander Peter Loughborough, who was in charge of the Royal and Diplomatic Protection Unit, and Commander Phil Gormley, who's now the deputy chief constable of West Midlands Police but who was then in charge of security at Heathrow and City airports, and also responsible for introducing protective security measures in response to the terrorist threat.

Later in the afternoon of 8 July Suzanna popped in again. The prime minister had returned from the G8 summit in Scotland and wanted briefing. He summoned me, with the heads of GCHQ, MI5 and MI6: we were getting unsubstantiated reports of other attacks being plotted, of mainline stations being targeted, and he needed to make sense of it.

We sat in the Cabinet Room at 10 Downing Street. Winston Churchill, Margaret Thatcher and others had made big decisions here. Now we were making critical decisions that would one day be judged in history books. I was moved by the sense that I was part of history.

The prime minister began by commenting again on the joy of the Olympic announcement being eclipsed by the sheer horror of what had followed the next day. We briefed him in turn, our comments to the point. I told him we were getting closer to identifying the bombers and this was a priority. I explained my strategy for deployments: we were at full stretch across the country and were creating a hostile environment for terrorists with high-visibility reassurance policing.

That weekend celebrations were planned in Whitehall to mark the sixtieth anniversary of the end of the Second World War. It was a warm evening and the windows were open. As we sat in Downing Street the sound of the bands practising wafted in. We discussed security for the event – the prime minister insisted the show must go on. Three years earlier he'd said the same when intelligence suggested a specific threat against him during the Queen's Golden Jubilee celebrations and we'd successfully protected him.

We also discussed how we planned to disrupt and prevent any possible further attacks. Tony Blair was keen we didn't react too fast without thinking: his advice was 'Don't rush and panic, slow things down, create headroom'. We agreed, and as intelligence sharpened up we could then be more focused in our direction.

We had already coined a new phrase: the 'new normality'. Already we knew things would never be the same – there had to be new means of security, such as concrete barriers around buildings, now that we faced the reality of suicide bombers in the UK. We would all have to put up with more intrusive security and more inconvenience.

The atmosphere was tense. I felt we needed humour to break the ice but it had to be appropriate. An off-the-cuff joke would not have gone down well – unless the main man came up with it. Someone asked Tony Blair whether he'd be going to Chequers that weekend, and he replied the family had decided to stay put in London – not least because the events of the previous week had precluded him from working on his in-tray, which was still full of other affairs of state.

'You're not going to get much sleep,' I told him, as 'We'll Meet Again' floated in to us.

'That's not my biggest problem,' he replied. 'I'm more worried about when Cherie starts singing along!' It was a light moment at the end of a sober meeting. The PM had contributed a little relief to a tense, high-pressure situation.

As I left the office at midnight on 8 July, news came through that Mohammad Sidique Khan had been identified as the account holder of a credit card found close to where the Edgware Road bomb had been detonated. I didn't know it then, but less than forty-eight hours after the attacks we were on to the leader of the suicide cell behind them.

It was useful information. Within days of the blasts it fell to me to brief my counterparts across the world. Most embassies in London bring in their own law-enforcement officers, mostly policemen and policewomen, to act as go-betweens, keeping their home countries in touch with what happens here, and we have the same in our embassies abroad. They're known internationally as liaison officers. We recalled ours from abroad to a meeting in London at which I updated them on events so far and passed on what we knew of those who'd planted the bombs in the hope that colleagues abroad could further our investigations.

My job was not to get in the way of those at the scenes of the bombs, because the last thing they want is a boss meddling or thinking they're Hercule Poirot solving the crime. It was not until day five, the Monday after the attacks, that I felt the need to encourage in person those working at the bomb-sites, and to find out if I could glean anything new from seeing them for myself. I decided not to go into the tunnels – that would be too disruptive for those working in them. Instead I opted for the bus scene. Some people might think, You're the man in charge, you're the boss, you should go to the actual scenes. Actually it takes more self-discipline not to visit them if the only benefit would be to get a feel for it. I didn't go into the tunnels until after they were cleared. My role was not to make an impression or to disrupt.

Martin drove me to Tavistock Square in our marked police car. We'd decided Monday would be a 'mobile' day for me – I would be out and about for most of the time. The temporary mortuary was the biggest and best equipped I had ever seen and I wanted to make sure it was running as well as possible, so we had visited it. Now we made our way to the south end of Tavistock Square – I purposely avoided the northern approach where the media were congregated on a twenty-four-hour watch. I gave my name to the uniformed female officer on the outer cordon. I was wearing a suit rather than police uniform and showed her my warrant card as proof of my identity. I then lifted the cordon tape, ducked under it and walked through the huge blue tarpaulin barrier erected to retain the privacy of the site, and out of respect for those killed as their remains were removed.

It is imperative to keep all evidence intact. Anyone

entering the cordon has their details recorded and one clearly defined route is taken by all, minimizing any disruption of evidence. The walk to the bus was at least three hundred metres. The blown-out windows and flapping blinds of nearby buildings reminded me of when I had visited the City of London Stock Exchange blast in the 1980s. Today I felt I was in no man's land – the public were not allowed here – and all I could see were the white-suited forensics teams working silently. I felt apprehensive and anxious. This was going to be an unpleasant experience. As I moved forward towards the mangled bus, the enormity of the situation really struck home. There was a calm that hung heavy with despair and sadness. All I could hear was the crunch of glass under my feet and, in the eerie quiet, the distant sound of police sirens elsewhere in the city.

What I found when I got closer was horrendous. It was like a series of still-frame photographs, surreal, very, very quiet, even though lots of people were about, some busying themselves gathering forensics, dealing with every awful new piece of evidence, others logging that evidence, or removing it, and more police officers manning the outer cordon. I'd seen the image of the bus on television but what I actually saw on the ground left me shocked and stunned. It was a full five days after the event. Yet horrifically they were still finding body parts hundreds of yards away in the park in the middle of Tavistock Square. I saw officers expert in this grim task, dressed from head to foot in white overalls, their mouths masked, their hands in rubber gloves, working from small cranes meticulously and gently sifting through the trees, removing body parts. I think everyone should know how utterly ghastly the effects of a bomb can be: only then is the callousness of those who plant them laid bare. I find it impossible to justify this kind of action in terms of religion.

Blood was spattered on the walls of the General Medical Council where, in the immediate explosion, those who were killed had hit the building and fallen to the ground. I cannot praise the forensics officers enough for the sombre, respectful way they carried out their task.

This was a scene of carnage with every complication. The blast area stretched some three hundred metres from the seat of the explosion in nearly every direction. And everything from the mangled bus to the outer extremities had to be pored over in fine detail during fingertip searches. I recalled how long it takes to comb through just one house at the scene of a domestic murder – you cover the actual room of the murder in detail plus the rest of house. It's very taxing. The scale of this, though, was off the radar.

There is a certain dynamic in the way a bomb explodes. People died according to where they happened to be sitting. Some who had sat very close to where the bomb went off literally walked away while others who were further from it lost their lives. The terrorists know this. In sadistic Al Qaeda training videos, easily accessible on the Internet, would-be terrorists are given such details. I have no doubt the 7/7 murderers viewed these videos: they are like a hideous form of the television advertisements the government put out in the 1970s to get us to 'Clunk-click every trip' and wear seatbelts. They showed dummies travelling in a vehicle at speed and braking, demonstrating what happened when you wore a seatbelt and when you didn't. The Al Qaeda training videos follow the same process. I've seen them. They are filmed in some makeshift barracks in a desert. They put sticks of metal in the ground representing people sitting in a bus and detonate explosives in different places; when the dust settles, you see which 'seats' have been destroyed and which haven't. Some of the 'buses' were six-seater, others fifteen-seater and so on. One image of the Tavistock Square bus bomb, which appeared in the newspapers, showed the front of the bus crumpled back. Just after the explosion on the upper deck a man who'd been sitting right in front of it had stood up. He survived although everyone around him was killed. The bombers had known where to put the devices to get optimum casualties.

It is almost impossible to describe what actually happened at Tavistock Square and at the other sites. Even now I can only imagine how overwhelmingly distressing it must be for those who survived the blasts and for the families of those who were killed. The bus bomb was the fourth bomb to explode that day. It wasn't until I visited the site and saw for myself the effect of the blast, and spoke to some of those who had witnessed what happened, that I really appreciated how severely traumatic the incident had been, not just for those directly involved but for those who had gone to help, including doctors and others inside the General Medical Council's offices. It would be another week of painstaking work by many dedicated officers before the site was cleared and open again.

My visit was brief, perhaps less than five minutes. I felt a little like an unwelcome guest, uncomfortable and uneasy, first because I was watching and everyone else was working. I didn't want them to feel I didn't understand what they were going through. Second, the sense that this was a place where people had lost their lives was intense. I wondered if I'd been voyeuristic in coming. When I got back into the car I remember thinking, I'm glad I've been, but am I one hundred per cent sure I needed to do that? I certainly gained a feeling for the scene close hand, and people working there might have been grateful I'd shown support, but I'm still not convinced it was needed.

I will never, ever forget what I saw when I visited the site of the bus bomb. A week later it crashed back when I came face to face with the families of those who had died at the meeting I described at the start of this book. It still distresses and chokes me. I felt no anger but I left more motivated than ever. This is my job, I thought, and we *will* get to the bottom of these attacks.

On day eleven I decided it was time to visit the Bomb Squad and other forensics officers who'd spent the best part of ten days underground searching for evidence. Much of that was now done and what they had found was being examined in pathology labs up and down the country or was housed at Scotland Yard. Officers who'd been underground were spending more time on the surface now, logging what they had found, examining it and following any leads it brought.

It was 3 p.m. on 18 July. The officers were on the top floors of Scotland Yard – the fifteenth and sixteenth, which were open plan. I saw a highly professional group of men and women, mostly dressed in black polo shirts, working quietly at whatever desks were free. They came under the umbrella of the Counter-Terrorism Unit. They were mainly of constable or sergeant rank and a substantial number had come from the military or Northern Ireland, although some were civilians with a scientific and explosives background. They were specially trained and their identities were always kept secret. Some specialized in explosives and were re-constructing the bombs to work out how they were made and how to make them safe if they came across similar devices in future. They would also find clues as to where the ingredients were bought, which would lead us to identify suspicious behaviour in future (why would a young man be buying vast quantities of peroxide, for example?).

Others were mainstream pathologists and forensics officers, trying to identify the terrorists, gather information on their route into London and their backgrounds in the hope of finding accomplices. They were also carefully logging every personal belonging they could find, to return to the families of people who had died or to the injured.

For several hours I passed from desk to desk listening to their often chilling words. Time and time again they described the intense heat of working in the tunnels in temperatures of more than 100 degrees Fahrenheit. There was little air, it was the height of summer, and the heat was compounded by the builders' lights they had to use. They had been dressed in heavy overalls and at times using heavy equipment to move the mangled wreckage of the trains. But the job was vital. It was one of those officers who had found the soot-covered gym passes that proved the vital clues in identifying some of the bombers. It was grimy, dirty, and very, very sad. Police dogs came down at intervals to deter rats.

All those involved knew they had one of most important functions in the investigation to perform. Every scene will provide clues, and without those officers' work the investigation couldn't flourish. They had to get the forensic clues, then identify the bombers, the 'recipe' and the bomb's ingredients. If there was so much as a fingerprint left they were determined to find it. Imagine trying to find DNA or a print in a tunnel in artificial light. They told me their work constantly reminded them of how it must have been for the people caught up in the bombs, travelling at the height of the rush-hour, stuck in hot black tunnels with little room to move or breathe, people close by, even on top of each other, all around.

Imagine being a survivor and able to walk. Passengers left

the train and started to walk back along the tracks. They would have heard the rumbling of a train travelling in a different tunnel but they wouldn't know for certain if it was approaching them. I believe the bombers would have checked the Transport for London website and chosen peak time to get maximum casualties. The devastation was clearly appalling. Months later I was travelling between Stratford and Mile End in the rush-hour, squashed among people standing up, and the train stopped in the tunnel for ten minutes. I shuddered at the carnage that would have been caused if a bomb had gone off then.

One officer was sitting at a desk with a picture of his family on it. He told me he'd been seconded without any notice from another force and hadn't seen them since he was billeted to central London eleven days earlier. I came to conversations like this offering sympathy and support but there was not one complaint from anyone in those vast offices across those two top floors. They were saying, 'It's kind of you to care, and it's not pleasant but it's my job. It's what I do and it's what I want to do. I'll be disappointed if I don't get to the bottom of it.'

Everyone played an important part in dealing with the bombs, but in my view those guys were real heroes. In the end it took them just three weeks to find out what the devices were and who was responsible.

I visited another group of people that day too – the officers scouring thousands of hours of CCTV footage. The use of closed-circuit television has dramatically changed the art of the criminal investigation. CCTV was first introduced in the 1970s and 1980s to combat crime and anti-social behaviour, but it has only really taken off in the last decade. I can hardly think of a big investigation recently where it hasn't had a major role to play. We started the 7 July investigation with nothing to go on at all – no clues. We had investigators at the scenes of the bombs. We also had people looking at those scenes and the areas around them on CCTV to find out what had been happening before the explosions. Some tapes took hours to check, others just a few minutes. By the end of the investigation the officers had watched 2500 items of CCTV footage – it took weeks. But it was bringing results within days.

By the morning of Tuesday, 12 July, five days after the attacks, we had established that three of the suspects came from West Yorkshire. We then received a report that four people had been seen putting on rucksacks at Luton station on 7 July. Luton is on the mainline into King's Cross. We grabbed CCTV tapes from there.

I'll never forget the breakthrough moment when Peter Clarke contacted me to say they'd found footage of the men they believed were the bombers. He walked into my office clutching a still photograph. It showed four Asian-looking men with identical rucksacks on their backs, walking, in King's Cross. They fitted the profiles of any number of young travellers on the Underground. A lot of people use rucksacks to carry computers and documents and on the day they would have blended in. But with the hindsight of knowing they'd been there just before the bombs went off, the skilled CCTV analyst scrutinizing that tape saw immediately that something was not right. The four were in pairs, like infantry walking into a war zone. Peter showed me the grainy still and I went straight back up to his office to view it on his computer screen, and to look through the series of stills around this particular frame.

Peter and I agreed that knowledge of the still should initially be restricted to him and his immediate team, our colleague Suzanna Becks, the commissioner, Sir Ian Blair, plus the person who'd found it and those around him. Operational security was very tight. But we were ecstatic. Peter congratulated the analyst and I went to brief Ian Blair. He, too, was very, very pleased.

Adrenalin surged. This, I thought, is where the job really starts. At last we could start piecing together the jigsaw. We needed to link the men in the pictures with those whose gym and credit cards we'd found in the trains. In fact, that one image would put us on the road to identifying the bombers, and finding their car and more explosives. It would lead us to CCTV pictures of the bus bomber going to buy a battery in King's Cross before detonating the bomb. We would work backwards using CCTV, discovering the time of the train the suspects caught, checking CCTV footage from Luton just before they would have got on the train. Bingo! That brought another shot of the four. Now we had to seize every bit of CCTV footage we could on every possible car route from West Yorkshire, where three of them lived, to Luton.

That picture rejuvenated the investigation. It gave renewed stamina to the CCTV analysts as they continued their painstaking task, resting only for a few minutes at a time to relieve their eyes as they hunted for more. They knew that as a result of this find the whole inquiry would open up. And it would not be long before we gave that still to the media – and sightings by the public would flood in.

Ironically, the set of stills also revealed, behind the four on the escalator, one of our own counter-terrorism officers on his way to work. He could not have known who they were – or even taken note of the men ahead of him. He wasn't caught in the attacks, but within minutes of that shot being taken the lives of those five people – the bombers and the intelligence officer – would become irrevocably entwined.

This country is alone in the world for the vast amount of intrusion we allow into people's lives with CCTV. In the USA and Australia, where civil liberties are of paramount importance, the police are unable to convince the public or the politicians of its value. In those countries they are in awe of the way we use it and the way, despite the protests of our civil-liberties groups, the public is largely supportive. I'm still surprised how in a relatively short time we have moved from being generally apprehensive about it to having accepted its widespread, almost Orwellian use.

At MI5 headquarters, the director general, Dame Eliza Manningham-Buller, and her team were poring over the stills too, working closely with our counter-terrorism officers to push forward the investigation. MI5 is the leading department on intelligence linked to national security within the UK. They decide who intelligence is shared with, and request detectives from Special Branch and Anti-Terrorist Branch if they want to develop their intelligence and need extra help – to spy on a suspect, for example, or trace his friends or bank records. They take the lead on intelligence-gathering and the police work to them. If MI5 acquires new intelligence – perhaps through surveillance of other suspects or from a double agent who is posing as a friend among a group of suspects – it may want to watch a new suspect. If it needs help in this it can call on the police who can do undercover work or trawl through bank-account details and mobile-phone records. At this stage, while we are still gathering intelligence to find out whether or not MI5 is right to be suspicious about this person, MI5 remains in charge of the operation and we take our orders from it. If it's decided there may be enough evidence to arrest and prosecute a suspect, or if that person might be a danger to society so that we need to arrest him or her and search their home, it becomes what we call an 'executive action' and the lead moves from MI5 to the police. We seek more evidence, carry out raids and make arrests. Then we present what we have to lawyers at the Crown Prosecution Service, who work out if we have enough firm evidence to prosecute the suspect and a fair chance of a successful trial. They will either say, 'Yes,' or tell us that we must release the suspect, or find further evidence that will stand up in court.

As soon as the bombs went off the DG knew her staff were in for the long haul, but they were not needed to help with the immediate emergency response: that was the work of others. On the morning of 7 July while the police, and almost every other department involved, were calling in all the staff they could get hold of, she ordered at least a third of hers to go home. The police run with an incident in an immediate way: we have a 'here and now' mentality that keeps us on the breaking incident. MI5 has a completely different mindset: it sends people home because it knows they'll be on the job for many months and wants them refreshed, recharged and mentally alert. Eliza Manningham-Buller was setting in motion a twenty-four-hour operation, putting staff on shifts for the duration – however long that proved to be.

Eliza is an awesome woman. Her decision-making is calm and balanced. She is incisive, yet approachable and humorous. Our backgrounds are so different yet I always felt we had known each other for years. Right now, though, her job was to find out what she could about the perpetrators. Were they 'clean skins' – people we'd never heard of – or had we come across them before? Were they suicide bombers who had also died in the explosions, as we suspected from early on, or had the bombs been planted by terrorists who made their escape before the devices detonated? Politicians and the press were asking these questions from the start.

United in our pursuit of the truth, the DG and I worked well together. On 27 July, nearly three weeks after the attacks, I instigated a face-to-face meeting of the intelligence chiefs to reprise where we had got to with our investigations. It was a working lunch starting at 12.30 p.m. and we had sandwiches on the table. Eliza was there for MI5, with her deputy Jonathan Evans, a serious and impressive man who took over when she retired in 2007. Sir John Scarlett, the head of MI6, came, and Sir David Pepper, director of GCHQ, where they intercept intelligence using state-of-the-art satellite and other communications technology. For the Met there were myself and my two deputies: Suzanna Becks to give the overview and Peter Clarke to update on the counter-terrorist operation. For an hour and a half we and the highest-ranking intelligence chiefs in the land discussed the suspects, their methodology and our most secret operational efforts to catch those who supported them.

After the meeting Eliza dismissed our backup staff and gently shut the door behind them. She dressed, spoke and carried herself with dignity and confidence. She wore smart suits in muted colours, often with a string of pearls. She had one of the toughest jobs in the country, in motivating her staff to take on life-threatening spying missions within our country, always juggling what was legally and politically acceptable in the pursuit of our national security. She was as tough as hell when her staff didn't deliver – I witnessed that – but they respected her. What I also discovered in those early days after the bombings was that she was compassionate. The combination made her a great and charismatic leader. During this period, her wisdom, strength and vision made her a role model to us all. I found her advice invaluable. She and I were well aware of the suffering of the victims, many of whom were now dead and some still fighting for their lives in hospital.

The police and in particular MI5 were coming under intense scrutiny on two fronts. We had collectively failed to identify, track and stop the bombers. Six weeks before the attacks, not only had the Joint Terrorism Analysis Centre (JTAC) reduced its assessment of the terrorist threat to Britain from 'severe-general' to 'substantial' – but on 6 July the newspapers ran reports claiming Eliza had told senior Members of Parliament in a private briefing that she didn't think an attack was imminent. No intelligence coming in to her or her analysts suggested otherwise.

She never lost her composure, her determined professionalism or her sensitivity to others. As she closed my office door that day she said simply: 'Andy, this is tough for us all. I want you to know you're doing a great job.' Then she walked across the room and embraced me.

Eliza and I maintained contacts with the Americans, which would become increasingly strong in the months post-7/7. One thing that worried me greatly on the day of the bombings was that one of my senior managers was on the wrong side of the Atlantic. Commander Janet Williams had just flown out for a routine visit to Washington. On the morning of 7 July when I realized she was in the wrong place my heart sank. She was head of Special Branch, which meant one of my two biggest units was without its boss – just as it faced its greatest ever test.

As the days wore on, though, this turned out to be a godsend. She and I could communicate by secure satellite telephone (yes, there is such a thing) and she was my link into the heart of American intelligence and politics. She went in person to see our counterparts with the New York Police Department (NYPD) to ensure we took on board any useful lessons learnt following the 9/11 Al Qaeda attacks on the World Trade Center. In the days after 7/7 she was able to reassure those Americans who were concerned about copycat attacks in the USA. She swapped information, circulated pictures of the bombers and the devices, and discussed their methods.

One American couldn't resist coming to the UK in person to see for himself what was happening. It was 19 July, a Tuesday, and at 3.30 p.m. I walked into the outer area of my office to find a tall, imposing figure standing there. I recognized him immediately – the silvery grey hair and dark bushy eyebrows, the thin, determined mouth and the hint of a twinkle in his eyes. He exuded energy. This was a man who had had brilliant careers in the military and as an investigative prosecuting lawyer covering some of the top criminal, terrorist and Mafia cases in the USA. A New Yorker and conservative Republican through and through, Robert Mueller was now head of the FBI, in charge of investigating terrorist and other serious interstate crimes against the United States. It came as no surprise that he would turn up to be briefed on 7/7. No one was as cool or as dynamic or as much of a workaholic as the director of the FBI. But he had only two hours to spare. My briefing was therefore clinically precise and factual.

After I'd given him my assessment I took him upstairs to meet briefly with the commissioner, then allocated a senior officer to take him to see the devastation caused by the bombs. Getting into the lift to go to Sir Ian Blair's office was like something out of a police comedy show. The lifts are a normal size so, with just the two of us, we should have easily fitted inside. But the FBI director had some of the biggest protection officers you ever saw – they towered above me and I'm almost six feet tall. And there were loads of them. I remember staring into this guy's chest as we all squeezed into the lift. When we arrived at the eighth floor, a strategic decision had to be made as to who moved first – we were all squashed in so tight we couldn't move.

This was the start of a regular contact. Mueller would arrive and drop in, often unannounced, when he was passing through on a mission elsewhere in Europe, or we'd meet if I was visiting the USA. My visits were usually planned in advance. I didn't have the luxury he was afforded, of a private jet that allowed him to get around *Thunderbirds*-style, as if the world was just a small country. He'd turn up at the Yard as if he was popping in for a cup of tea. His meetings, however, were no tea party. When you addressed him, it was always as though you were speaking directly to the President of the USA. He could sniff waffle at a hundred yards. As our contact grew, he became a strong ally and we frequently co-operated on terrorist investigations.

As Mueller left, Suzanna put her head round the door to remind me I needed to prepare for a meeting of the UK's top crime reporters. They always gathered downstairs in the Press Room on the ground floor, close to the main reception area at Scotland Yard. I put a quick call in to Peter to see where he was with the investigation, then phoned Eliza's office at MI5 and spoke to the office of her communications director to find out what he was briefing to his trusted correspondents. Dick Fedorcio, our director of communications, had turned up and filled me in on facts and figures – the number of detectives on the case, how many seconded from other forces, how many calls to our Casualty Bureau and the Anti-Terrorist Hotline and so on. We walked together, talking, and took the lift to the ground floor. We passed through the first security door, which separates the rest of the Yard from the press section. Only when it had closed behind us, locking us briefly inside a three-feet-square bubble, would the next open. We walked through to the small, slightly claustrophobic Press Room, with its intense blue soundproofed walls, grey blinds shutting out the daylight, and the rumble of chatter stopped.

I'd briefed the Crime Reporters' Association (CRA) almost daily since the explosions. Occasionally Peter Clarke joined me – he attended these sessions so rarely because I wanted to leave him clear to focus on the investigation into who the bombers were and where they had come from. The CRA is made up of a small group of trusted national newspaper and television reporters; there'd be persistent questioning that would ramble on for as long as I let it. The press were frustrated by the lack of information. For the first three days after the bombings, reporting the horrific raw facts was enough, but by day four they were interested in the investigation. At one particular meeting, under pressure from editors, they wanted precise figures for those killed and injured. We could only tell them we thought over fifty had died, but that total might rise. They wanted to know if the bombers were among them, and while we suspected this was the case we did not want to confirm it, or identify them as dead until we were sure, and had informed their families, who might not have known what they'd done and might find themselves in considerable danger. We needed to be very sensitive in handling them: we had to keep a very clear line between them and the families of those the bombers had murdered.

The press wouldn't give up. They didn't understand what we were up against. I decided to go totally off the record – knowing it would spark the usual minor stand-off.

'What exactly do you mean?' one correspondent asked.

'Non-reportable,' I said.

That wasn't good enough for veteran reporters from two of the broadsheet newspapers. 'If it's non-reportable I'd rather not know,' one said.

'Fine,' I retorted. 'You realize if you take that position you're implicitly proposing an option where you get nothing? Your problem, not mine.'

Mike Sullivan, from the *Sun*, and most of the rest wanted the opposite – they couldn't resist having the 'in' on everything even if they couldn't publish it. And they knew there might be a time when they could go public.

The squabbling went on for a good ten minutes – this often happened at these meetings – before we finally reached a consensus: I would fill them in but they would not report it. It was par for the course. The argument was nothing for me to get too alarmed about. In fact, it strengthened the relationship between the press and the police working on the investigation. And in the main the journalists were trying to do a good job.

I explained the problems with establishing identities when we were still finding bodies at the scenes of the explosions. In some cases we had to rely on DNA samples to identify people and we didn't want something so distressing to be published when a few families were still waiting for confirmation that a missing person had been killed. We knew, and the press knew, that some relatives were frustrated. But we, the police, would rather put up with wrath and complaints than publish information that would upset them even more. It must have been so difficult for those families, waiting, knowing, but not really understanding why we were unable to produce a body for them to identify and bury. In a sense the press were in the same position as I was. I couldn't give certainty to the families any more than they could to their news editor. Stalemate.

The CRA represents all the major newspapers and broadcasters, and had agreed to adhere to strict rules. Sometimes the journalists had no choice but to agree to be briefed on subjects we could not allow them to report because it would jeopardize a court case, undermine a future raid, or give away what we knew to the criminals in the case of a kidnapping. In telling the crime correspondents the details in advance, on a non-publishable basis, we believed there was a good chance that the story would be correct when eventually it could be published – at the end of a court case, for example, when legal restrictions are lifted. In this age of twenty-four-hour news, the television channels want the details ready to broadcast or put on their websites immediately that happens. Of course, there were times at these meetings when we added our own spin on events, but experienced reporters recognized this – and certainly didn't give us an easy ride. Our relationship was respectful but they still frequently published material highly critical of the Met.

I didn't give away secrets I was not supposed to, but if they were barking up the wrong tree when they questioned me I tried to steer them away from inaccuracies. Dick Fedorcio and I had set the tone for this on day one of the attacks. It was a system that would eventually bring trouble for me personally: our attempt to make relationships with the press more open, within professional constraints, proved a step too far for some of my colleagues, who regularly questioned our motives. Some eventually suggested that they were unethical – how wrong they were. I believed using the CRA was the best and most responsible way to ensure reporting was true and accurate. And to a great extent, in those early days, it worked. We also held open conferences for the rest of the press, taken by Andy Trotter, then deputy chief constable of British Transport Police, or Brian Paddick, a senior Scotland Yard officer at the time, and afterwards I often stepped in to brief the CRA further, in private.

I remember at that CRA meeting soon after the attacks we eventually returned to off-the-record-reportable-but-non-sourceable mode.

Rumours abounded on the identities of the bombers – the reporters were full of questions about them. Who were they? Why couldn't we confirm whether or not they were indeed suicides and that the bombers had died? What were we doing in raids in Leeds and London – surely we'd found something? I did my best but they left frustrated, though this was more than compensated for twenty-four hours later when we published the first CCTV pictures of the bombers.

I'd only been in my job for five months and was still getting to know the press, but in the coming months I would learn who among them I could and could not trust. I felt my relationship with them was of critical importance – I had to make it work. What they reported coloured the public's view of what was happening, and as part of our campaign of reassurance it was important to get it right. And while I focused on the CRA, I knew that was only a fraction of the work we were doing. Journalists from across the globe were in London to report the story.

Life at this point was taxing and tough, but also full and stimulating. Ten days after the attacks I nipped home for Sunday lunch. Martin drove me out to Essex, where I was reunited with my wife, Jane, and children, and picked up a dozen clean shirts. The family were preparing for our annual holiday, which was due when school broke up. It was the first face-to-face conversation we'd had since the attacks, and it was hard to have to tell them that I wouldn't be going with them. Mid-afternoon, I returned to Scotland Yard, reading the Sunday papers in the car, in time for a meeting of my Chief Officers Group.

Later that week I booked an extra seat on the plane my family were soon to fly out on. Then I phoned Jane and told her I'd arranged for her parents to go with her and our two children instead of me. Of course she was disappointed that I couldn't go, but she understood – she'd married a cop who lived the job and she had been prepared to accept the sacrifices that she would inevitably have to make.

My home was now the hotel, with my room right under the flight path for transatlantic jets. Every morning I went to the gym, showered, got dressed and waited for my driver. It was thought to be safer for me to travel by car because of my high-profile counter-terrorism role. As I waited I would sit at my ninth-floor window mesmerized by the planes, crystal clear in the sky, glinting in the sun as they passed, one after another, over the Tower of London – that iconic symbol of British tradition and history. I soon realized the gap between each plane was nearly two minutes and I used to count the time between aircraft as they made their way to Heathrow.

Over the months I watched London's new City Hall being built. It would become familiar to me as the Metropolitan Police Authority became increasingly involved in what we did. I saw the summer tourists queue for the Tower, then the Christmas parties in the hotel. I would sit in the foyer, which was decorated in red, black and gold with a huge chandelier – just like an Agatha Christie film set – with Kylie or some other superstar crooning softly from the speakers in the background.

I would occasionally grab a few moments to sit there, with

a glass of white wine and a BLT, and watch the world go by – a reminder that for most people it was business as usual. Despite our frantic work hunting terrorists, life was back to normal for most, which was what we wanted. Nothing brought that home to me more strongly than the event I witnessed there on 12 September, two months after the bombings. For some days the car park had been full of flash cars – Beemers and Mercs, with all the fancy extras. Now I discovered who they belonged to. England had won the Ashes that afternoon, and the boys were staying at the hotel, oblivious, I assumed, to all we were doing to keep them and the rest of the nation safe. Not surprisingly, the place erupted. The management laid on a champagne reception in the foyer. As I sat there, just to the side of the main door, I reflected on the irony of their win – a real show of British determination and resistance.

I stayed up late waiting for them to return. The wives arrived first, then the players – among them my cricketing hero, Freddie Flintoff. Some of the other guests and I went up to congratulate them. When I left for work at seven the next morning, the celebrations were still going on. Later that day the same guys were seen on television, meeting the prime minister at Guildhall, some struggling to stay on their feet.

I headed back into the frenetic round of briefings – as ever there was COBRA, with ministers and intelligence-agency heads, meetings at the Yard and with victims' families, then with the press. I regarded the endless meetings as a necessary evil – I had to be there but I would rather have been focusing on the investigation than the politics. What was worse, I felt duplicitous, privately cursing the number of official gatherings I had to attend yet forcing my own management team to hold endless meetings too. Some days I just wanted to stop the merry-go-round.

My concerns about the COBRA meetings did not diminish. They were extremely important events, bringing together the top politicians and law-enforcement chiefs in the land. It was a privilege to sit at the COBRA table and it brought incredible responsibility, yet the point-scoring was sometimes unbelievable. During debates on who should front press briefings, for example, I sometimes felt it was the mission of some civil servants to get their secretary of state or minister on television whatever the cost, even if, clearly, they were not the most appropriate spokesperson. At times it was a real bun-fight, and I felt for John Toker, the director of Counter-Terrorism Communications, who had to play the diplomat and sort it.

There was no doubt that the security of the country was uppermost in the minds of politicians, but after one particularly frustrating COBRA meeting, when I felt some were pushing agendas I couldn't understand and didn't always seem directly linked to operational matters, I got into the car and thought, I can't go back to the Yard. Instead I did what Dudley Moore did in *Arthur*: 'Take me to the park!' I told my driver. He knew I meant St James's, which was nearby. After that the park became a refuge. I often went there on the way back from COBRA to think, to piece things together, to quietly work out the next moves. Eventually that request to my driver was picked up by my office and became a euphemism when we needed to escape, especially in the evenings – 'Take me to the park,' we'd say, before we met up in the pub.

That day I stayed in St James's Park for about fifteen minutes. When I'd gathered my thoughts I went back to New Scotland Yard, the commissioner and the rest. Lo and behold, what I got when I arrived was a replica of the exasperating COBRA meeting I'd just left – more in-house fighting, positioning and bickering. I began to sense tension and loss of trust at the very top of the Yard. I was involved in it too and they probably felt I was being difficult and evasive – but it led me eventually to realize there must be a better, more independent and focused way of dealing with terrorism that didn't allow human vanities (mine included) or local politics to enter the fray.

There was nothing special about 20 July: it was dominated by meetings, the essential work of investigating the bomb attacks squeezed between them or delegated. At 8 a.m. I chaired a meeting of the Guardian Group, made up of some twelve people representing British Transport Police and City of London Police, the Met (usually me, Suzanna and the heads of the Anti-Terrorist Branch and Special Branch) and Ministry of Defence Police, who are deployed at military sites across the UK. We normally met every three months for breakfast to discuss the security of London and would sit at a conference-room table eating eggs and bacon while we reviewed the latest intelligence reports. It was a networking session, and a chance to spot weaknesses and plan exercises to rectify them.

That morning we reviewed the intelligence post-7 July and planned our response to further attacks. We also reviewed 'Kratos', which is the codename for the critical rules of engagement when using firearms, and sorted out who would be the Gold commander if there were more bombs. At that meeting we decided Kratos was fit for purpose. Less than twenty-four hours later we would discover how very, very wrong we were.

From 10.30 to 12.30 I attended the Chief Constables Council – a bizarre event made up of around sixty force leaders and senior officers from England and Wales, which was chaired by Chris Fox, the president of the Association of Chief Police Officers (ACPO). It was an unwieldy meeting by everyone's admission. There was a lot to get through and everyone wanted their twopenn'orth. Yet again it highlighted the problems in trying to persuade a large number of autonomous chief constables, who each had operational independence, to sign up to what was agreed and work together. It was a bit like herding cats: you can't get complete consensus. It's very rare that everyone takes the same direction, which is a nightmare when it comes to terrorism. With no single person in overall charge of UK counter-terrorism you have to corral all the chiefs to sign up to a policy. I was the UK police lead for counter-terrorism – but I couldn't force everyone to toe my line.

From there I went straight to a one o'clock meeting with the Home Office minister responsible for counter-terrorism, Hazel Blears. I'd first met her at a meeting in Norfolk when I was chief constable. I liked her no-nonsense approach. She had put me in my place when I had asked cheekily for more money from the national pot to run the force rather than raise it in council tax. Now we met most days at COBRA, but she wanted a one-on-one ahead of a roadshow the Home Office was doing to meet Muslim leaders up and down the country. I was keen for local police commanders to be kept in the loop when she was in town and for them all to present a unified message on terrorism.

At 2 p.m. I saw the chairman of ACPO's Terrorism Committee, Ken Jones, soon to become president of ACPO. Here was another chief police officer whose role could have allowed him to take a national lead – but, of course, he had no legal teeth or national remit. So, for now I decided to bulldoze myself into the role of national lead on terrorism. Ken would rib me that I was taking too much of a 'lone-shark' approach and told me I should be more patient. He was probably right but I was doing it for the right reasons.

The very next day the problems we'd so clearly identified with the lack of national leadership on counter-terrorism came back to haunt us with a vengeance. On 21 July 2005 there were four more attempted suicide bombings in London and we found ourselves carrying out the biggest ever terrorist manhunt, alongside the 7 July investigation.

Twenty-four hours after that, the Kratos rules of engagement for firearms officers were put to the test and failed. Police killed an innocent man in a train carriage full of commuters. The ensuing furore threatened to overshadow the events of 7 and 21 July and undermined the Met to such an extent that it would take many years to recover.

3. The 7 July Investigation

NEVER IN MY CAREER HAVE I KNOWN SUCH RESOURCES OR SUCH determination directed towards a criminal investigation: the one devoted to 7 July 2005 dwarfed anything – even those at the height of the IRA campaigns. I want to take you through that extraordinary investigation into the 7 July attacks and explain how we were able painstakingly to piece together the extraordinary and complex jigsaw that revealed who was behind them, and why they did it.

Within forty-eight hours of the bombs being detonated we had despatched a team north to supplement our work in London. It was already becoming clear that the indiscriminate atrocities of 7 July, which killed so many on that dull, showery July morning, had been planned and perpetrated from an unassuming suburb in Leeds. Over the coming weeks and months our investigations led us to realize that the bombers had indeed been inspired by, and had learnt their deadly skills from, Al Qaeda groups in the borderlands of Pakistan and Afghanistan.

Early on 9 July we were still focused on the UK. We put the Met police helicopter in the air, bound for Leeds. Detective Superintendent Dick Gething and Commander

John McDowall, both veterans of the Anti-Terrorist Branch, led the charge. They boarded at Battersea heliport and headed for West Yorkshire following the line of the M1. I chuckled when I heard how the helicopter had navigated its way up north: I'd assumed sophisticated sat-nav would do the job. In truth, though, nothing can surpass the human eye trained on the motorway as the best way of getting to your destination. Backup troops, in the form of other anti-terrorist detectives, made their way up by car. From then on, for two years, we maintained a presence in Leeds, linked to the Gold nerve centre of the investigation at Scotland Yard by daily video conference.

Gething and McDowall had been part of the main Gold command team that had been set up immediately after the attacks and sent to Hendon in North London. You'll remember we'd decided to put Gold there initially for fear that Scotland Yard could be next on the list if the attacks continued, but soon decided they were too far away from the central scenes of crime; the main command centre returned to its traditional home at Met headquarters in St James's.

Dick Gething was one of several senior investigating officers working on the attacks. His job was to act as a bridge between investigators at the scenes and the Gold command team. Every couple of hours the latter expected him to update them on what investigators at the bomb scenes and elsewhere had unearthed. But, like me in my dealings with COBRA, he was having problems with the team in Hendon and soon came to dread those briefings, not because they didn't get on but because a lot of the time he had nothing to say: in those early hours after the explosions there was little firm evidence to pass on. Worse, on day one, as Dick watched the night team in Hendon come in and replace almost everyone there, it dawned on him that no one had been earmarked to relieve him so he was stuck for the duration. Hardly was he back at the Yard, once Gold had returned there and he might have expected some respite, before he was sent up north.

The Leeds connection emerged fast. At 22.19 on 7 July, just over thirteen hours after the first attacks, the family of Hasib Hussain from Leeds phoned the emergency hotline, amid thousands of calls, to report him missing. At 23.40 cash and membership cards belonging to one Mohammad Sidique Khan and a Mr S. Tanweer were found at Aldgate. Detectives and police staff with expertise in tracing people began work on these – and other names that had emerged – trying to find addresses and family, checking mobile-phone and financial records. They were soon pointing to the West Yorkshire city.

Just over twenty-four hours later, at 23.59 on 8 July, another credit card belonging to Khan was found at the Edgware Road bombsite. The discovery sent a frisson round the investigation room – it was too much of a coincidence: the same person with possessions at two of the scenes? Why? What was more, we could tell by the way a blast affects those injured that the cards were close to the heart of the explosions. We began to ask whether Khan and Tanweer could have planted the devices and blown themselves up. Were we dealing with the first suicide attacks inside the UK?

On 9 July forensics teams painstakingly searching for evidence in the intense heat hundreds of feet below ground found more of Khan's possessions – he and Tanweer were fast becoming suspects. But we had to be cautious. As the terrible job of identifying the dead and monitoring the injured continued, we had to ensure we made no mistakes. We had to be clear about who the innocent victims were and who among the dead might have been the bombers. Clearly our priority was to deal sensitively and respectfully with the innocent commuters so tragically killed and injured in this appalling act of carnage, then separately and with speed to hunt for their murderers.

As our suspicions were raised as to the identity of the killers, we passed what information we discovered to MI5. Analysts there were combing through previous records, searching for clues as to who the bombers might be. Nothing had warned them that any attacks were imminent. As the day wore on, though, I took a call from MI5. They had been sifting through intelligence received in past months to check whether there might have been clues they'd missed and suddenly Sidique Khan's name was lighting up red. What a jolt that must have given the analyst who made the discovery.

When he checked the grainy pictures on the cards we'd found he realized that not only had MI5 come across Khan before but their undercover agents had photographed him as part of a surveillance operation. He had been filmed fraternizing with a group MI5 officers were watching as they hatched plans to plant a traditional fertilizer-based bomb at a club or shopping centre in London. Khan was with them but did not discuss the plot with them so had not been regarded as a threat. So, when the police had moved in to arrest the group he had been left alone. The job of identifying the people on the fringes of those plotters, including Khan, had been put on the back burner because MI5 were so stretched with other investigations.

Now, though, it was clear that Khan had passed beneath their radar. Ridiculously, the fact he had been covertly filmed by MI5 would not be made public for another two years although we and the media knew it. The surveillance pictures were a key element of the court case against the fertilizer plotters: if the jury in their case was told that one of the 7/7 bombers knew the suspects in the dock, it might prejudice the trial so it had to be kept secret until the case ended in 2007.

Two years on from the 7/7 attacks we, with MI5, had to defend why it appeared that we had let a potential terrorist slip through our hands. I don't accept that we did. The operation that Khan had appeared in was no different from many others in which the main focus was towards named targets even though others who were not known inevitably cropped up on the surveillance material. As with Khan, the unknown are routinely added to the list of 'nominals', and when the resources become available, research into them is conducted. There is a very fine balance between putting effort into the original operation and diverting resources away from it towards new people who enter the frame.

Unfortunately we will never have enough officers to cover every eventuality fully. Choices have to be made. A judgement is passed on each suspect as to risk and priority of either investigating or not. Khan was ostensibly an unknown when he entered that surveillance operation. It is easy in hindsight to say that efforts should have been directed towards learning more about him but that would have been at the cost of the original operation. And even if we had checked him out then, there is no certainty we would have continued to watch him up to the 7/7 attacks or learnt enough to avert the events. I believe we should stop wondering whether somehow we could have done so.

At this point in the investigation we all had to take a step back. Mohammad Sidique Khan was not an uncommon name among British Muslims of Pakistani origin: was it coincidence or was he really one of the 7/7 terrorists? And if he was, was he or was he not a *suicide* bomber? The men with whom he'd been covertly filmed in 2004 had not been planning to take their own lives but to kill and maim others by planting a bomb and detonating it once they had left the scene. The 7 July attacks had all the hallmarks of suicide bombs. I saw straight away that if Khan turned out to have been one of those terrorists there would be trouble because he'd been on a surveillance tape. But it was not something we in the police or MI5 could spend time worrying about that July.

Now our forensics teams made an in-depth assessment of the dynamics of the blast. In particular they studied the positioning of the bodies and the nature of the victims' injuries. It was easier to do this at the scene of the bus bomb than in the confined spaces of the Underground where the blast dynamics were more complex. It became clear very quickly that the device had probably been at the feet of one particular person who'd been killed in the bus blast, which drove us towards the working assumption that these had been suicide bombings.

Although the attacks may have been Al Qaeda-inspired, we conducted a text-book reactive murder investigation in which there would be no fast track to the final answer, just painstaking detective and forensic work, albeit on an unprecedented scale since we were dealing with mass murder. Yes, we had access to the very latest technology, but every lead still had to be logged, prioritized and followed through, every witness statement followed up. We were not working from intelligence but from evidence we collected at the scenes of crimes – the four bombsites. The investigation was led by the Anti-Terrorism Branch. MI5 worked in parallel, taking the evidence and looking for more intelligence on it that would lead us to the bombers or any accomplices who might still be alive – but this was largely responsive rather than a driving factor in our inquiries. Later they would also take what we found out from this inquiry and start horizon scanning – checking other plots that might be in the making.

MI5 were talking to us and to Special Branch in West Yorkshire, although they would later be criticized for allegedly not passing on the 2004 surveillance information about Khan to Special Branch, who might then have been able to identify and assess him.

We named the 7/7 investigation 'Operation Theseus', which excited the press: they started psychoanalysing it for hidden meaning. There was none. Hurricanes are named from an alphabetical list, and our investigations from a random selection that someone dreams up; Theseus was next in line.

The West Yorkshire force did not have a separate counter-terrorism unit but it did have a strong Special Branch, with a reputation for running a tight, efficient ship. There was the potential for conflict here but those we dealt with at West Yorkshire Police did not appear to have the reservations some other forces had about working with the Met. By the time our teams reached Leeds they'd made space for them and their equipment alongside their own officers so that they could work together. This was no mean feat: within a week we'd sent thirty to forty detectives to Leeds. Our Anti-Terrorist Branch had its own computer server to maintain security and secrecy, which had to be set up. We also had access to parts of the Police National Computer and we had set up the HOLMES software system – the Home Office Large Major Enquiry System, the norm now for big in-vestigations. It helped prevent duplication and meant everyone involved, including our colleagues in West Yorkshire, could access and cross-reference all but the most sensitive information to ensure no suspect slipped through the net.

HOLMES had been created in the wake of the Yorkshire Ripper investigation, which had generated tons of paper from which the senior investigating officer had had to develop lines of inquiry. Inevitably this had become a bureaucratic nightmare – some critics argue that the Ripper could have been caught earlier if the police had had a clear picture; instead they were overwhelmed. It had prompted the move from a paper-based to a computer system – namely HOLMES. Now we were back in Leeds – the backyard of the Yorkshire Ripper murders – for yet another landmark investigation that dwarfed anything that had gone before.

We put in place a tight command structure, which also helped avoid duplication. I was overall head, taking a strategic overview. Peter Clarke was in operational control, running the investigation from day to day, with Commander John McDowall as his number two; he was despatched to set up the West Yorkshire leg. Then came Detective Chief Superintendent Tim White, who co-ordinated the various seats of the investigation. He had a senior investigating officer, with responsibility for each crime scene and each arm of the investigation, reporting to him. Each SIO had a tight-knit team of investigators. Tim ensured that as new information emerged it was passed on as necessary for follow-up. We also had officers working alongside MI5 at their headquarters.

It was now two days after the attacks – a Saturday, but that was irrelevant to anyone involved. As our teams headed for Yorkshire, Peter Clarke and I discussed how best to ensure the operation up there ran smoothly. Peter was already pretty convinced Sidique Khan and Tanweer were two of the bombers, and he was now homing in on Hasib

Hussain, who also came from West Yorkshire. We both knew Colin Cramphorn, who was chief constable of the West Yorkshire force and a former deputy chief constable of the Royal Ulster Constabulary, who had considerable experience of dealing with terrorism. He and Peter went back years as they had started their careers together.

This proved a real advantage when they divided up the work on the ground. They decided that our teams would concentrate on the investigation, while Colin's would lead on community reassurance. He had dealt with the Bradford riots near Leeds four years earlier and understood how vital that role was. He did not want reprisals against Muslims, and he hoped to keep the large Muslim community in his area onside and calm. People would be shocked and confused when they discovered the terrorists came not from London but from their own city. They, too, would be touched directly by the London explosions.

One of the first joint operations was to organize a CCTV grab in Leeds – we needed to piece together the movements of the three suspects – and along every possible route from there to London: somewhere along the road the bombers would have been filmed. Now the investigation really took off. By Sunday, 10 July we had established that Hussain had travelled to London with Khan and Tanweer. We asked all service stations on key routes south to hand over any tapes and mapped their every move.

We discovered that Hussain had been using a flat at 18 Alexandra Grove in Leeds. It wasn't his normal home. He had rented it from an Egyptian chemistry student and we began to track that man down too. We discussed with West Yorkshire Police how we'd deal with the relatives of the men we were increasingly convinced were the bombers. Hussain's family, for example, would be grieving because we'd confirmed he was dead, but they had also to come to terms with the fact that he had been a terrorist who had planted a bomb that had killed and maimed: he had been a mass murderer. We worked together to remove the families from their homes to secure houses where they would not be found either by those seeking recrimination or by the press. We took them to different parts of the UK where they were not known – in effect giving them witness protection – as they would be vital witnesses in the inquiry. A bomber's wife told us she'd thought her husband was having an affair because his behaviour had changed and he was often away. The questioning of these witnesses had about it a dimension I had not experienced before. A bereaved relative requires a different kind of support from a witness, but both contrast starkly when that person may also feature as a co-offender who helped mount the attacks.

The nearest I had come to it was as deputy in command of a rape investigation. I accompanied the investigating officer to meet a community leader to ask for his support in collecting information from local people. His son was sitting in the room. Later the young man turned out to have been the rapist and was convicted. A slip of the tongue on our part might have given him information that could have helped him elude detection and ruined the case.

Meanwhile, as part of the 7/7 investigation a search of port and airport records showed that three men from West Yorkshire had left the UK shortly after the attacks on a flight to Canada – they were sent back and on 9 July we arrested them as they touched down. We and the Canadians had to divert resources into checking them out, but it proved to be one of many false trails. We also had a massive international search under way – our colleagues in police forces and intelligence agencies abroad were looking for any intelligence that pointed to accomplices abroad. The press were reporting that a mastermind behind the bombs had fled the country just before the explosions – another rumour that wasn't founded on any lead we were following.

We were getting to the point when we needed to search the homes and workplaces of the suspected bombers and decided it should be done simultaneously at all locations and without warning where possible. We did not want to alert accomplices and there was still one vital missing link: the name of the fourth bomber. The raids required massive resources: people to secure the buildings, armed backup and forensics teams. We also had to interview the men's families about their contacts, lifestyles and behaviour, and we needed their documents, mobile-phone and bank records.

The temptation is to rush into searches but as long as there is no risk to life that's not necessary. It's far better to take time in the planning and to carry out the work with painstaking and thorough care, ensuring every single item touched or removed is documented and accounted for, and that no clue is missed. By late on 11 July I was informed the search strategies were in place ready for us to move in on the homes of Khan, Tanweer and Hussain, the Alexandra Grove flat and other places. The bombers had lived with their families: we made a risk assessment and decided it was highly unlikely that they had left any dangerous explosives in their homes. The Alexandra Grove flat was a different matter. No suspect had appeared to live there so why were they using it? We were ultra-cautious. If we'd been in London we'd have sent in our own explosives officers first. Outside London the military did this job so we called in army bomb-disposal experts.

I had spent five days dealing with COBRA and briefing ministers. The next day, I thought, could be critical for the investigation. Suzanna, Peter and I gathered in my office at Scotland Yard on the evening of 11 July. We decided Suzanna would attend the COBRA meetings on 12 July, leaving me free for other meetings and to keep across developments in London and Leeds. I did not want to be out of contact or away from base.

By the time I got to work at 7 a.m. the raids, which had begun at dawn, were well under way. I ran through the diary with Suzanna: I had to chair a number of meetings to brief senior officers in the Met and from around the country so that they were all well prepared for any repercussions from the raids. We also knew there was the chance we would find information that could lead us anywhere in the country or abroad, and that we might be making arrests. The media were already getting wind of the house searches but they had not yet arrived outside all the addresses. If the raids had taken place in London you can bet some neighbour would have filmed and emailed the footage to the BBC or Sky – but this was happening in Leeds. Perhaps the communities we were targeting, which were mainly of Asian origin, felt under siege and did not want to publicize the unprecedented police activity on their normally quiet streets. It gave our teams a little longer to carry on with their work before a huge media presence was trying to film their every move. I phoned our press office and suggested they might put out an alert asking the press not to film or photograph the faces of our under-cover officers – I knew it wouldn't entirely eliminate the possibility but it was something.

Our raids on the homes of the three suspects threw up a mass of documentation that took many months to analyse, but by the end of the day, from talking to their families and friends and from the tickets, receipts and documents we found, we had the basics. Mohammad Sidique Khan, aged thirty, was the oldest of the three suspects. He'd been born and brought up in West Yorkshire and studied at Leeds Metropolitan University. He worked as a teaching assistant at a local primary school – the press would soon unearth video footage of him doing this, though in late 2004 he took extensive sick leave and resigned at the same time as his employers dismissed him. In 2001 he had married, and in 2003, as he appeared to become increasingly radicalized, he had taken his wife to Saudi Arabia on the annual Hajj pilgrimage, which is so important in the Muslim calendar. Also, in July 2003, he had gone to Pakistan. In June 2005 he had been on a white-water rafting trip in North Wales with Tanweer.

More sinister, Khan and the other two had travelled to London exactly a week before the bombings. We discovered this after ordering a further CCTV grab of the same places we had taken the footage from for 7 July but this time we asked for earlier tapes. To our astonishment we found the bombers on the same route. We had little doubt that this earlier trip had been a recce – a trial run for the devastating events a week later.

Twenty-two-year-old Shehzad Tanweer had also been born in West Yorkshire and studied at Leeds Metropolitan University. He was academically bright and very good at cricket and athletics. He lived with his parents and worked in his family's fish-and-chip shop. In 2002 he became more extreme in his observance of his religion, and in 2003 he developed a strong friendship with Khan. In April that year the two went on a camping trip, and over the Christmas holiday period of 2004/5 our police and intelligence colleagues in Pakistan established that he and Khan had been there together. In 2004 Tanweer had been cautioned for disorderly behaviour. He, too, had gone white-water rafting and on the recce in the week before the explosions.

Hasib Hussain was the youngest of the cell. He was eighteen, born in West Yorkshire, lived with his parents and was doing business studies at college. In 2002 he had done the Hajj with his family and had become increasingly religious afterwards. West Yorkshire Police checks revealed that he was cautioned in 2004 for shoplifting.

You cannot begin to imagine the number of new leads these searches threw up. We found out how the men had made the explosive devices, who had inspired them and how they had financed the bombings. We found signs that they had begun buying materials that could have been used for bomb-making in March 2005. Shop receipts showed unusual buying habits – we sent officers to the shops and seized CCTV from the streets outside. More receipts confirmed which service station they'd stopped at on the way from London and the route they had taken. But who was the elusive fourth bomber?

Our most extraordinary find that morning was at 18 Alexandra Grove, a modern ground-floor flat in a two-storey block in the north of the city next to the Leeds Grand Mosque. It is an area where a lot of students live in rented accommodation but one where the bombers would not have been recognized – it was some way from their homes. Our teams went in with caution. Eye witnesses had told us that people came and went all the time – but no one appeared to live there. By now we'd identified the Egyptian who'd been subletting the flat to the bombers for the past two months. He had gone back to his home country – highly suspicious, we thought, and asked our colleagues in Cairo to track him down and arrest him, which they did. Weeks later he would be released – he had had nothing to do with the plot but had simply leased the flat to the bombers.

Once the door to the flat had been forced, the first in was an army explosives ordnance officer, with our forensics manager who would ensure that this was maintained as a scene of crime and no evidence was destroyed in the search. What they found inside was astonishing: pots and tubs of a thick bubbling yellow liquid – a cast-iron bath was full of it. There was an almost unbearable rotting stench. The explosives experts knew immediately that we were dealing with something weird, volatile and unstable. Was it acid? Would it burn you if you touched it? They had no idea. Carefully, they took some small samples, sealed them securely into the back of a van and sent them for analysis. No one was prepared to move the bath or its contents out because they feared it might explode.

We'd found the bomb factory. It was very frustrating for our forensics teams, who wanted to go in and start combing the place. Instead for weeks we kept it sealed and guarded night and day while the chemical analysis continued and scientists tried to find a way of making the bubbling liquid safe. I think it took them six weeks. The bath dominated my COBRA briefings. Understandably no one quite grasped why it was taking so long to establish what was in it. I got the impression Charles Clarke and his ministers had real difficulty getting their heads round it. At 11 a.m. on 13 July I was back at COBRA briefing him and he kept saying, 'What is the stuff in the bath?' I said we had no idea but the experts were telling us not to go near it. 'Well, they must know something about what it is. What does it look like? Why can't they move it?' he kept asking, not just then but at meetings for weeks to come.

'Well, you know what it's like when you have a cheese and tomato pizza,' I said, 'all bubbling on the top when you take it out of the oven? Well, they say it's like that.' I must have said it a dozen times.

When our teams eventually got into the flat and were able to send off DNA samples from inside they quickly linked Khan, Tanweer and Hussain to the place, though forensic analysis of every tiny thing they found there, every fingerprint and speck of dust, would take nearly two years. We had scientists in and outside the police working on the liquid for months, establishing how the bombs were made. We traced the plastic storage containers the devices were constructed in through a public appeal. We found out when the men had bought them, and the ingredients they used, from receipts and till rolls.

We discovered that Tanweer and the fourth suicide bomber had bought face masks from shops and over the Internet, and had worn shower caps, but their hair was still bleached from the substance – they blamed chlorine in the local swimming-pool when their families asked why this had happened. We believe they must have carried out at least one trial explosion though we have no idea when or where.

But back to 12 July. It was a massive day for the investigation. As the searches took place the public, who were so important as our eyes and ears, came up with another breakthrough. Someone remembered seeing four people putting on rucksacks in the car park at Luton station. They'd apparently had two vehicles although one was now gone. The other was still in the car park, a Nissan Micra. A quick check with the licensing authorities showed it was a hire car, and a check with the owners revealed that Tanweer had rented it.

We had to treat the vehicle with extreme caution. We sealed off the area and the bomb-disposal teams moved in. They carried out nine controlled explosions. Inside the car we found containers of the bubbling liquid we'd found earlier that morning in the bomb factory in Leeds. Later our scientists would establish the bombs left behind were smaller than the devices used for the actual explosions – perhaps they had been backup in case things went wrong. This was the car the three from Leeds had travelled down in, early on 7 July. We also found what looked like the components of more bombs. Had there been a fifth bomber? We were on the threshold of a major development.

Meanwhile it didn't take long to trace the other car that had been seen in the Luton car park with the bombers. CCTV helped us locate it – a Fiat Brava. It had been towed away because it didn't have a valid parking ticket. The discovery of this car in a compound nearby was another huge breakthrough. It would lead us at last to the identity of the fourth suicide bomber. We found a handgun inside the car, which was registered to one Jermaine Lindsay – he must surely have been the fourth bomber. The Police National Computer showed the vehicle had been used in an unsolved burglary eight weeks before. We established that Lindsay had met up with the three from Leeds in the early hours of 7 July at Luton station.

By lunchtime on 12 July the CCTV teams had pulled out two very big trumps. First they'd found the initial CCTV images of the bombers on the day of the attacks and as I described earlier Peter Clarke had rushed down to my office to show me – it was a great result. One of our analysts had recognized Tanweer from his driving licence. The shot showed all four perpetrators. We needed to get them out to the press as soon as possible. It was chilling to think that an hour or so after these images were taken all four had been dead, having carried out the worst act of terrorism on British soil in modern times.

We took a CCTV grab of the route they must have taken

through King's Cross station from the Luton train to the various Underground lines they were heading for, and found images. Then came the second CCTV coup – pictures of the four at Luton station a little earlier on 7 July. There also appeared to be a fifth man just behind them. Had he been with them? We needed to find him fast. Was he a fifth bomber? That would fit with the extra bombs in the car at Luton, or maybe he was supposed to clear up the flat in Leeds. It didn't take long to pick him out – he passed through Luton station most days and was a regular commuter who, that day, had happened to be walking just behind the bombers. We eliminated him.

All these developments in the investigation left me with a lot of juggling to do. Throughout the day I chaired meetings with officers from around the country and internally. I invited representatives from the different foreign embassies in London to be briefed so that we kept communication and information-sharing at the top of our priorities. Community issues were paramount and we arranged meetings with leaders. Once again we went through all the security options to ensure we had every base covered. We updated police forces on what intelligence we had and the findings coming from Leeds. We warned of a further upsurge in phone calls from the public as soon as we put out the CCTV pictures of the bombers. We discussed the possibility of further attacks.

The next day, six days after the attacks, Jermaine Lindsay's wife reported him missing on the hotline. We sent a search team to their home in Aylesbury. That he was missing, combined with his link to the car, DNA and a wife who could confirm he was the fourth man in the CCTV photographs meant we could now prove his identity. We learnt he was nineteen, not of Pakistani origin like the rest but Jamaican-born; he had come to the UK with his mother when he was a year old. He lived in Huddersfield in Yorkshire, and when he was fifteen he and his mother had converted to Islam, when he had adopted the name Jamal. He was often in trouble at school – on one occasion for handing out leaflets supporting Al Qaeda. He had taught himself Arabic so that he could read the Koran in its original language.

When he was sixteen his mother had gone to live with a man in the USA, leaving him behind; those who knew him saw this as traumatic for him. He left school, continued to live in their home in Huddersfield, married a British convert to Islam, whom he'd met on the Internet, and moved with her to Aylesbury. In 2004 when their first child was born he was eighteen and had a job as a carpet fitter. But he had also met Mohammad Sidique Khan, and in May 2005 he arranged the rental of the Alexandra Grove flat. CCTV pictures showed that he, too, had been involved in the recce trip to London the week before the explosions.

By now the names of the four terrorists were seeping out in the press but so far we had not confirmed them officially. Over the next few days DNA test results came through, placing the men close to the seat of the explosions at each site and we went public with the names. On 14 July, a week after the explosions, we found more of Khan's belongings at a third scene, that of the bus bomb in Tavistock Square. It was as if he'd handed the others a calling card to leave behind. Had he, the oldest, been the cell's ringleader?

The day after we'd moved in to search Lindsay's house, a couple of bank investigators turned up because his cheques were bouncing. We also asked our financial team to work out how the attacks had been financed. Had someone bankrolled them? Our people pored over the four men's bank statements, tracing back every transaction, and produced a set of accounts that put the cost of the bombings at just under eight thousand pounds, including the trips to Pakistan, car hire, rent on the flat, the bomb-making equipment and travel within the UK. It seemed Khan had funded most of it. He had multiple bank accounts, each with a small amount of cash on deposit, credit cards and a personal loan of ten thousand pounds. Towards the end he had defaulted on his loan payments and was overdrawn. Lindsay had paid for various items with the cheques that had bounced. We paled: if it was so cheap to mount such an atrocity, how long would it be before another cell did the same thing? At that point we knew nothing of the imminent 21/7 attacks.

As the investigation continued, we learnt that the bombings had been planned with military precision. Khan was the cell leader and Tanweer his lieutenant, but all four were involved in the planning. They were disciplined, covering their tracks cleverly, never doing anything that made them stand out as potential terrorists. When they disappeared for a long period they explained it away as a visit to friends or to the gym. And the bonding sessions – camping and white-water rafting – appeared innocuous enough.

All of them bordered on extreme in the practice of their religion: they were fervent in their Islamic beliefs and keen readers of the Koran. Three of the four were born in the Beeston area of Leeds, a relatively poor area, and appear to have developed a sense of injustice. Criminal psychologists studied what we could learn of their lifestyle and behaviour to try to understand what motivated them. I helped the government and civil servants compile a 'Narrative' of the events of 7 July, which concluded they were driven by 'fierce antagonism to perceived injustices by the West against Muslims and a desire for martyrdom'. A suicide video made by Khan, which appeared on the Arab television station Al

Jazeera on 1 September 2005, supported this view – he talked of the importance of martyrdom and then said, 'Your democratically elected governments continuously perpetuate atrocities against my people all over the world. And your support of them makes you directly responsible, just as I am directly responsible for protecting and avenging my Muslim brothers and sisters. Until you stop the bombing, gassing, imprisonment and torture of my people we will not stop this fight. We are at war and I am a soldier.'

The sight of him spouting that in a broad Yorkshire accent was abhorrent not just to us but to most Muslims. We and MI5 studied every tiny aspect of that film, trying to deduce where it was made and who had videoed it. But there were few clues. We think it was probably made on his last trip to Pakistan – hence it was not released in the UK – but we can't be sure.

Now we asked our Special Branch liaison officers in the British embassy in Pakistan to help fill the gaps concerning the trips the bombers made to Pakistan. What did they do? Whom did they meet? We worked closely with Pakistani intelligence too. It was clear that the men did visit family and friends on those trips but there were holes in their itineraries.

We found that in July 2003 Khan made a trip to a remote part of Pakistan close to the Afghan border. He went again from November 2004 to February 2005 with Tanweer. On their return we can assume they began to plan and prepare the 7 July bombs.

We also discovered through their phone and email records that the group was in touch with people in Pakistan between April and July 2005. But whoever they were communicating with covered their tracks well – we couldn't identify them, and that is frustrating. Tanweer's suicide video also appeared on Al Jazeera on 6 July 2006, more or less the first anniversary of the attacks. In his threatening, sinister message, he said, 'What you have witnessed now is only the beginning of a string of attacks that will continue to become stronger until you pull your forces out of Afghanistan and Iraq. And until you stop your financial and military support to America and Israel.'

I am proud that since then we have prevented many of those attacks taking place with our robust investigative work.

There were many aspects to the 7/7 investigation but it was the CCTV pictures that gave us the strongest insight into what had happened on the day. CCTV uses video cameras to transmit a signal to a specific or 'closed' set of monitors. Nowadays it's not just the authorities – police, government and the military – that use CCTV to fight crime: private enterprises, like banks, car parks, shops and, increasingly, individuals, use it to protect their businesses and homes. The arrival of digital video recorders means hours, even years, of recording can be stored live.

In the early days CCTV had a bumpy ride – it had the ring of George Orwell's Big Brother and clashed with our traditional principles of civil liberties. There was also an operational argument against using it: some feared it would displace crime to locations where there was no CCTV. It's fascinating now, thirty-odd years later, that displacement is much less of an issue. Civil-liberties groups still complain, but the wider public seems to accept that there are cameras everywhere. CCTV is part of everyday life and people expect it to be a principal means of investigation – they'd be angry if we didn't use it to catch criminals. When it comes to catching the terrorist, I'd say that, alongside financial, mobile-phone and computer data, CCTV is our primary means of investigation and a key source for creating lines of inquiry. Despite its presence – sometimes obvious, sometimes discreetly hidden – it's amazing how often criminals are oblivious to it. It's the same with mobile phones: everyone knows their data can be tracked, that they can be eavesdropped on, but they are still indiscreet – it's as if it's in the criminal psyche to court risk. Of course, the 7/7 bombers didn't care about leaving clues and being filmed because they planned to be dead after the event.

The footage we seized meant we were able to piece together the final hours of the four bombers.

At 3.58 a.m. on 7 July 2005, in Leeds, a CCTV camera in Hyde Park Road, close to Alexandra Grove, captures a light blue Nissan car with three men inside it – already, we assume, stuffed with explosives.

At 4.54 a.m., CCTV cameras at Woodall service station on the M1 capture the car again as it stops for petrol. Tanweer is dressed in a white T-shirt and tracksuit bottoms, dark jacket and a baseball cap; he looks straight into the camera as he pays.

At 5.07 a.m., a red Fiat Brava arrives at Luton station. Jermaine Lindsay is captured on CCTV several times as he gets out, paces up and down, checks the timetable in the station and moves the car.

At 6.49 a.m., ninety minutes after the arrival of the first car, the Micra arrives at Luton station and pulls up next to the red car. The CCTV pictures show the four men looking into the boots, and putting on heavy rucksacks.

At 7.15 a.m., CCTV cameras show the four clearly in one frame going into the station.

At 7.21 a.m., they're filmed again, heading towards the Thameslink platform for trains to King's Cross in London. Tanweer has changed into dark trousers. Analysts say that the way he's carrying his rucksack suggests he finds it heavy.

We estimate each rucksack contained between two and five kilograms of explosives.

At 7.40 a.m., the train pulls out from Luton station with the four men on board.

At 8.26 a.m., the four are captured on CCTV leaving the Thameslink platform and heading for the Underground. Eye witnesses claim they saw the men hugging each other at about 8.30 a.m. seemingly happy and even 'euphoric'. Khan takes a westbound Circle Line train, Tanweer an eastbound Circle Line train, while Lindsay and Hussain head for the Piccadilly Line.

At 8.50 a.m., Liverpool Street station, CCTV pictures show the train leaving the platform. Forensic evidence suggests that Tanweer is in the second carriage from the front, his rucksack on the floor beside him. He detonates a bomb between Liverpool Street and Aldgate stations, killing seven people and himself; 171 are injured. CCTV shows smoke billowing back onto the Liverpool Street platform and there is chaos.

At 8.50 a.m., Edgware Road station, Mohammad Sidique Khan is also in the second carriage from the front, as forensic evidence suggests, the rucksack on the floor beside him. He fiddles with it and detonates the bomb, killing six people and himself; 163 are injured.

At 8.50 a.m., Jermaine Lindsay is travelling from King's Cross to Russell Square. Forensic evidence suggests he is in the front carriage, standing; there are 127 people jammed into it. Lindsay detonates his bomb killing twenty-six people, including himself; 340 are injured.

At 8.55 a.m., Hasib Hussain is forced upstairs as King's Cross station is closed. His mobile-phone records show he tries to contact the other three bombers. We can only assume he must have realized the others had gone through with detonating their bombs yet CCTV pictures show him relaxed. He's filmed, primed bomb on his back, going into Boots and then WH Smith, rubbing shoulders with people buying their daily newspaper. He is clearly visible buying a battery. We will never know why he did this. We can only speculate that he was unable to reach his intended target underground. Perhaps he had tried and failed to detonate his bomb – hence the need for a new battery.

At 9.06 a.m., CCTV shows Hussain going into McDonald's.

At 9.19 a.m., he takes a 91 bus to Euston, where he changes on to a 30. Forensic evidence puts him on the top deck, the rucksack on the floor beside him. The bus is crowded.

At 9.47 a.m., in Tavistock Square, the bomb on the number 30 bus explodes, killing thirteen people, plus Hussain; 110 are injured.

The investigation into the events of 7 July, Operation Theseus, was unprecedented in scale. We seized and examined in minute detail more than six thousand hours of CCTV footage. We seized, decoded and examined 142 computers and hundreds of pieces of hard- and software with them. We logged 33,554 exhibits, or pieces of evidence, and took 15,798 statements.

So far, we have followed up 19,614 leads and arrested eighteen people suspected of helping with or having prior knowledge of the attacks. And to this day the investigation remains open.

4. Politics and Terrorism: the Games People Play

ON THE MORNING OF 7 JULY, AS THE AWFUL SCALE OF THE suicide attacks unfolded, I remembered the prophetic words of my predecessor. Sir David Veness was a legend in New Scotland Yard, a man with real presence. He was a combination of elder statesman and ageing film star, with silver hair flopping over dark eyebrows and a fixed expression of determination. He was enthusiastic, compassionate, humorous and honourable, and had a strong sense of public duty, all qualities that seemed to shine through his eyes, however serious he was. He seemed never to take a holiday. We knew he was on annual leave when he turned up for work in a sports jacket rather than a pin-striped suit.

He was completely dedicated to his profession. After ten years of managing some of the most difficult investigations in Specialist Operations he had earned a reputation as a steady, reliable hand and his word was respected. He went on to become under-secretary general at the United Nations, in charge of security. For me, succeeding him meant taking on the job of a lifetime. So, when we shook hands at the conclusion of his handover to me on my first day his comment had sent a chill down my spine: 'Andy, it's not if but when,' he said, then leant forward and added, 'We're at war, you know.' Was this delivered for effect or bravado? Given his reputation and professionalism, that was unlikely. But I remember thinking optimistically that he was a wise old owl being cautious. Now I know how short of the mark my perception of the situation was. In the next three years I was to oversee investigations into some of the worst atrocities ever to hit the UK in peacetime, when the police, the intelligence services, government and other partner agencies were stretched to their operational limit and the political and media pressures were unprecedented.

As I took up my new post, before I became aware of the weight of the challenge I faced, I had one essential piece of housekeeping to attend to. Sir David Veness's office was notorious. Anyone opening the door was met by a sea of documents – papers and files, newspapers and books – in piles taking up nearly all of the available space, some of them three feet high. You couldn't get near the cluttered desk – and I don't remember a computer though there may have been one. There was usually an easel with a world map on it strewn with strategically placed coloured pins. Negotiating the maze to draw the curtains wasn't an option. In the middle of this sat Sir David, immaculately dressed, occasionally smoking a cigar, overseeing the security of the nation. In this apparent chaos I know he saw absolute order. He knew where everything was. This was his ivory tower, where he did his brilliant strategic thinking.

I prefer a completely different atmosphere in which to operate. I am fanatically tidy: I like papers to be filed away, I store little, and I like space. So when I took over, I asked for the office to be refurbished. I didn't think that was unreasonable, given it hadn't been touched for twenty years. When colleagues visited after I was ensconced, they couldn't believe it was the same room. It had been decorated light and dark blue. The blinds on the windows were modern and you could see how enormous the window actually was. The office looked four times bigger. Instead of papers and books there were walls and pictures, a clear, neat desk and a comfortable area with blue leather chairs, a sofa, and a large dark wood conference table. It may have lacked the character it had had in David Veness's time, but it suited me and this was where I held all my meetings, formal and informal.

You entered it via an outer office, where my staff sat, and at the far end there was a small dressing room, which was also modernized – the old bath now replaced with a shower. I kept suits there and would pitch up on a Monday morning with fifteen newly ironed shirts. The press gave me stick for the cost of all this, but it was necessary, given the huge number of high-level meetings that would be held in that room as the terrorist threat unfolded.

It was in those rooms, where I would spend much of the next three years, that I learnt not just about terrorism but about the politics of policing and, in particular, the internal politics of the Met. At times I would come to wonder who the real enemy was. It should have been straightforward – Al Qaeda or any of its splinter groups – but a host of political battles was intertwined with the complexities of the heightened terrorist threat. In any senior position you expect political squabbling but I was taken aback by its intensity and how high the stakes were. The notion of trading politics with national security and public safety seems pretty warped. There were rows over planned new anti-terrorism laws, epitomized in debates over whether terrorist suspects should be held for ninety or forty-two days, or whether we should maintain what was then the status quo, which was fourteen days. There were Whitehall battles over who was in charge, as major decision-making had to take into account the egos and career aspirations of colleagues and civil servants. Add to the mix the shenanigans of the Met and Association of Chief Police Officers, and you had an amazing cocktail of politics.

On top of all this, there was the ever intrusive yet necessary media circus. It was never clear who the ring-master was. There were certainly plenty of monkeys and clowns, but it was abundantly apparent the media could never lose since every player on the field exploited them, including me.

Not only would my time in the job lead me through a life-time's worth of policing a new terrorist threat, bringing me into the most intimate contact with world leaders and counter-terrorism chiefs, but it would also to teach me that, however united we appeared to be in our determination to fight terrorism, there were large areas in which things were simply not working – where personalities and personal agendas were actually obstructing the counter-terrorism offensive and where the structures in place were failing. I had taken on the job with a mission to modernize, but within months that had become a side issue compared with the affairs of global significance that I was forced to confront and advise on almost daily. Time and time again, what I per-ceived as trivialities would get in the way of my efforts at tracking terrorists. I was to leave the job with a strong sense of frustration – and the determination to fight to change those structures that I believe allow personal or political interests to undermine the wider security of the UK.

I make these observations with the intention of trying to expose in a constructive way how ridiculous the games can be in the context of fighting terror. I wholeheartedly endorse our democratic society, and to argue for a complete truce on political manoeuvring would be as ridiculous as the actual games. However, the personal agendas, egos (mine included) and career aspirations that so often influence behaviour and decision-making could be curbed.

When I joined the Met I had already known Sir Ian Blair for several years before he became commissioner. I had worked alongside him when he was deputy to the former commissioner, Lord Stevens, who had flair and vision, and was a strong leader and a good role model. Stevens created an environment in which it was tough to work for him yet he remained approachable – though you wouldn't want to screw things up. Behind him he needed a deputy who dealt with the detail and Ian Blair did that brilliantly. He made things happen: he delivered a new IT system across the Met, for example, and continued the work of Lord Condon and Lord Stevens in driving forward an anti-corruption agenda. He was inclusive, too. I worked then as Ian Blair's deputy and considered him a friend. When I became chief constable of Norfolk we kept in regular, though not frequent, contact, and when he became commissioner I was delighted when he brought me on to his Management Board as assistant commissioner in charge of Specialist Operations.

Over the months, though, I believe he started to become distant and aloof. I often discussed my perception of him with my colleagues on the board and learnt that others shared it. It was so frustrating: we all wanted him to succeed, but I believe that he became so isolated from some in his top team that he did not seem to notice he risked making dangerous enemies within his own top tier. I think this was a key factor when he resigned in 2008 because the Mayor of London didn't fully support him: I did not see many senior colleagues stepping in to take his side. The departure of Ian Blair was dreadfully sad not only for him and his family but also for the Met. He earned the label in the press of being gaffe-prone, and by the end I believe he didn't have a hope in hell of shaking it off. It must have rocked his confidence although he didn't show it. Ultimately, the politics he appeared to enjoy at times finally turned against him.

At the beginning of 2005, though, Ian had pulled together a new management team that was oozing potential. We were full of optimism and enthusiasm. We had a new commissioner in Ian, chairing the Management Board, as well as a new deputy in Paul Stephenson, brought down from the north after his success in driving the Lancashire force to the top of the police league tables, and three other new people were promoted to the board as assistant commissioners: Alan Brown, in charge of Service Improvement – within months he found himself in charge of the Gold incident room after the 7 July bomb attacks; Steve House, who was given Central Operations, controlling pan-London services like firearms, public order, dogs and the Vice Squad. I was heading up Specialist Operations, covering counter-terrorism, Special Branch, diplomatic and royal protection, security at Heathrow and City airports and protection of the Palace of Westminster. Continuity from the old regime came with Tarique Ghaffur, who was head of the Specialist Crimes Directorate, and Tim Godwin, who ran Territorial Policing. We were the five assistant commissioners of the Metropolitan Police. I remember thinking, Ian's doing a fantastic job here – there's a real blend of expertise and experience. We believed we had five years together ahead of us. No one had ugly aspirations to go anywhere else – Ian was the boss, and we were not expecting further promotion. It felt really good. So why did things go so badly wrong?

I had my first Management Board meeting when I was still closing up shop in Norfolk. Once he'd taken the helm at the

Met, Ian had been very good with Her Majesty's Inspectorate of Constabulary and had agreed to second a senior Met officer to take control temporarily as chief constable up there so I could get away while they were still looking for a replacement. He needed me quickly as Sir David Veness had already accepted his new post at the United Nations. Ian had been commissioner for just a few weeks. He arranged a two-day planning and bonding session for the assistant commissioners at a conference centre in one of the outer London boroughs.

That conference should have rung alarm bells. It was here I learnt for the first time of his plans to remove Suzanna Becks from her post as deputy at Specialist Operations, once I took over as boss – and I had my first contretemps with him in my bid to keep her. We also discovered that there'd been another weekend away with a group of his lower-ranking allies when they'd planned forward strategies. I found that a bit strange. Where did it sit with what we were doing? Were we a second tier of activity? If you have a top team you trust, how do you proceed when there's already been a conference with the number twos? Quite frankly, at the time no one really gave it a second thought: we were pretty buoyed up and ready to put our stamp on the Met.

It was clear to Suzanna Becks and Peter Clarke, and indeed to my predecessor David Veness, that Specialist Operations needed an overhaul. The structures weren't right. The separation between the Anti-Terrorist Branch and Special Branch was not good: it was difficult to keep on top of budgets and there was a lot of duplication and waste. Within a year the two sections would merge to form Counter-Terrorism Command. Ian Blair supported the change. He had got the top job as commissioner in part on a streamlining ticket and had planned to cut and redistribute budgets substantially, enabling him to put more bobbies on the beat in the London boroughs. To achieve this he commissioned a Service Review to help him restructure and modernize the Met.

At first we all thought the level of savings he intended was manageable, and the journey we embarked on to reconstruct the Met was in my view absolutely right. Five months down the line it became clear the objective was still correct but that some of the detail would have to go. The reason? As so often happens, unforeseen circumstances got in the way. The 7 July bomb attacks forced us into the biggest criminal investigation in British history and any control of budget was lost.

But instead of being flexible in the light of this momentous change in the threat, most of us tended to soldier on as far as possible to meet the level of savings pledged. Now, though, we were trying to work miracles. The July bomb attacks turned out to be just the start: later, we had a copycat set of bomb attacks to deal with, we killed an innocent man, mistaking him for a suicide bomber, and we carried out a mass raid on a house looking for bombs and got nothing but trouble. Despite all of this, we were still ploughing on with budget cuts and restructuring without fully grasping that things around us were crumbling. It was a crazy situation. I still wonder why I didn't say, 'What are we doing?'

It would have been sensible for Ian to renegotiate the objective with the chairman of the Metropolitan Police Authority (MPA) and tell him publicly that the cuts were no longer achievable, that the MPA would have to adjust its expectations big-time. Instead we on the Management Board found ourselves pitted against one another as we clashed and fought for diminishing funds. It wasn't personalities or people that were the problem. It was the budget. We should have been putting all our energies into terrorism but my colleagues and I wasted precious hours in surreal debates because the Met had committed to cuts it couldn't cope with. Attacks on the scale of 7 July had not been adequately factored in. In the circumstances, trying to stick to the original plan presented too tall an order and inevitably created strife within the team.

Not only had Ian agreed cutbacks, but he'd also committed to increasing the number of bobbies on the beat. He had pledged that every one of the 624 wards in London would get a dedicated team of one sergeant, two police constables and three community-support officers – subject to finance. He also promised he would do his best not to keep pulling them away for other duties when there were big events like football matches or demonstrations. They would be available for their beat 24/7.

So, we had to reduce budgets *and* put more police on the streets. But who or what would pay for them? Assistant Commissioner Alan Brown, in charge of the Service Review, had identified some £150 million worth of savings that could be made, including selling off old police stations – but it still wasn't enough if you took into account the other things we all wanted. We raised our concerns in no uncertain terms.

Critically, in my view, the tensions irrevocably damaged the relationship between the commissioner and the UK's highest-ranking Muslim officer, Assistant Commissioner Tarique Ghaffur, just when we needed him to help bring onside moderate Muslims, as we tried to root out the terrorists who chose to hide in their communities. Tarique had already restructured his Specialist Crime Directorate. His department had reduced the murder rate in London. He was now focusing on gang culture, and gun and knife crime.

He came to the Management Board with a plan to sustain the reduction in the murder rate and to reduce gun and knife crime and gang activity. But it was going to cost money so he was blocked. Despite his previous successes he was told he couldn't have the funding for his new offensive. Not only that, but he would instead have to make serious cutbacks: in particular, he was to lose some two hundred officers, including detectives, from his murder squad. Tarique was deeply unhappy and took a very strong stance against Ian. He explained that his team was reducing the murder rate and beginning to understand gang culture, and warned that if they cut down on manpower in these areas the murder rate might increase again and gangs spiral out of control.

Sir Ian argued that he was putting extra police into the community as part of his ward scheme, which might help to nip gang culture in the bud. This included moving some detectives who were centrally based into the boroughs. Tarique said extra bobbies and detectives on the beat wouldn't stop the gangs – that would happen much more gradually. Would detectives be more effective at the centre investigating after the crime or in the boroughs trying to prevent it? I wholeheartedly supported the commissioner's ward-based policing plan – in combating terrorism you need community-based intelligence. Some questioned the merit of putting all our eggs in one basket when terrorism was not the only show in town and knife and gang culture were emerging problems. But in the end, having listened to the arguments, I was persuaded that the gamble was worthwhile. I sided with the redistribution of officers on to the beat at the cost of the Specialist Crimes Directorate. With hindsight I regret it. I should have bowed to Tarique's specialist knowledge. After all, I would have been fed up if colleagues had ignored my advice.

So, Tarique lost the argument and thus a chunk of his staff. What was more, he was soon moved from the job he loved in Specialist Crimes to lead another directorate. He was told this was part of the restructuring process. Within three years murders were up again while knife and gun crime and gang warfare were indeed – in the view of many in the press and the public – out of control. In my view the relationship between Tarique and the commissioner would never really recover. No one is suggesting the Met restructure alone increased knife and gun crime and gang culture. There are lots of reasons why crime gets worse – other factors could include social deprivation, poverty, alcohol and drugs, for example.

I could be accused of being too smart after the event, but much has been learnt from that period: first, you need to keep your top team on board, balance your resources to cope with all eventualities, and be ready to change direction completely if something, such as the 7 July attacks, strikes out of the blue. When something happens that hadn't been anticipated and has a profound effect on the initial planning regime, you must say, 'Whoa! Time out. Let's reassess.' I believe we all thought we did that, but if that's true the record shows we didn't do it very well. We muttered our concern in the corridors but, despite our macho airs and graces, some of us didn't have the strength of character to say no.

To me, this was inextricably linked to a further distraction from the job of tracking terrorists: the increasing politicization of policing. On Sir Ian Blair's watch, as he pushed through his ward-based policing plan, politicians became increasingly involved in deciding how London was policed. It began with our relationship with the MPA.

Half of the MPA's members are independent, and half are

elected politicians who represent political parties and are members of the London Assembly, led by the Mayor of London. MPA meetings are usually open. When issues like the Met budget, police numbers and general security are discussed anyone can go along, including the public and the media. Sir Ian would go to these meetings accompanied by whichever of us was relevant to the subject under discussion – it was a bit like the chief executive of a private company going to the monthly board meeting. Initially only a small number of journalists would turn up. Unless there was something significant on the agenda most would rely on information supplied by the Press Association. But over time Sir Ian made a series of controversial comments publicly. For example, when talking to the MPA about 'institutional racism' in the media coverage of crimes, he said that 'almost nobody' could understand why the murders of two ten-year-old schoolgirls in Soham became 'the biggest story in Britain'. After this comment was published and read out of context, the national press were turning up at the meetings too – no doubt in case he made another gaffe. Sometimes there'd be a bank of cameras with the satellite channel Sky TV even broadcasting live at times. The scrutiny was intense. What used to be a discursive style at the MPA meetings became more inquisitorial: Sir Ian would be questioned forensically on every new initiative. Were some of those on the MPA playing to the power of the cameras in the knowledge that their constituents or political masters might be watching? And did this affect how they treated us?

It may sound facetious but I felt going to the MPA must have been like being in the *Big Brother* house. As on the TV show, the MPA included an amazing mix of backgrounds, personalities and beliefs. There were cameras and people spying on you from every direction and you knew your every movement might be analysed by psychotherapists – the *Daily Mail* once did an analysis of why Sir Ian pushed back his cuticles until they apparently seemed raw. Every now and then the MPA would vote someone out – well, publicly reprimand them. And every Friday morning Sir Ian visited the MPA equivalent of the *Big Brother* 'Diary Room' when he had his weekly chat in the MPA chairman's office.

The trouble was that the politicization didn't stop with the politicians. Throughout his time at the top Sir Ian was criticized – rightly or not – either for getting too close to the politicians or for being too political himself. Personally, I think he may have been too soft on them, allowing them to get too involved in policing. All chief constables, for example, are accountable to a Police Authority but as they are operationally autonomous it should be inconceivable for them to seek Police Authority approval to move a chief superintendent, say, from one district to another. When I was chief constable of Norfolk I'd privately look for the Police Authority chairman's endorsement when I employed officers. It was politic and courteous to do so. But it was never *his* decision – it was mine. I remember once in Norfolk eyebrows were raised when I moved an entire top team out of a division because they were ignoring continual efforts to help them improve performance. My chairman told me it was a radical move and warned that I might face a backlash within the force – but he never said, 'You can't do that.'

At the Met, though, a different system was agreed when it came to senior appointments. The MPA had set up a 'Sounding Board', a committee that considered and commented on these appointments. I felt it was incredibly powerful. If that committee didn't want someone it could effectively, in my view, put its foot down. Equally I can think of at least one instance when it wanted someone in a specific job and got its way. Some members of the Sounding Board were also members of the London Assembly, local politicians, elected by the people of London, mostly along party political lines. Can you truly dissociate all Sounding Board members from political gain? Surely some must have considered the effects of their decisions on the people who voted them into power. I see this as another sign of the politicization of the police.

The MPA were right to demand that Sir Ian Blair should reduce the Met's budget and stick to his pledges – but I believe that he should perhaps also have done more to resist their interference and maintained complete autonomy over relevant appointments, advising the MPA of whom he'd chosen, but not involving them so much.

Ironically political intervention eventually brought Sir Ian down. When the Conservative MP Boris Johnson became Mayor of London, he made clear to the commissioner that he did not have full confidence in him and Sir Ian felt obliged to resign. The move put a strain on the mayor's relations with the home secretary but that didn't stop Johnson assuming the chairmanship of the MPA, asserting himself on the policing of London.

The replacement of Sir Ian with Sir Paul Stephenson in 2009 brought a real opportunity for the Met's strained relationship with the MPA to be resolved. At Sir Paul's press conference on his appointment he stated he was not going to be a celebrity in the role. It was a signal that he planned a new, less public style, with a strong focus on basic policing. However, if I was in Sir Paul's position, with Boris Johnson at the helm of the MPA, I wouldn't be so certain that politics would not once again rear its ugly head. In fact it's already beginning to happen.

When I was in the Met, Sir Ian's problems went wider than

the MPA. The difference between operational policing and the political side, it seemed, was becoming blurred. As early as April 2005, just before the general election, he publicly stated his support for Labour's controversial plan to introduce identity cards. He then allowed political posters to adorn police protection vehicles used by politicians in the election campaign. The argument that the cars were armoured and therefore ministers had no other option but to use them was, in my view, shallow.

By now the world and their aunt were flexing their muscles over terrorism. The motives ranged from political positioning to a genuine need to oversee and manage the agenda. Groups vied for primacy over counter-terrorist activity. The chairman of the MPA chaired a counter-terrorism committee made up of people from the Police Authorities in London, Birmingham, Manchester and Leeds. The Police Authorities' chief executives also joined in to give welcome scrutiny to our work. But the Home Office stepped into the fray, too, almost as if in competition with the Police Authorities, setting up a Capabilities Board chaired by a high-ranking civil servant. They saw their task as checking what we were doing in building greater capability and argued, quite plausibly, that as they were providing the funding they should scrutinize the spend. They even put two members from the Police Authority counter-terrorism committee on the board. The arrangement was crazy: we had two forums sitting to discuss the same issues but neither felt able to merge into one group. Each wanted its own identity – but for what? I think it could only have been for political advantage and posturing. I rest my case.

Imagine if I'd sat down with a high-ranking and presumably highly intelligent Home Office official and said to them, 'I've got an idea. Why don't we set up two bodies to meet and discuss nigh on the same things? We'll even put a handful of the same people on both.' I reckon the official would have said, 'You're mad – that is neither cost-effective nor efficient.' It seems blindingly obvious to me that we should have had one committee made up of all the stakeholders.

There is hope, though. A couple of years later when Dr John Reid had taken over as home secretary and declared parts of the Home Office 'not fit for purpose', Charles Farr was brought in to create a new Office for Security and Counter-Terrorism. He is a senior Whitehall official with a distinguished career behind him in security and this was an important job. He was appointed director general, and took under his wing parts of the Cabinet Office and the Home Office. His department focuses on policy, deciding how the government should go about dealing with terrorism. It also decides how government spending on counter-terrorism should be allocated – how much the police, the Home Office, MI5 and so on should get. It drafted a new strategy, named Contest, which has four planks: Prevent, Pursue, Protect and Prepare. 'Prevent' involves work by the government on why people become radicalized, then turn into extremists and terrorists. 'Pursue' aims to disrupt terrorist networks and bring perpetrators to justice. 'Protect' advises on how the country can defend itself against physical and electronic attack. 'Prepare' is about making proper assessments of the risk from terrorism and putting in place adequate measures to respond in the event of attack.

From my perspective this was a great idea. Here was a guy with no history of working in a mainstream government department, a fresh pair of eyes. He had bundles of energy and commanded immense respect across all agencies. To date, he has already turned round the malaise and lack of action and diminished the turf wars between departments. He has more to do, but he has created an office with the potential to bring much-needed changes across government.

But in 2005 government duplication was only the half of it. We were and are little better in the police service. The Met commissioner has principal responsibility for terrorism yet each chief constable is operationally independent (a recurring theme of this book). Some chiefs don't like the Met. They view it as arrogant and detached from the difficulties of policing a county force. Equally, the Met views county forces as detached from the difficulties of policing the capital and can be dismissive too. Both have their own committees. I have been in both camps and believe they are both right. The commissioner was strident in establishing his leadership role but in practice each independent chief constable could, and at times did, thwart him. Two bodies to discuss the same thing, one to look at operational issues the other for overview, would be fine – but within the police we had four committees. Peter Clarke and I had to navigate all this. Officially I was the national police lead to Counter-Terrorism, and he was national co-ordinator for Counter-Terrorism Investigations, though, of course, we had no legal sway over chief constables.

How did I cope back in 2005? I took a pragmatic view. I turned up at all the different committees where required. When I went to the Capabilities Board, the Home Office committee, I had to make them think everything in UK policing terms was meeting their Home Office agenda. A couple of days later I'd be at the joint Police Authority meeting where they thought they were in charge even though the Home Office paid. Then I would have conversations to keep the chief constables and their Police Authority chief executives happy – I'd listen to what they said so that I could consider how we might develop operationally, only to go back to the Yard and be told by the commissioner, 'I don't care – this is what I want.' Add into the equation British Transport and Ministry of Defence Police, intelligence agencies, and even Her Majesty's Inspectorate of Constabulary and you can see that the politics was a nightmare. The whole system was open to turf wars and clashes of ego. With no clear command structure, when things went wrong and there were serious implications – guess what happened. Not many of that lot could be seen for the dust.

And trouble did lie ahead, for reasons of Politics – with a capital P. In the early days after the 7 July attacks, Sir Ian Blair and I worked closely together in trying to fill the gaps in police powers in the face of the heightened terrorist threat. But in the scramble to acquire new powers we found ourselves caught up in a highly damaging political controversy. Under Sir Ian's leadership the Met became increasingly embroiled in political affairs at national level. Whether consciously or not, he led the way in this, but I became enmeshed too. In retrospect I think we should have been more detached from Parliament and government. Instead, as we sought new powers to tackle the new terrorist threat to the UK, we were caught up in a politically charged argument for which we would later face fierce criticism. Sir Ian, in particular, was said by the press to have become too close to his political master and namesake, Tony Blair. It was a charge he was never really able to shake off and undermined the independence he needed to show as Britain's highest-ranking police officer. To this day I know our hearts were in the right place but in the blinkered race to gain new powers we did not anticipate the side effects of our actions.

It started less than a month after the bombings. The prime

minister, Tony Blair, was still pained that London had been targeted by terrorists to such devastating effect. He took the bit between his teeth, determined to do everything possible to stop it happening again. He asked us at the Met if we were happy with the powers we had to tackle terrorism. Before the attacks we'd been mulling over ideas with a view to a new Terrorism Bill. Part of my job was to take a long-term, strategic view of what we needed to fight the new threat and to deal with no-warning suicide bombs aimed at killing the maximum number of innocent civilians. We had moved on from the IRA threat and I firmly believed we needed extra, legally binding powers.

What we didn't expect was the speed at which the prime minister now decided to push this through. He held a press conference announcing, 'The rules of the game have changed.' He said he would be introducing strong measures to tackle extreme, violent radicalism and to stop terrorists in their tracks. He gave Whitehall twelve weeks to draft new laws with our help. Then he took a well-earned holiday and left us to work out the detail.

I have never known legislation to emerge at such speed. Perhaps we should have taken notice of warnings in the press that this might be a knee-jerk political reaction and could backfire. Even the Home Office appeared to have been caught on the hop. Nevertheless, I was keen to help colleagues in the Home Office frame a new Terrorism Bill and that was what we did. Encouraging and helping terrorists became an offence, as did publishing terrorist material and distributing it on the Internet and elsewhere. There were new powers to make it easier to stop and search. We made terrorist training an offence. And since our intelligence was suggesting Al Qaeda had the will, though not the wherewithal, to carry out radioactive attacks, we added as a precautionary measure offences relating to radioactive materials and nuclear sites.

There was one further clause, which, to our surprise, caused most controversy. If we arrested someone on suspicion of terrorism we could only hold them for up to fourteen days before we had to charge or release them. We wanted longer. I believed then, and I still do, that ninety days is needed. Let me explain why. We were increasingly finding sophisticated IT equipment and encoded computers: it might take far longer than fourteen days to decipher them. On 6 October 2005 I sent the home secretary, Charles Clarke, a letter formally outlining my position on this.

Soon after that the Home Office drafted a bill proposing holding terrorist suspects longer before charging them. The heads of all the intelligence agencies, MI5, MI6 and GCHQ, and I were invited to a full cabinet meeting to discuss it. It was a daunting prospect. I remember walking through the door at Number 10, Downing Street. We signed in with the commissionaire, and handed over our mobile phones. Everyone who visits is surprised by how deceptively small the prime minister's residence looks from outside and how massive it is inside. We were led down the main corridor towards the Cabinet Room. To my right I always glanced at Churchill's armchair, which is displayed as a museum piece, and as we arrived at the door I looked up at the great staircase lined with portraits of past prime ministers.

Inside the room, with its long table, I remember I sat next to Gordon Brown, then chancellor of the exchequer. Tony Blair walked in last – as ever stern, charismatic, slightly intimidating, though of average height, his navy suit and shiny black shoes without a fleck to blemish them. We were now, we believed, at the endgame of the process. The prime minister went through the proposed Bill meticulously. It was a serious, focused meeting, spiced with a sense of urgency. We knew from intelligence reports that other plots were in the planning and wanted the new powers in place ahead of the game. We did not want to be introducing them hastily in the middle of a new crisis.

When we got to the idea of holding suspects for ninety days without charge I outlined the case – as I would many times in the days to come. I believed the increase would give us a vital tool in hunting terrorists. In the modern age if we arrested a terrorist suspect we had endless hours of CCTV to review, phone records and mounting numbers of computer hard drives to examine, with extremely difficult crime scenes to comb through scientifically, all of which took time. Modern technology required an up-to-date response and we could no longer guarantee our ability to cover all eventualities within a fourteen-day period. Our biggest fear? If suspects walked free, the safety of the UK might be jeopardized.

I explained that I believed ninety days was the right length of time – we had not plucked it out of the ether as a bartering tool. We had seized five thousand hard drives and eighty thousand videotapes after the 7 July bombings. In one case the material on a computer hard-drive disk we'd found would be sixty thousand feet long if it had been printed out. Equally, the increasingly international nature of terrorist networks posed a greater language difficulty, and a greater need to gather evidence from abroad. Terrorist networks were increasingly complicated. I explained that it had taken us almost eight weeks to analyse material we had found that was linked to the July bombs in a rubbish dump in Dewsbury, near Leeds. Imagine the pressure we would be under if we had to do searches like those within fourteen days of arresting a suspected terrorist. It would not always be possible.

The prime minister and his colleagues raised the thorny issue of civil liberties. He in particular knew his plans would not please civil-rights groups. How could we justify holding somebody in a police cell for three months if they turned out to be innocent? Would that not be an infringement of their human right to freedom and privacy? I admitted there might be times when this would happen but we also had to consider the right of ordinary people to be safe. The two things had to be balanced. We'd taken legal advice, and lawyers involved in drafting the Terrorism Bill had put in place safeguards to try to prevent innocent people being held too long. Anti-terrorist officers would not be allowed to subject a suspect pointlessly to endless questioning on the same topics. The suspect would only be re-interviewed when new evidence came up. Police would apply to a senior high-court judge every seven days to extend custody, probably at closed hearings so the judge could evaluate the reasons for the suspect's continued detention without charge. Given the problems and the complexities of the new reality, we felt the ninety-day rule would be justified. I told the prime minister emphatically that this was not a bargaining tool: we were set on ninety days. He asked if I would go on the record and public with this and I said yes.

Tony Blair was convinced. The cabinet approved the Bill and details were published. That's when things started to go wrong. As the time for the crucial vote on the ninety days drew near, it was clear that opposition MPs would not vote for the ninety days – and many of the government's own MPs were against it too. The commissioner briefed political correspondents at a lunch, rather than the crime correspondents we would normally brief. Then, just days before the vote, I was persuaded to go into the House of Commons to brief wavering Labour MPs. It was a clumsy intervention and, with hindsight, I believe it was a step too far. MPs from the main opposition parties, the Liberal Democrats and the Conservatives, accused the ruling Labour Party of using the police to further its political agenda. The implication was that, at best, we'd shown weakness in allowing ourselves to be led into the fray but at worst we were under the government's thumb.

I went to the meeting at Charles Clarke's request. I don't think even he realized just how big a deal my going there would be. It was two days before the vote and he said it would be really helpful, that several MPs would benefit from a little more explanation, so would I mind popping along to the House at 6 p.m. one evening? It was dark by the time I reached St Stephen's Entrance and passed through the customary security. I made my way through the ornate yellow stone corridors to one of the committee rooms. To my shock I was not confronted with a handful of MPs but fifty. Charles Clarke chaired the meeting, his Home Office minister Hazel Blears at his side. I did not see there was anything wrong with meeting MPs – we do it all the time. In hindsight, it seems an incredible admission, I had missed the facts that it was so close to the vote, that we were dealing only with the government and, of course, that we were firmly planted on their side. I was available to all politicians and I waited to be invited to meet any of them. David Davis, the Conservative home-affairs spokesman, who was opposed to ninety days, did not receive a briefing from me. But it played out in the press as interventionist lobbying, when our intention had been to explain why we needed the new power.

I was not given an easy ride at the meeting. The MPs in that room were sceptical. They wanted clarification and explanation. Coming out afterwards I began to realize we were potentially crossing the line between independent policing and politics. And it wasn't just me. Now, ironically, I'm questioning the politicization of policing yet on that occasion I had a big hand in the process – an own goal, I know, but if we don't admit these things, how can we stop it happening again? I'd like to think the senior politicians involved also understand now that we went too far. I don't think they wanted to hang us out to dry. But it clearly didn't work.

Sir Ian Blair had encouraged and supported me in meeting the MPs. But I suspect conversations were going on at a higher level to which I was not party. I wonder if he was positioning the idea of ninety days in much bigger forums. If the commissioner speaks in favour of something like this it's highly influential. It created a ripple effect across the country – chief constables in the regions took real note and many threw their weight behind him publicly. ACPO wrote to the chief constables asking them to make sure their local MPs understood the arguments. Was this, some asked, yet another sign of political pressure on the police to intervene?

By now the wave of opposition to the Bill had grown to gargantuan proportions. The other elements included in the draft were largely ignored. The *Independent* newspaper ran a leader article describing the ninety-day idea as 'dangerous, draconian, illiberal and unnecessary'. The Tories called for an inquiry into how the police were used to lobby MPs. Ministers jumped to our support, proclaiming we had simply given expert advice.

The debate over ninety days was fierce, but so was the criticism afterwards of the role we'd played in it. We'd been drawn into it and got our fingers badly burnt. I'm the first to hold up my hands and admit I didn't think through the consequences of what we did. In retrospect I was naïve, but I did it with the best of intentions.

Despite our intervention the government lost the vote. We failed to convince MPs of the need for it, although they did vote through a compromise, increasing our power to hold terrorist suspects from fourteen to twenty-eight days. But this fell far short of the ninety we wanted and the process left the credibility of the police dented on two fronts: our operational advice that ninety days was needed had not been accepted, which showed a lack of trust by MPs in our judgement, and we'd been allied with the political process, which undermined our independence.

The vote took place on Wednesday, 9 November 2005. It was Tony Blair's first defeat since he had come to power in 1997 – and it was the worst defeat for any government in more than twenty-five years.

Very soon afterwards I was due to attend another cabinet meeting and the irony of this was not lost on me as I gathered in the outer lobby of the Cabinet Room with the heads of the intelligence agencies. We were due to give a routine update on the terrorist situation. When we'd finished there was an adjournment for coffee before ministers returned without us to continue with other business. To say I was nervous was an understatement. I imagined Tony Blair would be uneasy after the humiliating defeat of the night before. But during that break he wandered over to me, gave me a firm handshake, and characteristically shrugged his shoulders. He tilted his head to one side, gave a wry smile and remarked that it had been a pretty tough night, but the result was what democracy is all about. That was what this country stands for. He might have been smarting but he certainly didn't show it. To my surprise, he was not angry and I realized I had not got the measure of the man until that moment.

When the government revisited the plan three years later in 2008 I was astonished. People hadn't bought into the idea in 2005 when the 7 July attacks were so fresh in our minds so why would they go for it now? There had been no new pressing incident to catapult people to a change of heart. At Scotland Yard, far from trying to rejuvenate the issue, we were still bruised from the political mauling we'd received first time round – why would we want to go there again?

The plan put to Parliament in 2008 didn't go as far as ninety days but suggested increasing twenty-eight to forty-two days. It was flawed: it had too many built-in hurdles. They were aimed at pacifying opponents but would have made it unworkable. For example, the home secretary would have to obtain independent legal advice to prove there was a sufficiently grave threat to justify the use of the forty-two-day power. If that hurdle was cleared, he or she would have to make a written statement to Parliament and then, having been shown the independent legal advice, Parliament had seven days in which either to approve or dismiss the application.

This would have amounted to political interference in an operational matter – and might have marked the end of the operational independence of the police. How confident could we be that every politician could put to one side their political views when judging the necessity of extended detention in any particular case? I am not convinced that they could.

But it didn't end there: if Parliament approved longer detention, a judge would then be required to agree the grounds before issuing a warrant for further detention. Let's get real. This system was far too convoluted to work and would bring with it a massive amount of paperwork for the police and the Crown Prosecution Service, who would have the unenviable task of preparing the documents to service the monster.

If it had passed, it would have given MPs a greater say on whether a suspect could be held for that long, and police officers would have been form-filling and preparing a politically acceptable case to persuade MPs and ministers to invoke the forty-two days instead of concentrating on their terrorist investigations to save lives and solve crime. The plan was to make MPs responsible for gauging the gravity of the threat, with the extension only being available in 'exceptional circumstances'. But that had never been our argument for extending detention limits: extra time was needed because the investigations were so complex and on such an immense scale.

By now Gordon Brown was prime minister and the case for extension had not changed. The government had expressed no interest in revisiting the issue, and the police were not asking them to. Brown and the new home secretary, Jacqui Smith, had been in office for a matter of weeks when the Bill was introduced in Parliament – were they looking to make their mark on the security front? I'm still wondering whether the issue was being used as a political football. When I saw it had narrowly won support in the House of Commons I was moved to re-enter the debate just before the House of Lords voted on it. I had left the police and was therefore better placed to offer my opinion. I was convinced the redrafting was a complete mess and felt it imperative that I should expose this – which I did in an article published in *The Times* on 6 October 2008.

My concerns were not those of the shadow home secretary, David Davis, who resigned over the forty-two-day detention plan to 'take a stand' on the 'relentless erosion' and 'slow strangulation of fundamental British freedoms' by the government. He argued that it was a fundamental right not to be held for long periods without charge or trial. He forced a by-election on the issue and was promptly re-elected as Tory MP for Howden and Haltemprice, but did not win back his post in the shadow cabinet. I have every respect for an individual who does what he feels he must do but, in my view, David Davis overreacted. The debate certainly pushed the boundaries of civil liberties, but that was always intended to be balanced against the terrible threat to public safety. A lot of people will have forgotten why David Davis resigned and, sadly, he's now in a less prominent position and thus less likely to be able to influence the debate as much. My anxieties were over the detail of the proposal, not civil liberties.

I remain convinced that the police will soon need the power to hold suspects for longer and that the government should legislate for that power now rather than in the middle of an emergency – just as I argued back in 2005. I have been involved in nearly every terrorist investigation since then and we have already had to use the full twenty-eight days – though not often. But the 2008 Bill was not the answer – not least because it was detached from the operational needs of the police. Instead it was about politics and wouldn't work.

There was one other festering distraction from the job of hunting terrorists. It took precious time from the critical work of investigations and would eventually be a factor in my decision to retire. It was over the issue of expenses and performance management. We were told that the Met was old-fashioned and needed to modernize. In Specialist Operations I decided I would publish my expenses every month openly on the Internet, and encouraged those around me to do the same. I was given a corporate credit card. Ignorance is not of course a defence in law. But I admit I didn't know that Met rules prevented me using it to pay for meals inside the M25 – when you had a meal nearer base you had to pay on your own card and claim it back. To this day I don't know why. On top of that I had the right to pay my staff small bonuses. Instead of giving a cash sum I sometimes took them out for a meal – if ever there were staff who gave their time and dedication to protecting the UK it was those in Specialist Operations dealing with terrorism. My senior team didn't have a holiday in 2005 and I didn't think it unreasonable to boost morale and make people feel valued by taking them for a meal at a fixed-price-menu restaurant.

When I took all my top team out at Christmas 2005, the total lunchtime bill for twelve people was in the region of thirty-five pounds a head. I thought it was worth every penny. The MPA audit department took a different view: they began a secret investigation to find out if I had abused Met funds. If I'd labelled the meal a business Away Day and claimed it differently I'd have been fine. On my return from holiday in August 2007 I discovered that the head of Audit was scrutinizing my use of the budget. No one had bothered to write or speak to me about it. The commissioner refused to get involved and then, to my outrage, it was leaked to the newspapers. Was someone trying to discredit me or my department? I felt obliged to take my eye off the day job, find out what was going on and start defending my position in readiness for an internal inquiry.

I was delighted when it was decided to appoint an independent chief constable to conduct the investigation as my confidence in internal systems had been undermined. Eventually he concluded that all my expenses were reasonable and justified but I had claimed them in the wrong way thereby contravening the rules. I agree with that finding. He concluded that the rules should change, allowing the type of thing I had done and nowadays it wouldn't be an issue. Yes, of course, there should be scrutiny but what a waste of everyone's time.

Over the years I learnt to cope not only with the politics of policing the state, but also with the comparatively petty internal politics of the Met. In describing what I see as the ugly side of life and the 'games people play' I am not expressing any regrets or distancing myself from that behaviour – I needed to do the politics to survive. I was privileged to work in the Met and on such an important agenda, helping to protect this country from the terrorist threat we face. I believe politics is a necessary component of a functioning organization and of government – it would be fanciful to try to argue for a truce. However, unless there is a demarcation between the healthy state of politicking and the politics I have sought to reveal in this chapter, there will always be the potential to damage and even derail a mission. One thing is for sure: on the security stage, that drive for political advantage has to stop.

5. 21/7: a Race Against Time

JUST WHEN YOU THINK THINGS ARE BEGINNING TO SETTLE, JUST when you feel life is resuming some kind of routine, just when you think your fears about another attack are unfounded, it all comes crashing down again. Nothing about this war on terror is predictable, and we had certainly not then reached a state of complacency. It was two weeks to the day after the 7 July attacks, and I still worried there might be further atrocities. But so far these had not emerged and I tried to put my concerns out of my mind – after all, we had every contingency in place if something did go wrong.

I had a long-standing appointment with my dentist back home in Essex and decided to keep it. I walked in at 10 a.m. with a huge sense of relief. The rush-hour was over and there had been no explosions in London or anywhere else. Maybe, after all, the attacks of 7 July had been a one-off. We had enough on our plate dealing with that investigation. I had just taken a call about the substance in the bathtub in that flat in Leeds, still bubbling away as our scientists tried to figure out what it was. We were in the middle of intense interviews with the families and friends of the bombers, and at a critical time in identifying all those murdered in the four explosions. Our forensics teams were still working in the intense heat below ground searching for evidence at the bomb scenes.

I'd been coming to this dental surgery for years and wasn't prepared for the change in their attitude to me: 'Hey, Andy, we keep seeing you on the telly over the bombings.' I hadn't given a thought to the implications of the TV appearances as far as my life was concerned; my only considerations had been about the impact that what I said would have on the bereaved families, the public and other terrorists.

I kept an eye on the television mounted on the wall as I waited to go in – and I remember that as the hygienist scraped and scrubbed away she joked about how I needed to be spruced up in case I had to rush back to do another press conference. The irony of her comment was lost on both of us.

I was back at Scotland Yard by 11.30 a.m. In hindsight I thank God I didn't hang about at home any longer – I would have been beside myself if I'd still been out of London and something had kicked off. Soon after I arrived my inner management team gathered in my office. We were concerned about resources – several Underground stations remained shut as forensic work continued and nearly everyone involved on the investigation was exhausted, but we had been told no further help would be available from forces elsewhere in the country. We would have to manage with the manpower we had. We had no idea that within an hour our calm would change to frantic urgency as we stretched the resources we did have to encompass what was to become the biggest manhunt in our history.

I've thought long and hard about how to reproduce the tension, the stress and the nervous excitement – for this short period life was a rollercoaster moving at high speed, with hourly twists and turns, incredible peaks and troughs of emotion. I had real trouble sleeping even though, like most others involved, I was extremely tired. The following excerpts, compiled from my diary and other records, give an idea of the pace and the developments in this extraordinary investigation.

Thursday, 21 July 2005
12.25 Another bomb scare – we've had hundreds recently. This one is near the BBC at Shepherds Bush Underground station on the Hammersmith and City Line. The station is evacuated.

12.30 The Oval Underground station on the Northern Line is evacuated. Suzanna Becks pops her head round the door and warns something might be going on – assures me she's keeping an eye on it.

12.45 Warren Street Underground station in Central London on the Victoria and Northern Lines is closed – the ambulance service is *en route*. Sky TV and the BBC start broadcasting reports of 'incidents' on the Underground – possibly 'explosions'. No sign of casualties. I have that awful feeling of *déjà vu*. I think, Not again, and feel fear in the pit of my stomach. The adrenalin starts pumping but I hold back. I know my team and others from the emergency services will be responding. I start to think about managing the work-force, jotting down who to bring in, who to divert, if we suddenly find ourselves confronted with another set of bombs.

13.20 Nearly an hour since the first explosion and the Met is buzzing. Officers who, after two weeks of living out of suitcases, had been sent home for a couple of days this morning have been asked to turn round and come back to London. The value of the pound begins to fall against other currencies as the financial markets respond to reports of bomb attacks – I shake my head and my heart sinks. This is the stark impact of a terrorist attack, already hurting the nation's economy though we still don't know how serious it is.

There is smoke at Warren Street and eye-witness reports of small explosions at each station with bubbling liquid spilling out of bags. An off-duty fire-fighter reports an odd smell at Warren Street. He's talking with our investigators – fantastic witness – saw what happened, confronted the would-be bomber who, he says, tried to detonate a device. It went off like a firework, scaring the shit out of everyone in the carriage and causing mayhem and panic. Then a bubbling liquid spilt from the man's rucksack across the floor. He argued with the guy. I'm reminded of the liquid still bubbling in the bathtub. Now the emails and calls are coming in thick and fast. I approve reallocation of resources as I watch developments unfold on the TV screen on my office wall. I am more tense than I can ever remember being. My senior colleagues confirm three explosions on Underground trains – no serious injury. I hope against hope the inevitable next call will not come.

13.30 It does – a 999 call reporting an explosion on a bus, the number 26 in Bethnal Green, East London. People on it try to bundle the bomber down. They hurt his arm but he escapes. Is this a copycat of 7/7, or part of a wider, prolonged set of attacks? We press the counter-terrorism button big-time and launch the widest manhunt we've ever known. MI5 puts every government, law-enforcement and transport organization on the highest security by confirming the official threat level to the UK has been raised again from 'Severe' to 'Critical', which means further attacks could be imminent. Transport for London invokes 'Amber Code', its plan for evacuating passengers from the Underground and suspending services.

With potential failed suicide bombers on the run, I make what some would see as a controversial call to the military. No time for being precious about who owns this investigation, we need all hands on deck. We, the police, have lead responsibility but, as with hijacks or sieges, I see there could come a tipping point when we need to hand over to the military, which could include Special Forces – the SAS. I remember it happened during the siege of a hijacked Afghan aircraft that landed at Stansted airport in 2000. We could find ourselves in a standoff today with dangerous men. My counterparts in the military put a backup response team on standby.

Downing Street calls – the prime minister is convening an urgent meeting of COBRA for 2.30. I speak with the commissioner. Sir Ian Blair says he will attend. I want to stay at Scotland Yard. The head of the Anti-Terrorist Branch, Peter Clarke, is away so I need to be hands-on.

14.00 In the USA the White House puts out a statement saying they are watching developments. We advise Tony Blair to cancel a visit he's planned to a school in East London. John McDowall, deputy head of the Anti-Terrorist Branch now tells me four bombs planted on Underground trains and a bus have only partially exploded; a bubbling liquid is seeping from the devices. The bombers have fled. The attacks have every sign of being Al Qaeda-inspired. He is concerned at reports of fumes – we need to test for dirty bombs. We send in experts to check for signs of nuclear, biological, radiological or chemical attack.

14.28 Two hours after the first explosion the TV pictures show there is a sense of panic in the crowds being evacuated that wasn't evident at the time of the 7/7 attacks. People are afraid we're witnessing a repetition – they don't know what's going on. The commissioner goes public: these are 'clearly very serious attacks'. He announces the transport system is to shut temporarily. He goes into COBRA with the prime minister and other senior intelligence and political figures. I see maps showing the extent of evacuations round the stations and we decide to widen the cordons round these areas while we check for dirty bombs. Television pictures show police trying to push back crowds in Shepherds Bush – a female detective, hair tied back, dressed in T-shirt and jeans, is speaking, holding up her warrant card, shouting for attention, appealing to the crowd for witnesses. Brave woman – is she one of ours? Somewhere nearby a bomber will surely be hiding like a cornered animal. Radio contact with those at the scene suggests he made his getaway along the track – his bomb was detonated at a spot above ground.

15.03 This is a race against time. I'm conscious every second lost is a second more for the terrorists to escape and possibly regroup to bomb again. The terrible video pictures of the awful, awful carnage inside the burnt-out carriages after the 7 July attacks flash before me – the haunted eyes of the bereaved. It must not be allowed to happen again – we must get to the bombers before they get back to us. They gave no warning: they clearly wanted to kill, maim, and blow themselves up. They will be humiliated – determined, perhaps, to try again. The risk is too high to run a covert manhunt. We must identify, trace and arrest them fast.

We need the public's eyes and ears. We appeal for photos and mobile-phone footage from the public – we didn't do this immediately after 7/7 and crucial photo evidence was sent instead to the papers and broadcasters. This time we set up a website so people can email it to us. We divert officers from other work to collect CCTV footage. We put all ports, airports and other police forces on standby.

We alert Europol and Interpol, the European and international police agencies that were created to apply unity within policing that cuts across borders and boundaries. The UK seconds officers to both agencies and for some this is a real career move. Sadly, both organizations have been dogged with criticism that they do not appear to achieve the results you would expect from such a big investment by the governments who sign up to them. I have some sympathy with this view: they can be very bureaucratic and it's often easier to bypass them and deal directly with individual forces from specific countries.

We send out every Automatic Number Plate Recognition vehicle we can find. ANPR is a really effective tool in the armoury of serious-crime prevention and detection. It operates across the UK and is a combination of fixed and mobile cameras that record every number plate which passes them. It has a computer database connected to other police databases, ensuring every link with each car that passes can be made. Retrospective analysis can be conducted to elicit who was near a crime scene at specific times, and if we want to analyse the movement of suspects around the UK, ANPR can plot their journeys by logging their number plates as they move. We may not know the bombers' cars now, but if they are escaping in a vehicle, we need to have a record of this. Once we do know their vehicle registration number, we can check back on the ANPR system and detect their movements. The ANPR computer could lead us to them.

15.22 Nearly three hours after the initial explosions, we establish no dirty bombs and no chemicals at Warren Street – thank God. We send in our forensics teams. They find the mysterious bubbling liquid. Still dressed in anti-contamination suits they secure it in bombproof containers and send it to Porton Down in Wiltshire where government scientists will examine it. One complication ruled out – but another appears: a man with a rucksack trying to get into Downing Street. We discover Tony Blair is at home. We arrest the man.

I talk to the commissioner. We agree public messages of reassurance. Sir Ian Blair says there's no sign of unconventional or chemical attack. Tony Blair calls for calm and normality.

16.20 We receive a report that one of the failed bombers may have gone injured to University College Hospital in Central London. We send armed police, who arrest two men nearby at gunpoint. The strategy is no risks: if we're suspicious of people we have to pick them up in the interests of public safety.

20.49 Over eight hours since the explosions. All those arrested so far will be released. We've established that the man arrested near Downing Street and the two near University College Hospital are not terrorists. The bombers are still at large.

I compare with 7/7. Similar targets, similar bubbling explosive mix, but it appears that this time the detonators didn't work – why? Different bomb-maker? If the two cells are linked, these failed explosions will give us huge insights into the 7/7 bombers. This has all the hallmarks of Al Qaeda. But we have to find the 21/7 bombers in case they're successful next time round. We have advantages. Already we're getting amazing CCTV of some of the devices actually being detonated and clear pictures of the bombers before and trying to escape. We have DNA, fingerprints, the bombs, and eye-witness descriptions. The men have left personal possessions with possible names on them. We have an alarmed public and we will use them to help find the bombers.

I have a scrum-down with Suzanna and John McDowall. I admit I'm nervous. We didn't see 7/7 coming – we hadn't seen this one either. What next? I report I've spoken to MI5 and they're on the job. Operationally people might feel the bombs' failure to go off would make the job of the police easier. In a way it does – but when you have dead bombers on site you know there's no huge rush. In this case we're up against it.

22.00 It feels like Groundhog Day. This morning we had five major crime scenes from the 7 July attacks (four bomb-sites and the bomb factory). Now I have to take people from these ongoing searches and put them on our four new crime scenes. Send in forensic and counter-terrorism investigators, secure the sites, search for evidence, fast-track the CCTV search, find new offices and lead the manhunt.

The surge in work exceeds any planning regime we'd envisaged. And we have a massive confidence problem. We have to help stabilize the nation. COBRA meets. Those attending are worried that this is a massive blow for the transport system – numbers using it were already down post-7/7. Who believes we're on top of things now? Scotland Yard, Whitehall, the media, the public in the UK and worldwide are in shock and disbelief, in fear and full of apprehension. We need to reassure – show we're on top of the game. I ask Suzanna to appeal again to every force to pull out the stops, to push for high-visibility policing, to warn that arrests could well take place on their patch.

Friday, 22 July
CCTV pictures and gym cards found at one of the bomb scenes have led us to an address in South London where we think one of the bombers lives. We put the block of flats under surveillance, call in firearms officers.

9.30 A man who looks like him leaves the flat. We are on tenterhooks. The man is followed – he heads for Stockwell Underground station.

10.06 He is shot dead on an Underground train by police marksmen who believe he is about to detonate a bomb. For several hours we believe he is one of the four bombers. Later we discover he's not. It's a complete nightmare – will it stop firearms officers taking defensive action when they do come across the real bombers? Now I have a ninth crime scene, an investigation into our actions and a major distraction from the manhunt for the bombers. Meanwhile the manhunt for the 21/7 bombers continues.

10.40 As I deal with the aftermath of the shooting I see on the television that the number 26 bus on which yesterday's bomb was detonated is being removed from Hackney to a secure warehouse where our teams can work in privacy.

11.00 Reports of a bomb at the massive East London mosque. We evacuate the area and send in our explosives experts. We find nothing.

12.20 Transport for London have worked round the clock to reopen the transport network. The Northern and Victoria Lines start running again.

14.00 We have clear CCTV pictures of the four bombers – separately – minutes before they tried to detonate their bombs. We need to get them out urgently. Every lost minute gives them more time to get away. But the morning's shooting needs urgent attention too. Leading Muslims accuse us of operating a shoot-to-kill policy. Of course we will shoot to kill if we believe it will save lives – but now I cannot be distracted by that philosophical debate. We must find the bombers still on the run. The world's press is gathered at the Queen Elizabeth II Conference Centre off Parliament Square – but we delay our press conference until 3.30. Intelligence is coming in thick and fast – from MI5, Special Branch, our counter-terrorism officers and members of the public. We have suspected names of the bombers from items left at the scenes and have traced them through searches of computer databases held by police, Department of Transport driving records, banks, mobile-phone and other private companies that carry out credit ratings. They have thrown up several possible addresses where the men may have lived. We get the warrants to raid them.

14.15 I receive a text confirming our teams with armed backup are beginning raids on three addresses in West London. We send in firearms units and explosives experts. They're not there.

15.35 The commissioner and I begin our press conference. Our CCTV pictures of the four bombers, showing them minutes before they tried to murder innocent commuters on the London transport network, are broadcast live around the world. I am relieved. Ian talks a little about the police shooting earlier. He also says we are facing 'the greatest operational challenge ever' against 'unknown threats'. I confirm the devices were home-made and that we have begun raids on addresses in London.

18.00 We get a possible sighting of one of the men at Snow Hill station in Birmingham and it's evacuated. We arrest another man in London. We're rounding up contacts of the suspects and people who meet their descriptions if sighted by the public. The Bomb Squad go to Birmingham but later it proves a false alarm – the man's released.

Saturday, 23 July
The manhunt brings more arrests and more raids, more bomb scares, more evacuations. Warren Street station reopens. I'm frustrated. We're working flat out but it's forty-eight hours after the attacks and the bombers are still at large – could be anywhere in the world by now. With every passing hour we learn more about them from neighbours, friends and family, from CCTV, their phone and computer records and from the public. We've had 400 calls so far. Interpol and Europol follow up sightings abroad – but nothing concrete emerges on where they are.

15.00 Since the Shepherds Bush bomb was detonated on a stretch of line above ground, we bring in massive cranes to lift the carriage out and take it away to analyse it in a private hangar, so that the station can reopen.

Incredibly a fifth bomb, discarded, still gurgling under a bush on Little Wormwood Scrubs a mile or so north of Shepherds Bush, is found by a member of the public – probably been sitting there for two days. Was there a fifth bomber who bottled it? Our experts move in, wearing protective gear, and film it. I see their footage. It's just like the others we'd seen, and as I'd described to the home secretary in COBRA. The device is like a pizza that's still bubbling when you take it out of the oven. As with the substance in the bathtub in the Leeds bomb factory, we daren't move in yet. Another major crime scene, more resources, more CCTV grabs. Where will it end?

19.30 Peter Clarke has curtailed his short break abroad and is back. I am relieved to see him – I need his steely focus, his lateral thinking.

Sunday, 24 July
Three people in custody. None of them are the bombers but may be linked. I'm distracted because families of the 7 July victims will visit those bombsites today and I am to meet them for the first time.

12.00 It's a harrowing experience, to meet the bereaved families, because I feel we let them down by allowing the bombs to get through. As a father I find it hard to imagine the depth of their grief. While I'm with them, explosives experts carry out a controlled explosion on the discarded bomb on Wormwood Scrubs. It doesn't cause a major blast. Like the others, it's in a round plastic storage container about a foot deep – the sort of thing you keep flour in.

Information comes through from our Anti-Terrorist Squad detectives who specialize in bombs and blasts, working with scientists. Looks like the explosives consisted of chapatti flour mixed with liquid hydrogen peroxide, detonated by a booster charge made of electrical items bought from the high-street chain Maplin. Shopkeeper in Green Lanes has told us he sold them the flour on 18 July. Seems only the caps of the detonators fired, causing an explosion like a firework. Main bombs didn't explode – possibly because of poor quality of hydrogen peroxide and the ratio of ingredients was wrong. I shudder to think how many people would have died if they'd got the bomb recipe right. Same recipe as 7/7 except 7/7 used black pepper and this lot used flour as base for explosives. Recipe is highly dangerous and unstable and we'd never seen anything like it before 7/7 – surely must be linked?

Monday, 25 July
Breakthrough! Combination of items left at scene, eye-witness reports and phone calls from the public, mainly from neighbours who recognized them from CCTV pictures. We've got firm names on two – looks like an African cell, Britons of Somali origin, not Pakistani like the 7/7 bombers: Muktar Said Ibrahim, also known as Muktar Mohammed Said, who, we believe, tried to blow up the 26 bus, and Yassin Hassan Omar, believed to have detonated the failed bomb on the Underground at Warren Street. We have their mobile numbers – but they've stopped using them – their phone and utility bills, car registration numbers, addresses (lived in council houses – we put these under surveillance). We're on to them. First question for members of their families who did not phone us when we issued the CCTV pictures: why not? Suspicion will, of course, be that they were harbouring them. We think we have names for the other two bombers – Hussain Osman, the Shepherds Bush

bomber, and Ramzi Mohammed who, we think, planted the bomb at the Oval.

14.50 Press conference – go public with the first two names. I'm really concerned the bombers could be regrouping. I must keep this uppermost while the team get on with the investigation. Have we got the right security in place? I believe the bombers are still in the UK – massive security at ports and airports. No intelligence suggesting they're abroad. Will they try to attack again? Suicide bombers want to lose their lives and in their view be martyrs, so there's every reason to believe they might strike again. Warn of this at a press conference.

Haven't been able to trace where the plastic containers holding the bombs were bought and need this to help track the bombers. Go public with a similar one – show it alongside the CCTV of the bombers. Soon we get shopkeepers phoning who think they sold them – send officers to check. More raids.

Call comes in from family of Muktar Said Ibrahim, who say they're shocked, haven't seen him for months and will co-operate with us. We despatch senior detectives to take statements. Tread carefully – they may be completely innocent [as in fact they turn out to be] or they may have known something and hidden it. At this point we don't know if they are witnesses or suspects.

Tuesday, 26 July
All names confirmed now. Address used by two of the bombers comes through from the public: grim high-rise rented flat in Southgate, North London. Tip-off from neighbours. Omar has lived there since 1999. Send in our explosives experts – it's crammed with stuff for making

bombs, nearly two hundred boxes of peroxide, four hundred litres, normally used to bleach hair. Same as used by the 7/7 bombers. Not in an unstable form like the bomb factory in Leeds but similar ingredients. Send the stuff to the scientists checking the 7/7 substance and get one of our men who's seen the Leeds bomb factory down to look at this – hope he'll spot similarities.

Allocate a small team of detectives to reconstruct a bomb using what we've found to see if feasible as an explosive device and find out why it didn't explode fully. Find a lot of Al Qaeda propaganda – tapes of radical preaching by extremists like Abu Hamza, whose Finsbury Park mosque had been closed down after terrorist propaganda was discovered there.

Info from neighbours gives description of car they used – old white VW Golf. Some remember which year it's registered – put info out to all cops on the beat. Big brownie points for a PC who spots similar vehicle parked oddly, unmoved for several days. Send experts to make safe and remove it for forensic examination. Where are the bombers themselves?

Find discarded 'New York' T-shirt that the Oval bomber was wearing – left in a street nearby. Find his car parked near Stockwell where CCTV shows two of the bombers got on to the Underground. CCTV pictures unbelievably clear, which means very accurate reporting from the public.

Peter and I decide to bring in the help of staff from the Kidnap Unit who have specialist skills and techniques in dealing with live crimes. An added bonus is that the superintendent in charge of the unit used to be my staff officer – she knows how I work and will manage and smooth through decisions and actions.

I doubt there's an officer in the Met who doesn't want to

be involved and help in the July bomb investigations. I am grateful to every one of the hundreds working on it. There will no doubt be criticisms of some of our actions after the event – tough: we don't have time for soul-searching now. I know every officer's heart is in the right place and I appreciate that.

Caretaker of flats in Birmingham has called a police contact as he's found ten large bottles of hair dye, which can be used to make explosives. Establish Omar may have used the flat. Put this and two other locations linked to his family and friends under covert surveillance, with help from West Midlands Police and MI5. I give the go-ahead to raid overnight.

We are closing in on the bombers. We have ruled out some addresses as we've raided them. Now we're down to twelve where we think the bombers may be hiding – some are their homes, some the homes of friends and family who might be harbouring them. We put them all under major covert surveillance – dozens of officers watching each in shifts, some on foot, some in vans, some in nearby flats, listening to what's happening inside, tracking phone calls made. Armed officers at every scene – these men are highly dangerous, the officers watching them extremely brave.

Of the twelve addresses, seven are in West London fairly near Paddington, three in the West Midlands, two in Spalding in Lincolnshire. We have been granted seventy-eight search warrants – that's seventy-eight cars, business and residential addresses, etc., where we think the bombers may be or have been – and are working through them systematically.

Take stock: we're planning our biggest ever deployments, worrying intelligence still coming in from all sides, now dealing with the repercussions of shooting an innocent man at

Stockwell. The Independent Police Complaints Commission is demanding information as they must investigate our actions and we're obliged to service them.

We now focused on one of the addresses the bombers may have used in West London. It wasn't the official home of any of them. Could be somewhere they're lying low or a bomb factory – need to check it out.

23.00 More sightings – on a train *en route* from Newcastle to London. We despatch to Grantham in Lincolnshire, pull two men off the train and arrest them under the Prevention of Terrorism Act. [Later this proved to be another false alarm.]

Wednesday, 27 July
4.30 *a.m.* I get a text. Yassin Hassan Omar has been arrested. We believe he planted the failed bomb at Warren Street Underground station. We are jubilant, relieved but pragmatic: his three co-conspirators are still at large. West Midlands Police got him during raids on the houses we'd been watching in Birmingham along with three others we're questioning about harbouring a suspected criminal. I have deep respect for the twelve anti-terrorist officers from West Midlands Police who went in, throwing gas cylinders into each room before they entered. They cornered Omar fully clothed standing in the bath wearing a rucksack. They thought it was a bomb – one officer released the safety catch on his gun but another got in first and shot Omar with a Taser, stunning him for long enough to arrest him – my God, that could have triggered the bomb. Luckily he didn't have a device. I wonder if they used the Taser because they were worried about killing an innocent man as our firearms officers had last Friday. Omar, apparently extremely violent

– clearly prepared to die – came very close to being shot.

We raid flats where we believe members of his family may live and make arrest.

This manhunt is like a yo-yo. Just when you're up something brings you back down to earth with an almighty bang. Uncorroborated intelligence received overnight indicates an attack on the rail network within the next week. The intelligence suggests a number of potential targets. We can't ignore it – if we do, the consequences could be dire. It's a no-brainer – I'd rather be criticized for creating inconvenience than for causing loss of life. Also suggests other parts of the transport infrastructure are targets. There's logic to it – the attacks on the Madrid rail network in 2004 were part of a plan for a wave of attacks. And the 7/7 and 21/7 attacks were on Thursdays. Discuss with MI5. This compounds my fears of further attack.

Suzanna in early – goes off to fix meetings for me with senior officers from the Met and other forces, with the intelligence agencies, transport bosses and the prime minister. Get update on further raids planned – looks like we've got new leads on at least one of the other bombers. Need to find armed backup for some of the raids from outside London.

8.00 Meet with my Chief Officer Group involved in Operation Theseus. Right now we think the two cells, 7/7 and 21/7, are linked. Discuss this and the methodology of the terrorists.

8.30 Now I plan the biggest operation of my career for tomorrow. I take it to the commissioner. Sir Ian Blair is sounding off at the risk of using a Taser on someone carrying a bomb. We move on to my belief there's a strong chance of another attack tomorrow – today's arrest could be a further trigger for that. He is as tense and determined as I am not to see more attacks. Gives his support for overwhelming high-visibility armed-police operation, but he says we need to brief the prime minister – need to convince the PM this will not alarm the public. I argue it's better to inform the PM of what we're doing rather than ask for his consent. This is squarely an operational decision, albeit with potential political implications. It just means more care is needed. We don't want to get embroiled in debates with politicians about civil liberties, just to get on with the job.

9.00 If the last five days have been crazy, the next forty-eight hours will be off the radar. I brief the Met's Management Board on my plans – tell them I believe there could be more attacks tomorrow. I want armed coverage at every station in London and every station leading into London: I estimate six thousand officers are needed, many of them armed, to stop the bombers moving and to reassure the public. Call an emergency meeting of senior officers from every force in the country as need their armed officers on this as soon as possible.

10.15 Peter Clarke comes to my office for a pow-wow with John McDowall and Suzanna Becks. The four of us thrash out our plans for the security operation, then Peter and John head back to run the investigations. Suzanna and I take on the task of bringing the regions and government on board.

11.00 Meet and brief colleagues from the other London police forces and MoD Police, plus Met senior officers who will be in operational control of parts of tomorrow's operation, followed by a meeting with intelligence chiefs.

12.30 Heads of the UK intelligence agencies gather in my office. Not for the first time I'm humbled by the awesome brains in the room. After two weeks of working closely with Eliza Manningham-Buller, in particular, she continues to be challenging and at the same time very supportive of our joint ventures. Our relationship is building strong bridges in the interaction between police and MI5. If you have two people at the top of their organizations obviously getting on it strengthens relationships throughout both – our staff see us co-operating and working well together and trust permeates from top to bottom.

The three intelligence chiefs agree that the intelligence we have, though not conclusive, merits my massive security plan for tomorrow.

13.00 Big developments in the manhunt through the afternoon with new leads on the other bombers: possible sighting of one at Luton airport. Get air exclusion zone, effectively closing airspace above the airport while we arrest him – keeping the press choppers well away from the area. At first we're optimistic we've got the right man – but, no, damn it: another false alarm. The man is innocent so he's released. Raid addresses in North and South London, arrest three women in Stockwell. Anti-terrorist detectives will start questioning Omar, who was arrested in Birmingham but has now arrived at Paddington Green high-security police station in London. Could he lead us to the others? Will release new and very clear CCTV pictures of the Shepherds Bush bomber later – Peter will do the press conference.

14.30 Attend COBRA: brief ministers and leading civil servants in broad terms of tomorrow's security operation; MI5 briefs on the intelligence supporting the possibility of attack. Chairing, Charles Clarke asks if we should close the entire transport network. I realize just how high the stakes are. He adds that this is essentially a political decision and the impact would be so great it's one for the prime minister. I will meet Tony Blair later.

15.30 Brief the Met's Management Board. Have conversations with Chris Fox, the ever-helpful president of ACPO, who agrees to try to persuade other forces to get involved.

16.00 Assistant chief constables from seven forces in London to discuss latest intelligence, arrest plans, building public confidence and minimizing effects on the economy. I chair. We must agree tactics for tomorrow's mega security operation – they must deliver visible reassurance and deterrence, and allow us to identify, arrest and obtain best evidence. Need huge police cover in London including on trains and stations. Outside London, police coverage must be on rail and other transport routes into the city.

The meeting demands sustainability of manpower must be linked to intelligence, which is now flying at an alarming rate. I explain strongest suggestion is of an attack on a railway station, but can't rule out other transport infrastructure. Not clear when and we couldn't tell if the bombers on the run were involved or another cell. Police activity could displace this by either time or location. Meeting agrees level of activity deployed will be a one-off – not repeated on other days.

We agree to put armed police across coach stations, and bus, rail and Underground networks in and out of London, focusing on escape routes as well as arrivals, from 6 a.m. to 20.00 tomorrow. I leave Andy Trotter, then deputy chief constable of British Transport Police, to iron out specific tactics and divvy them up among forces.

17.00 Downing Street. Brief the prime minister in person. He rules out closing the entire transport system – a political decision. It would be easier to shut it down and cheaper for policing – but the political fallout in terms of damage to the economy is a key concern for him. Explain the intelligence: it's not totally reliable but we can't ignore it. Explain why we need overwhelming armed security: the *modus operandi* on 7 July was that they entered by train from Luton; if attacks are planned for tomorrow we want to deter potential bombers from travelling by rail. If a cell is on the way to London by train it will be met by armed officers. Anyone carrying a bag or rucksack in tomorrow's rush-hour will be considered for searching, however much it slows things down. Question is, am I displacing the bombers on to the roads? PM seems to understand the plan is horrendous resources-wise, and a logistical nightmare.

The PM agrees with our plans, and sees this as an independent operational decision which should be left to the police. Great: his support means we don't have to get involved in long discussion to persuade his ministers at COBRA, just explain it to them.

This is where the line between politicians and operational policing should be drawn. Aware critics in- and outside government will argue it's taking away civil rights for the police to go so heavy-handed into dealing with the threat – to which I say, 'If terrorists are travelling around the country with bombs, are you telling me the protection of civil rights is a greater objective than our ability to stop someone in the commission of atrocity? We must do all we can to deter them, and that includes making them aware they might be stopped. My job is not to worry if we're civil-liberty compliant.' If they're worried, they should complain to Parliament which made the laws. 'I've been given a power by Parliament and I am going to use it. It means we have the power to deploy armed officers and to stop and search in every station in the country if need be.'

18.10 Andy Trotter presents me with the tactical plan. We draft a message to put out to all forces of action to be taken tomorrow. All systems go.

Thursday, 28 July
06.00 The biggest ever armed operation to protect the people of London and beyond is under way – highly visible armed and unarmed police and community-support officers in large numbers at every station and Underground station, on the trains and on the streets of London, at ports and airports, outside key buildings like power and nuclear stations. We raid two addresses in South London and arrest nine men under the Terrorism Act – none of the suspected bombers is among them.

10.30 I get a text. There's been an extraordinary revelation at Paddington Green police station about how one of the bombers got away after last Thursday's failed attacks. Three bombers are still on the run but we have one in custody, Omar, and some of his relatives. Through them we've established he escaped dressed as a woman clothed in black from head to foot in his girlfriend's mother's *burka* – the black head-to-toe gown some Muslim women wear. Apparently he carried a white handbag. Quickly find CCTV footage of him in his camouflage at Birmingham coach station.

Relief – so far no bomb attacks during rush-hour.

11.45 Major development: intelligence from surveillance on a block of flats near Notting Hill in West London suggests the bombers may be inside – men seen going in with provisions. Peter Clarke and I meet in my office to review the logistics we've drawn up for raiding the flat. We must not get it wrong this time after the disastrous and sad shooting at Stockwell last Friday. Peter alerts firearms and surveillance teams and heads over to MI5 to discuss with colleagues there – this raid will be a joint operation. It's a week since the bombers tried unsuccessfully to detonate their bombs in London – they've probably still got explosives and we *must* get them before they try to bomb again. Need to be careful in case they've wired themselves up and will blow the place up if we go in as happened when Spanish police moved in on the Madrid bombers. Frustrating but we can't risk bursting in without thought.

12.15 We discover that one of the suspected bombers, Hussain Osman, has a father and a brother living in Italy. We alert Interpol and the Italian police. Find CCTV, which could be of him catching a Eurostar train from Waterloo, bold as brass, two days ago. Italian authorities now monitor a call on a mobile from Milan. Timings fit with the route of the Paris/Milan/Rome train – must be heading for Rome. Italians, working now with MI5, put a brother of his, who runs an Internet café in Rome, under surveillance.

15.00 I drive to the Cabinet Office for another COBRA meeting. It's tense. The politicians want to know why we can't just break into the flat now. I explain we've got it surrounded but can't take risks. We ask the Home Office to start checking out extradition proceedings with the Italians – my hunch is we'll get Osman in Rome and we want him back here fast.

18.30 New Scotland Yard. There are now more than a thousand officers involved in the investigation. We're getting leads from all over the world. We call in 250 officers. I remind them this is the biggest ever manhunt in UK criminal history – and potentially the most dangerous. We detail a plan for moving in on the flat should we decide to. Surveillance officers have seen no movement in or out – but they know someone's in because they've seen shadows across the drawn blinds.

20.00 We arrest one of the wives as she returns from work – no resistance. Most of these bombers had small children – how could they plan to kill and maim?

Still no sign of movement from the flat we're watching in West London. Neighbours suggesting they've heard banging – is it barricaded? Surveillance suggests at least two people inside moving around.

Midnight I return to the hotel, relieved because no attacks today. Is that because of our mass presence on the streets or was the intelligence wrong? What if we're barking up the wrong tree and the bombers are about to detonate explosives in some packed nightclub? I feel exhausted and have a restless night. I'm mulling over all we know – is there something we've missed?

Friday, 29 July
5.05 A reminder that the investigation into the 7 July attacks is ongoing – in real terms it's still in its infancy. For the first time since those attacks more than three weeks ago Edgware Road Underground station reopens. Forensic work in the tunnel there is finished and the men and women who've been down daily for the past three weeks can have some respite.

They have done a magnificent and very difficult job. I am back at base by 6.30 a.m. Scotland Yard is already buzzing. I see several teams of firearms officers in their flat caps coming in for breakfast in the canteen. I ask for an update from Peter on the 7/7 inquiry which cannot be sidelined – we owe it the families of those who died.

9.30 Eureka! We get a call out of the blue to the Anti-Terrorist Hotline: a member of the public claims two people fitting the descriptions of two of the suspected bombers, Muktar Said Ibrahim and Ramzi Mohammed, intermittently live in the West London flats we have under surveillance, though haven't been seen going in and out for a week. [Later we discover they used the flat as a base when they wanted to meet or get away from their own homes for a while.] Things start moving.

9.35 We have a top-level meeting with the commissioner. Peter attends with the head of the Firearms Branch. The commissioner gets the home secretary on the phone and tells him we plan to move in. We leave the commissioner's office and press the button.

10.00 Police teams begin quietly evacuating the area round the flats. I sit in the office – nervous. A crime reporter calls me on my mobile. I tell them to keep close to what's going on and they push me for more but I don't give it. Suzanna comes in with tea for us both and sits with me. I get a text from Peter: the two armed raids are under way, one at Tavistock Crescent, West London, the other at the Notting Hill address. We're tuned in to the conversations from the Gold command centre. Horror of horrors, two children move across the line of fire of our marksmen covering the flat – I pray that the bombers don't appear now. The operation is frozen. The children move on, oblivious, and our officers take up their firing positions again.

11.30 A second team has gone into Tavistock Crescent – one arrest.

Now another nightmare moment: the press arrive at the Notting Hill flats. I don't know why I'm annoyed and surprised – these days, the public seem to be on to the media the second they see anything out of the ordinary. Suddenly I'm watching the drama unfold live on Sky TV – the roadblocks, the neighbours coming out, the streets of police vehicles on standby along with the Fire Brigade and Ambulance Service, lines of armed and unarmed officers, the Bomb Squad. Peter calls me, furious – it'll jeopardize the whole operation. I phone Dick Fedorcio, head of communications, and he's already looking up the phone number of the head of news at Sky to complain. I phone the crime correspondent Martin Brunt directly on his mobile and he promises to do what he can. The camera team must have bought up some of the neighbours overlooking the flat – they've got a prime view over the balcony of the address we've surrounded. If we can see what's happening on TV, the suspects inside can too. We've lost the element of surprise. We can't wait any longer.

Reports now from neighbours of police in full body armour using explosives to break through the door of the flat. They throw in canisters of tear gas. Armed police follow in full CBRN suits in case there are any radiated weapons or chemicals inside. Eye witnesses tell the press that officers shouted to the two suspected bombers by their first names, telling them to strip. That's in case they've got explosives attached to their bodies, hidden under their clothes. The officers confirm to our Gold control room on their police radios that they've identified two of the bombers. They are Muktar Said Ibrahim, aged twenty-seven, who is suspected of trying to detonate a bomb on the number 26 bus, and Ramzi Mohammed, the failed Oval bomber. But the two have barricaded themselves into one of the rooms. We don't know if it's wired with explosives. There's a stand-off.

Our officers in the flat begin the delicate task of trying to coax them out. This is dangerous work – they must know the bombers could detonate an explosive at any point. Outside, neighbours are interviewed on television. The stand-off lasts nearly two hours.

Suddenly it's over. The two men, so clearly recognizable from the CCTV pictures, appear stripped to show they're not hiding weapons or explosives, wearing only underpants, on the walkway outside their flat. Now I'm seeing all this unfold on TV too – the men arrested, led away and filmed, their every movement broadcast across the world. They put their hands in the air. I'm relieved but drained. Seems they had been at the flat all the time, gone there soon after their failed bombings and hadn't left since. Three down and one to go.

I see reportage of comments from the commissioner confirming what I already know – that the costs of this investigation are astronomical.

13.54 Undercover teams have been following two Somali women. They have travelled to Liverpool Street station and are trying to buy tickets for the express service to Stansted airport. Uniformed backup police now move in. The women are suspected of being related to one of the bombers. They appear to try to escape but are wrestled to the ground and arrested. Later it emerges they are not involved – but it's not long before we find other women who are family members of one of the bombers. They are charged under the Terrorism Act for failing to disclose information likely to help the police.

14.45 I discuss press messages. We go public confirming two suspected 21 July bombers are among those we are holding. We confirm two men were held at one address and a third at a second address after raids in West London.

15.30 The adrenalin is running high. Covert operations are now turned into overt ones: we order that those under surveillance must be brought in for questioning. We get word things are moving in Rome. They're close to locating Osman. Police begin to raid a number of homes in the suburbs.

In the UK we are piecing together how he escaped even though he is one of the most wanted men in the world. He did it with the help of his wife, who drove him to her sister's home in Brighton and gave him a new mobile phone. Later he returned to London and, travelling on a brother's passport, made his way to Rome.

17.35 I receive a phone call from the Italian police officer in charge of counter-terrorism. He tells me they have arrested Osman in the suburb of Tor Pignattara.

18.00 Giuseppe Pisanu, Italy's interior minister, goes on television to announce the arrest. He says it's the result of a 'truly praiseworthy' international operation. Hussain Osman was the bomber who tried to blow up an Underground train in Shepherds Bush eight days earlier. I call Dick and tell him to announce we'll be seeking Osman's extradition under the European extradition warrant process, which came into effect in Italy yesterday.

19.00 I receive a call at my desk. I suspect it is one of the crime reporters trying to establish the facts, many of which are still only just emerging. It's not: it's from SO13 to say Muktar Said Ibrahim, who allegedly tried to blow up a number 26 bus in Hackney on 21 July, has formally identified himself to detectives who are beginning arrest procedures at Paddington Green police station. As I take the call I watch crime correspondents on television reporting from outside the station.

20.00 We have an identity for the man we arrested at Tavistock Crescent. He's Wahbi Mohammed, aged twenty-two, the brother of Ramzi Mohammed, and we think he dumped the bomb in bushes on Wormwood Scrubs. [Later we would find out that he was involved but he had not dumped the fifth bomb: questioning and forensic examinations will reveal that another man arrested, Manfo Asiedu, helped set up the plot and it was his bomb that was dumped on 21 July.]

I am astonished and relieved: all of the bombers have been captured alive. My phone doesn't stop pinging with congratulatory texts. In particular I see one from Catherine Crawford – she's the chief executive of the Metropolitan Police Authority, which will have to scrutinize our behaviour over the tragic shooting of an innocent man last week. To have her support so close to the shooting is important. I also consider her a friend, so from a personal and professional perspective I'm pleased.

I walk down the corridor from my fifth-floor office to meet colleagues in the Kidnap Unit who have been carrying out critical work for us round the clock. Without them we would not have had the result we did in arresting the terrorists. The Kidnap operations room spans two adjoining offices. I find it buzzing with an atmosphere of excitement mixed with relief and exhaustion – like a marathon runner who's just crossed the line and is now recovering from the race: a feeling of satisfaction, laced with tiredness. I know in this age of political correctness what I then present to them could be frowned upon but I arrange anyway for several bottles of wine and beer to be delivered to their office to kickstart their celebration at the closure of their part in the operation.

It's the first of many congratulatory messages owed. I email and speak to our teams across London and beyond. I phone Italy. Every last person involved in the manhunt deserves thanks. I speak on the phone to the commissioner, who is due to go on leave tomorrow and will be able to take his holiday as planned.

There is a real sense that we have completed a good day's work, and put a worldwide stamp on the reputation of British policing and the profile of New Scotland Yard. [This will be brought home to me some months later when I'm invited to speak about the investigation to a group of American police chiefs. They appear to be in awe of what has been achieved and say as much.] I'm very proud of the New Scotland Yard team.

Over the next few weeks the Italians proved what good partners they are to work with. They arrested some members of Osman's family and saw that he himself was speedily extradited to the UK. However, I'll never get my head around the quirkiness of their criminal-justice system. Peter and I would crease up each time we saw on television the defence lawyer holding a press conference on the steps outside the police station after each police interview with Osman. He went into the detail of what was discussed and the explanations given by Osman, although the interviewing process was ongoing and he had not been charged. Apparently this is common practice in Italy. Bizarrely, these early disclosures had no detrimental effect on the prosecution of Osman once he was back in the UK. But I can't see it catching on in the UK. Our legal system doesn't allow any public disclosure in case it prejudices the trial.

I felt it very important to recognize the Italians' hard work and later decided to visit the investigators and present them with our police commendation certificates, which acknowledge and reward good work. Andy Slater, one of my staff officers, and I went to Italy; we also used the trip for meetings there with MI6, the British ambassador and other key government officials.

Through an interpreter we staged a semi-formal ceremony where I presented each officer who'd been involved with his commendation certificate – to their obvious delight in this very British tradition. This was followed with a few glasses of Italian red wine and pasta – post-investigation celebrations don't differ the world over.

Like the 7/7 inquiry, the 21/7 investigation continued not just for months but for years. The sharp focus of the initial manhunt and our utter dejection when we killed the wrong man were followed by our dogged determination, with lawyers of the Crown Prosecution Service, to put together the tightest of cases, collecting every tiny bit of evidence we could find in order to punish the perpetrators. When they were finally convicted the trial judge described what they'd done as 'A viable, indeed very nearly successful, attempt at mass murder . . . it was long in the planning . . . designed for maximum impact . . . part of an Al Qaeda-controlled sequence of events . . . At least fifty people would have died, hundreds of people would have been wounded, thousands would have had their lives permanently damaged, disfigured or otherwise.'

We know members of the 21/7 cell, like the 7/7 bombers, were in Pakistan during the winter of 2004/5, and it was shortly after they returned that both cells began planning the explosions.

As the investigation continued, and through interviews with the others, it became clear that the 21/7 ringleader, the man who'd thought up the plot and put it together, was Muktar Said Ibrahim. It also emerged he had crossed swords with the police and MI5 before and, once again, we found ourselves criticized for having failed to stop him earlier. He'd been filmed at a camp in the Lake District we had under surveillance. He'd been questioned as he flew out to Pakistan with extremist literature and a large amount of cash, and had been charged another time for distributing extremist literature in Oxford Street. Did we, as some allege, allow him to slip through the net? We have learnt many lessons from what happened then. The police and MI5 now constantly reassess those who are peripheral to other investigations. Where we can't bring a successful conviction we can disrupt activity through new powers such as control orders. We have got better and we are stopping many more plots.

But we should not forget that Muktar Said Ibrahim was a determined killer, whose sinister, callous wish was to perpetrate a worse atrocity than the 7 July attacks. The bombs he and his co-conspirators made were laced with screws, which would have torn into victims' flesh, had the devices exploded properly.

The four failed bombers, Muktar Said Ibrahim, Ramzi Mohammed, Hussain Osman and Yassin Hassan Omar, have been jailed for life, and told they must spend a minimum of forty years in jail. The fifth bomber, Manfo Asiedu, involved in the planning but who lost his nerve and dumped his bomb, has been jailed for thirty-three years.

Those who helped the plotters have been jailed too. Adel Yahya, Wahbi Mohammed, Abdul Sherif, Siraj Ali, Muhedin Ali and Ismail Abdurahman have been jailed for between six and seventeen years.

Wives and girlfriends who harboured them or knew of their plans have also been punished: Yeshi Osman, Hussain Osman's wife, was jailed for fifteen years. Her brother, Esayas Girma, and sister, Mulu Girma, were jailed for ten years. Mulu's boyfriend, Mohamed Kabashi, was jailed for ten years. Fardosa Abdullahi, Yassin Omar's fiancée, was jailed for three years.

6. When Things Go Wrong: Stockwell

LET ME TAKE YOU BACK NOW TO 22 JULY. WE WERE LIVING IN unprecedented times. Tension was high. We were juggling investigations that were moving at an incredible pace. We were edgy, worried that other bombers could still be at large. The pressure we were under was without parallel.

We were still in the early stages of the investigation into the 7 July killers, the biggest terrorist investigation we'd ever undertaken. It was the day after the four 21 July would-be suicide bombers had attempted to carry out copycat attacks so we were also in the middle of the biggest manhunt in our history. I was in overall command of both and, suddenly, things went very, very wrong.

At first I didn't realize the magnitude of what had happened because I was preoccupied with the bomb investigations. I certainly did not anticipate the weeks and months that I would spend soul-searching after the events of 22 July – or the damage it would do to the Met and to individuals within it, including me. It was a bitter, tragic tale that unfolded against the backdrop of the race against time to trap the bombers, a catalogue of misunderstandings, compounded by rash and, with hindsight, wrong decisions on the part of some police officers. At the centre of it all, the sad and violent death of an innocent young bystander brought untold grief to his family thousands of miles away.

During that period, we were dealing with a crisis of such magnitude, and we were so nervous, that at one point we actually locked down key buildings in central London for fear of further suicide attacks. It happened in the Government Security Zone. MI6 headquarters, in Vauxhall, is on the south-western edge, and the zone runs north across the Thames, up round Victoria station to Buckingham Palace and east along Pall Mall, taking in all the buildings of Whitehall new and old, including the Houses of Parliament, the Cabinet Office and Downing Street. This is a security hotspot – there is more covert and open surveillance there than almost anywhere else.

A photographer appeared to be acting suspiciously near the MI5 headquarters in Westminster. To this day I don't know what he was actually doing but he was on the move close to a number of iconic buildings, including Buckingham Palace, the Houses of Parliament and New Scotland Yard. Within minutes someone pushed the equivalent of an intelligence alarm button and we had lockdown. MPs, the Royal Household and the police found their buildings completely sealed. I have never seen anything like it before or since. I was at Scotland Yard and hundreds of people were coming and going all the time. Suddenly, behind the reception area, inside the reinforced-glass security doors that staff pass through to get to their offices, two huge steel doors came clunking down, closing the building. For ninety minutes nobody could get in or out. It happened on a Friday night, when we normally went to the pub to debrief. It was a sign of just how tense the situation was.

In the early hours of 22 July 2005, a global manhunt for the would-be suicide bombers of the day before was well under way. The UK was on full alert, ports and airports were on standby, and police leave cancelled.

My predecessor, Sir David Veness, and the former commissioner, Lord Stevens, had worked hard to prepare an operational plan to deal with suicide bombers. It used two key scenarios: one in which we'd had time to plan how we'd confront a person we knew had a bomb or a vehicle-borne device; the other, the more complex of the two, when we couldn't plan in advance but were confronted without warning, spontaneously, by a person with a bomb or a vehicle-borne attack. Neither was deemed more likely than the other. Operation Kratos was the codename for plans to deal with the latter, i.e. a spontaneous attack.

A Kratos was everyone's nightmare, whether you were the firearms officers tasked with weighing up the circumstances and deciding in a split second if a shot to the brain stem is justified, or whether you're the designated senior officer (DSO) in overall command of the operation. Since I had become head of Specialist Operations I had decided we should double-check the strategy handed down by the previous team, but my colleagues and I could come up with no other more suitable options. However distasteful the words sound, when you're confronted with a spontaneous suicide bomber who could kill at the push of the button, there can only be one response: kill or be killed.

During the night we phoned Cressida Dick and asked her to be our Kratos DSO – she would co-ordinate the use of firearms teams, if they were needed, under the Kratos rules. Cressida was one of a new breed of police officer, an Oxford graduate with accountancy experience who was fast-tracked through the ranks bringing much-needed management skills. She had commanded firearms teams and was a trained hostage negotiator, and one of the few senior police officers entrusted with taking the helm in life-threatening situations involving decisions on whether or not to shoot to kill. She was one of our coolest and most experienced officers and I was relieved that she had been chosen for this challenging role today. Where the possibility exists of a firearms stand-off, it's normal to call in a DSO. As such, Cressida would be the operational decision-maker, co-ordinating surveillance and firearms teams and other officers who were on the ground.

True to form, she turned up not at 7 a.m., when she was asked to, but at five. Already hundreds of officers were on the treadmill, working long shifts round the clock. Forensics teams were sifting through evidence from the aborted bomb attacks of the day before. Specialists were studying the lethal cocktail of explosives, which, thank God, had not detonated. And officers were combing tape after tape of CCTV footage taken from the three Underground trains and the bus on which the failed bombs had been left.

The scale of police mobilization was unprecedented. Officers seconded from around the country were staying in hotels – some way out in the Home Counties – and working on the multiplication of aspects in the 7/7 and 21/7 investigations. John Bunn, a veteran of the Anti-Terrorist Branch from the IRA days who had since retired, was brought back in to oversee and co-ordinate those seconded from other forces. He and his team managed all their professional and domestic needs. He commands huge respect across the police service and although I know he would have liked to be closer to the actual investigation, his 'civvie' role was just as important.

Peter Clarke was on his way back to the UK from his family holiday. His key function was running the Anti-Terrorist Branch, and with him away Commander John

McDowall was in charge. John had spent the previous two weeks in Leeds following up leads after the 7/7 attacks but now he was back in the hot seat. I wanted to give him as much support as I could as he was also one of our designated Gold commanders, taking the initiative in deciding what resources were needed hour by hour. He and the team were doing a fantastic job: they had already found CCTV pictures from the day before which they believed showed each of the four failed bombers. At 2.15 a.m. on 22 July they found a gym pass at the scene of the Shepherds Bush device. They now compared the photograph on the pass with the picture of the man caught on CCTV who, they believed, had planted the failed bomb. The two matched and now they had a name – Hussain Osman – to go with the photograph. Swift inquiries at the gym brought an address at Scotia Road in Tulse Hill, South London. Intelligence came through that a second bomber also had links with the flat. I left them to it. Tomorrow was going to be a busy day and I had to think strategically, take a look at the bigger picture to ensure everything was covered.

At the back of my mind I was worried that there was now another group of traumatized members of the public – people who had been on the trains, who had seen the bombers detonate the devices and had believed they were about to be blown up. Also the 21/7 attempts would have brought vivid memories of what they had gone through to those injured or bereaved by the 7/7 explosions. I had called a meeting of our family-liaison officers for 7.30 a.m. and returned to my hotel for a couple of hours' sleep.

I got back at 6.30 a.m., and despite the lack of sleep I did not feel tired – there was too much to do and yet again the adrenalin was pumping. I was very concerned that the bombers might strike again – would it be in this morning's rush-hour? Scotia Road had been put under surveillance, though anyone going about their business in that part of London wouldn't have known it. Osman could still be in hiding there and we didn't want to alert him. Our Red surveillance team (they're always named by colours) had moved into the area to wait for official authorization of the operation. It had come at 6 a.m. and by 6.04 they were covertly watching the flats in Tulse Hill from positions outside and inside the block. Close to the flats we had a van with an officer inside filming, and all those watching the building were in constant communication with the control room at Scotland Yard. I was very aware that as we tracked the bombers we had men and women on the ground risking their lives, determined to stop the terrorists striking again.

I was all over the building now, catching up on the intelligence, and with officers responding on the ground, briefing the commissioner, keeping the civil servants from the Home Office at bay, fielding calls from my counterparts abroad and talking with MI5. John McDowall had set up an operational chain of command, which was, of necessity, complex. There were two of us in overall command: Assistant Commissioner Alan Brown was Gold commander, dealing with the day-to-day policing resources. He also liaised with the other emergency services. I was Gold in control of investigating what had happened: my job was to find the perpetrators of the attacks of 7 and 21 July. On 22 July we brought in a third Gold commander to deal with the specific developments in the manhunt for the 21/7 failed bombers. This was John, whose key focus on the morning of 22 July was the Scotia Road flat.

Commander Cressida Dick, our DSO in the control room, assumed overall Silver command of the firearms and surveillance operations, putting into practice the Gold strategies that Alan, myself and in particular John McDowall had planned. She could find herself making life-and-death split-second decisions. Two other senior officers were designated Silver commanders: Detective Chief Inspector Greg Purser would manage the incident on the ground because it was so dangerous and we needed someone of high rank out there, and Detective Superintendent John Boucher stayed in the control room. Two tactical advisers were brought in to advise the firearms teams on the ground and officers in the control room. I approved the entire chain of command and the people who'd been put into each position.

Through the night a separate support team at the Yard had worked at getting the various authorizations we needed for the manhunt. We'd set this team up after the 7 July explosions to work full-time on these hugely important though rather bureaucratic duties, seconding people from all over the Met to help, including from our top-secret hostage-negotiating unit. It was yet another sign of just how massive our response to the bombings had become. We needed authorizations from the Home Office for the phone tapping. This was critical now we were getting the names of terrorists who were on the run. We needed police authorization to use arms, and to put specific buildings and persons under surveillance. Senior police officers unconnected with the investigation have to give these operational authorizations; they scrutinize our plans to ensure that they're justified.

John McDowall had worked out a firearms strategy that I approved. He had obtained verbal permission the night before for the surveillance team to be armed. The written permission came through at 5.45 a.m. So the surveillance team at Scotia Road was armed. And it had specialist snipers from the firearms unit to support them, and to make any arrests so that the undercover status of the surveillance teams was protected. But things did not go to plan.

At 6.50 a.m. John McDowall chaired a briefing for all the senior officers involved to outline his plans. I went in and out of it, leaving the room at one point because details of the type of bombs the terrorists had tried to use the day before were coming through from our scientists. I came back to pass on the information so that those on the ground knew what to spot if there were further attempts to plant bombs. Cressida was subsequently briefed personally by John when that meeting ended, as she had missed part of it. At this second briefing they talked through and agreed exactly what their (John and Cressida's) individual roles were to be in delivering the overall strategy. They were two professionals who knew how important it was to have clear lines of command and control – they would not have time to be disputing things later.

With the Red surveillance team already watching the flat, at 7 a.m. the backup firearms unit came on shift at their headquarters in East London. They were warned they could find themselves in a critical situation. They collected their weapons and were sent to Nightingale Lane police station, two miles from the surveillance operation in Tulse Hill, to await further instructions. By 8.45 a.m. they were on site and ready to go. They were briefed by the Silver commander on the ground, DCI Greg Purser. He described the type of explosive the terrorists might be carrying and warned it could be hard to detect. He told them that the men they were hunting were 'deadly and determined'.

Meanwhile I was tied up with my 7.30 meeting. The family-liaison officers were critically important in ensuring that the victims of these attacks understood what we were doing to bring the bombers or their accomplices to justice. It was two weeks since the 7/7 bombings and those involved had been getting their lives back into some sort of perspective when along came the 21/7 attacks. I wanted to know how they were. Did they need more of our time or specialist help? I had a meeting pencilled in to meet the families. We decided it should be a priority and fixed it for the following Sunday – 24 July. We had learnt from our counterparts in the USA after the 11 September 2001 attacks on the World Trade Center in New York that it was very important to maintain strong contact with victims and the bereaved families of a terrorist attack. In the UK this had been common practice with serious crime but that is very different from a terrorist attack. In terrorism there are almost always going to be more victims who will have greater need of support and counselling. There is a higher chance that someone may fall through the net. This will make them feel detached from the authorities. It can even be more traumatic than the terrorist event. We knew we needed expert help and advice to strike the balance between giving a factual briefing and providing counsel and support.

Officers at the meeting said some of the families were angry that for the second time in two weeks we had allowed the bombers to get through. Now we had run out of experienced family-liaison officers and agreed to put out pleas to other forces for help.

I slipped back to my office just after 8 a.m. Suzanna came in and told me what I already knew: that the Home Office and other senior officers in the Met were desperate for information and clarity about what was happening. We didn't know for sure that Osman was in the flat and I had to resist filling in the gaps with speculation. I had to be very cautious and self-disciplined. We decided Suzanna would take over various meetings I'd arranged that day so that I could keep an eye on the manhunt. I needed to ensure intelligence agencies in America, elsewhere in Europe and beyond had received the CCTV photographs of the 21/7 bombers and to work with our director of communications and the commissioner to decide when and how we would publish them in the UK.

I felt it was of critical importance to get those pictures out to the public. We didn't know what frame of mind the would-be bombers were in, so soon after their failed attempts. We had to assume they would be humiliated, possibly psychologically disturbed and trying to fulfil their plan to carry out a series of potentially devastating suicide bombings. Only two weeks ago fifty-two innocent commuters had been killed and we could not let that happen again. Even if we arrested Hussain Osman in the coming hours – in the unlikely event he had gone home after his aborted bomb attempt – we would still put his photograph out in the hope the public could bring in more information about him and the others.

I spoke to John McDowall by phone. He told me the surveillance team had reported people were coming and going from the flats as they left for work. One of the team wanted the bus routes in the area suspended to make it harder for anyone to escape, but after discussion at the Yard we decided against this in case it alerted the terrorists. The message, though, didn't get back to those on the ground, who wrongly assumed the request had been met. It was one of a series of misunderstandings.

We discussed what would happen if the terrorists were in the flat and found out they were surrounded by armed police. I couldn't get the memory of Madrid out of my mind. Once again I remembered the detail – 191 people had been killed in train bombs in March 2004, and when police moved in on a flat where the suspects were holed up, the terrorists blew it up, killing themselves and a policeman, and injuring thirteen more officers. What if these terrorists had wired up Scotia Road? What danger would that put our officers and the public in? Now, potentially, we faced a similar scenario. Should we or shouldn't we move in on the flat? We decided not to go overt, but kept covert positions on and near the premises.

The control room for the operation was on the sixteenth floor at Scotland Yard. This facility is old and therefore some of the new technology is missing. That said, for run-of-the-mill operations in the past it had been sufficient. It was due for refurbishment and refitting but there had been no urgency for this project as no one had imagined we would be facing the magnitude and diversity of events we found ourselves confronted with in July 2005. I was confident that the room could cope with any one of the three events we were now facing – the two bombings and a police shooting. But I am now aware that three within just over two and a half weeks left it inadequate. This control room is actually made up of two adjoining rooms. One is the hub of activity and the other is for command-type meetings.

In the main room, along one wall, there was an impressive set of screens, flashing updates on what was happening. Below, four officers, headphones plugged in, were listening to what surveillance officers were surreptitiously reporting through tiny microphones hidden in their clothes. Their words were logged into a computer and immediately came up on the screens so other officers in the room could see what was going on. Behind the four listeners sat another row of officers, and the commander, Cressida Dick, stood to one side with her advisers and their loggists – junior officers who kept records of the communications and decisions made by their seniors.

Now they sent in a second Special Branch surveillance team – the Grey team. They were also armed with pistols and set up a second cordon round the flat but further away than the Red team already on site. And that was when things began to go wrong. There were two surveillance teams on site and the firearms unit had not arrived. It was 9.33 a.m. A young man emerged from the Scotia Road flats and walked past the undercover police observation van towards a bus stop. Inside the van the surveillance officers were furiously photographing him. Those outside were sending fast messages to the control room – the man was white, one said, complexion like a light-skinned North African, said another, eyes with a Mongolian look, said a third. He was five feet eight inches tall, dark hair, stubbly beard, wearing a blue denim jacket, blue jeans and trainers. But could they identify him as the man in the grainy photograph they held? Was he Hussain Osman? One reported back by radio he was worth another look; someone else said he couldn't identify him as such. The surveillance teams were now communicating with each other by mobile phone.

At 9.39 a.m. the man they were following got on to a number 2 bus. One of the surveillance officers boarded it with him.

I don't know exactly when I popped my head into the control room but I remember I saw pandemonium. It was too small – chosen because it had communications with other security agencies – and it was noisy, with people talking all at once and too loudly, making it tough for the officers whose job was to listen to and log the conversations on the ground. I spoke to Cressida, checked she was OK. She was fighting on all sides to keep on top of everything, but she kept her cool and her voice low. They simply did not yet know if they had the right man.

An entry made at 9.46 a.m. in one of the control-room logs states: 'Not identical male as above discounted. Surveillance team to withdraw to original positions.' It's not clear where this information came from, but it seems to show lack of certainty about the man's identity.

At 9.47 a.m. the suspect got off the bus at Brixton Underground station. He walked twenty metres towards the station, then turned and ran back to the bus he'd just left and got on it again, making a mobile-phone call at the same time.

You can imagine the chatter back in the control room now. Those tracking him did not seem to notice, or at least did not report, that Brixton station was closed. Instead they began to describe his actions as nervous. Cressida Dick's own loggist noted: 'It is him, the man is off the bus. They think it is him, and he is very, very jumpy.' Still officers on the ground disagreed about whether or not he looked like Osman. Now Cressida called in the firearms unit to arrest him.

At 9.55 a.m. some of the firearms officers say they heard over the radio that the man on the bus had been positively identified as Osman. They had arrived near Scotia Road but now got back into their cars to follow the bus.

At 10 a.m. the man got off the bus at Stockwell station, still followed by a team of undercover officers. One saw his face close up and reported it was possibly Osman, although he had less facial hair than in the photograph, which had been filmed on CCTV fewer than twenty-four hours earlier. So, no surveillance officer had positively identified the man as Osman, yet in Scotland Yard those running the operation had a perception that he had been identified as the suspect.

Cressida did not want him entering the Underground – there was nothing obvious in his appearance to suggest he was carrying or hiding a bomb under his clothes but it couldn't be ruled out. He disappeared into the station followed by five surveillance officers. One minute later the firearms team arrived. From the Scotland Yard control room Cressida ordered them to 'stop' the suspect. The man himself was still oblivious to the fact he was the focus of such scrutiny. As he got to the bottom of the escalator he ran to catch a train that was about to leave. The surveillance team ran after him on to the train.

Upstairs the first firearms officers vaulted over the ticket barriers and twelve of them raced down the escalator to the waiting train. In the control room there was silence: the communications system didn't work underground. Only later would they find out that as the firearms officers reached the train the doors were being blocked open by one of the surveillance team.

'He's here,' he shouted, and pointed to the man, who got up and walked towards them. The surveillance officer pushed him back into his seat. The first two firearms officers ran on to the train, convinced he was a suicide bomber about to detonate a bomb and murder everyone in the carriage. It was 10.06 a.m. They fired seven bullets at point range into the man's head killing him instantly. Two other shots missed.

There have been several reports into the way the manhunt was set up and carried out. The Met has been criticized for lack of clarity in the command structure, for choosing a control room that was too small and for failing to supply adequate resources or adhere to procedures. I do not agree with everything everyone has said. Nobody deliberately set out to be lax or to thwart the manhunt in any way. Everyone went to work that day to protect the people of London. Whatever our rank, we all desperately wanted to get this right. Sadly, others felt we failed to do this. There were no other jobs in policing on that day that carried so much responsibility. If you were a surveillance or firearms officer you thought you were dealing with a suicide bomber, a scenario never before experienced on the streets of the UK (two weeks earlier on 7 July we became convinced pretty quickly that the bombers had killed themselves – we did not have the major manhunt we had now). If you were a senior officer in command you were overseeing an operation in action where the stakes could not have been higher. None of my colleagues involved are looking for sympathy, just understanding of the complex incident they were trying to resolve peacefully to save lives.

I don't remember the exact moment I was told he was dead. I know that some time between ten and ten thirty I phoned the commissioner and briefly filled him in. I asked my deputy Suzanna to step in and chair the weekly Security Review Committee meeting, which I was supposed to lead at 11 a.m.

As if things weren't already bad enough, with suicide bombers operating for the first time in the UK, now, tragically, we had a fatal police shooting to contend with. Could things get any worse? I remained calm. I have lived through police killings before and have learnt you don't get all the facts immediately and things are rarely as they seem initially. You have to wait. Yes: I asked myself what the bloody hell was going on – were we on top of things? We were still trying to work out what had happened with the bomb attempts of the day before and were in an intelligence vacuum: nothing of substance was coming through on the wanted men, nothing to suggest we'd come across them before, and now someone was dead who might or might not have been one of them. Our resources were knackered and stretched to the nth degree. I remembered that, three years earlier, when I'd been deputy assistant commissioner at the Met in command of corruption investigations, I had managed fourteen deaths of people in police custody and two fatal police shootings within a five-month period. I was very experienced at this and knew the score. Patience and focus on the job in hand were vital; never reach conclusions till you have firm evidence. I now know that type of experience only holds good on your CV. It's worth nothing when you're facing the chain of events that my colleagues and I were now confronting.

The shooting happened just as we finally pulled together clear CCTV photographs of all four wanted men. By lunchtime on 22 July it was very much a live event. We still didn't know if the man we'd shot was one of the four, an associate or, heaven forbid, not linked at all. But despite the shooting we could not be sidetracked from our focus on the manhunt. I believed we should hold a press conference and publish the CCTV photographs of the four bombers so that the public could help us identify them and spot them if they tried to attack again.

Publication of the pictures would inevitably bring a massive response and we needed to warn forces up and down the country, who would have to gear up for a surge in phone calls. There would be sightings – real or imagined – not just in London but elsewhere. We sent them an advisory message, telling them we planned a press conference. We said it wouldn't dwell on the shooting but on the images of the bombers. We knew that at least three of the men, if not all four, could be anywhere in the country or abroad. Every force should check its ability to deal with reported sightings: they might be called on to invoke the Kratos rules and bring in armed backup to make an arrest if a terrorist turned up in their force area. We could not emphasize enough that these men were an extreme threat, willing to endanger the lives of many people and blow themselves up in the process.

Forces would also need to think about how they'd cope if there was an arrest or crime scene in their area: their forensic capability would have to be bigger than almost anything they'd come across before. London was jumpy, which was making the rest of the UK jump: other forces had to know what they were up against. We decided to circulate an internal video of the volatile peroxide mixture we'd found in the bath in Leeds. We wouldn't go public with it yet, but it would help police officers visualize the deadly cocktail of explosives in case they came across similar.

Next we organized a community assessment: what had been the impact of all this on the Muslim community in particular? Our searches for the bombers inevitably focused on Muslim areas where the men might hide. Would those living in these areas feel under siege? How much further damage to community relations would the shooting do? There were already reports of people referring to it as an execution. We needed to get specialist community officers out there talking to prominent people. What about the rest of the country? It was pretty difficult to reassure the public we were in control when we'd had a second set of bomb attempts, had four bombers on the run, and now a police shooting. How much more could we or the public take? And where would it end?

At some point during the day the commissioner, Sir Ian Blair, pulled me into his office and told me he had decided to try and stop the Independent Police Complaints Commission (IPCC) taking control of the latest crime scene – it happens automatically after a shooting by the police: independent expert investigators come in to find out what has taken place and whether or not the police were culpable in any way. Sir Ian had written to them, aiming to keep them away from the scene for the time being. This was a monumental decision. I remember feeling very surprised that he had taken this action. He was normally a cautious guy who, in my experience, rarely took risks, especially when they could have serious repercussions. As far as the police were concerned, the buck stopped with him, and if the risk proved a bad one he would have to take the blame. He had certainly not consulted me before sending his letter so I had to assume he had consulted others – not least the man to whom it was addressed to: Sir John Gieve, the permanent secretary at the Home Office and, as such, the highest-ranking civil servant there. Looking back, I wish I'd been more challenging. I didn't deliberately push Sir Ian to the wolves by not questioning his action more strongly; I simply assumed that he had cleared it. I was wrong. Where I really do kick myself is that I always used to remind others not to assume anything.

In my view, that letter was dynamite. It was dated 21 July, the day before the shooting, which was clearly an error as it was about the shooting so couldn't possibly have been written beforehand. In the letter Sir Ian suggested suspending Section 17 of the Police Reform Act, 2002, which gives the IPCC the right to enter the scene of a police shooting. He wrote to Sir John:

> The only choice an officer may have is to shoot to kill in order to prevent the detonation of a device . . . There is much concern about revealing either the tactics that we have and/or the sources of information on which we are operating . . . I have therefore given instructions that the shooting that has just occurred at Stockwell is not to be

referred to the IPCC and they will be given no access to the scene at the present time. The investigation will be carried out by the Met's own Directorate of Professional Standards. This investigation will be rigorous but subordinate to the needs of the counter-terrorism operation.

Sir Ian had taken a colossal decision, but he was the boss and he'd already made up his mind. By then, I believe, the letter had already been sent and he was merely informing me about it. It caused controversy, and within days we had reverted to the status quo and the IPCC came in. I believe the incident put the Met at loggerheads with the IPCC, souring its relationship with them; it would take many years to undo that. I wonder if some feel I was the instigator of that letter because I was head of Specialist Operations and my department would retain control of the scene. For years afterwards I felt I got undue grief from the IPCC as a result, which was regrettable as I had been the senior officer helping to advise them on the creation and introduction of the IPCC and had felt I enjoyed a good working relationship with people there and with their predecessors at the Police Complaints Authority.

Soon after this, during the afternoon of 22 July I went over to the Queen Elizabeth II Conference Centre a few hundred yards from New Scotland Yard where the assembled press corps was waiting. Irritatingly the planned conference kept being delayed and the two hundred or so journalists from across the world, including a bank of camera crews ready to transmit it live, were fractious. Eventually we were all gathered. I was there with Dick Fedorcio, and the commissioner turned up with his press officer, Joy Bentley. It was nearly 3.30. The four of us sat huddled outside the room to set the strategy for the press conference. Dick told us we'd be entering from the back and would have to walk to the side of the audience up to the stage. 'I'll introduce the press conference,' he suggested. 'Ian, can you give the broad overview, and Andy, the details. There's a huge screen behind you and while you speak the CCTV pictures of the four bombers will appear on it. Is that OK?' It was a sensible plan.

We opened the door and Ian went into the room. Bulbs flashed, cameras whirred. I walked behind him, thinking, Oh, God, this must go well. We need all the help we can get. I was worried I'd do one of those Spotty Dog-type walks, all stilted and strained, where your right arm and your right leg move together instead of opposites, which is more natural.

Dick did the introductions, then Ian set the scene. We expected him to be pretty constrained, outlining that the purpose of the conference was to publicize the four photographs. He started as expected – and then he went off piste. I nearly fell off my chair when he started addressing the shooting, telling the assembled reporters, 'The information I have available is that this shooting is directly linked to the ongoing and expanding anti-terrorist operation. Any death is deeply regrettable. I understand the man was challenged and refused to obey.'

This was news to me – the man when challenged refused to obey? Where had he got that from? I couldn't recall any conversation when that was shared as verified fact or speculative information – and even if that was known, there was no way we would have shared it at a worldwide press conference so soon after the event. It was earth-shattering. My first thought was that I must have been out of the loop – maybe there was information I wasn't aware of – which made me uncomfortable. I still didn't know for sure whether or not the man we'd shot was linked to the bomb attacks. Yet this planted a seed in the minds of those who attended the press conference that we might have killed one of the bombers. We did not want complacency on this. If it turned out he wasn't linked – which was a possibility – we would face the marathon task of adjusting and realigning the public's view. Worse still, in saying the man had been challenged and refused to obey, we had painted him as non-compliant, implying he was a bomber, thereby opening the way for a major complaint from the dead man's family if he turned out to be innocent. At this point I had no reason to believe this was so – but there was still an element of doubt.

I had to keep people focused on the manhunt. We needed to know more about the men on the run. What had they been doing before the attempted bomb attacks of the day before? Did they have accomplices? Instead we had given the press a great big carrot and they took it with relish. I thought gloomily that tomorrow's headlines were now more likely to be of the aftermath of the shooting than of the four bombers.

Only two weeks earlier we had talked long and hard about how we should handle the press in the wake of the 7 July bombings. Dick, Ian, others and I wanted to control the messages that went out. We knew we needed to limit the appearances Ian made: he would not be effective if he was over-promoted. On the counter-terrorism side, I realized that on straightforward operation issues, updates on the investigations, Peter Clarke should now come forward more and face the press, but when it went wider, with the multiple bombings, and when politics bore on the event, I would appear. We would both intermittently brief the Crime Reporters Association (CRA). It worked, and we established a good battle rhythm.

The press conference of 22 July should have been the same. We had been absolutely clear about its aim even though it had veered off course. We should have been on the front foot. Instead, for the next twenty-four to forty-eight hours, we were running to keep up. We should have been focused but instead we had gone off at a tangent.

When it came to my turn I presented the photographs. You could have heard a pin drop as the four appeared together on a massive screen above us. I thought it looked very dramatic and professional. I glanced down and saw in the front few rows the crime and home-affairs reporters from the tabloid and broadsheet newspapers and the main British television stations. They were scribbling furiously. But when it came to questions it was clear we'd lost them. They were following up on Ian's comments on the shooting: 'Was the dead man one of the four bombers, or was there a fifth?'

We were all over the shop. Of course Ian had to touch on the shooting – any report of a police killing would ordinarily attract a high profile and media interest so at some point it would have had to be addressed in the media. It could have been batted away neatly in this conference but now we were in deep with it. What Ian had said started a chain of events that would bring major criticism of the force, not least of him and me.

I left the press conference and made my way back to Scotland Yard. It was clear that we needed to identify the dead man fast. Assistant Commissioner Alan Brown was dealing with that. At my office I was met by one of our press officers, Paul Halford. His girlfriend had just telephoned him – she'd been the press officer at an internal meeting of the Gold command team trying to identify the dead man. He told me what she'd apparently said: 'You need to know they think the man we shot may *not* have been one of the bombers.'

I was due to brief the CRA. In a big conference you don't have the intimacy to exchange points and I wanted to make sure they were absolutely clear about the messages we were trying to get across. But first I had to check what Paul had just told me. My mobile-phone records show I had three calls around this time. I had made one to the Home Office, where I checked with civil servants whether the home secretary had any questions following the press conference. I was told he was busy but they'd tell him I'd called. We spoke for less than a minute. There was a missed call or text from Suzanna.

I also spoke with John McDowall. He was still acting as my second deputy and head of the Anti-Terrorist Branch until Peter returned, and I'd been out of circulation for two and a half hours: I needed an operational update from him. The last thing I would do was go into the CRA meeting without knowing developments. The call to John was no more than two minutes long. Neither he nor I can remember exactly what was said. What I do know is that it would be inconceivable for John to have told me that we had definitely identified the dead man as either a bomber or an innocent man. First, his identity was not confirmed until the early hours of 23 July so it would have been impossible to state either way, and, second, had there been any true concerns the call would have been more than two minutes long. I am adamant I would have met him to discuss anything that was significantly different from the information we had been running with at the press conference. Even if Paul Halford's comment was true, we still didn't know if the dead man could be linked to the bombings in a different way. As far as we were concerned, he was linked to the suspect address in South London. I decided not to discount any theory until facts were known: keeping an open mind is one of the most basic rules for any detective.

I went into the CRA meeting. To my frustration all they really wanted to know about was the shooting, and I couldn't be conclusive on that front. All I wanted was to get them on track in the hunt for the four bombers, but it was almost impossible. In hindsight, I was probably wrong in thinking otherwise. After all, the shooting was so newsworthy.

Reports of the exact words I used at the briefing vary. I was repeatedly questioned about the dead man. According to Paul Halford, and to a verbatim note made by one of the journalists, I said the dead man was 'not believed to be one of the suspects'. I am convinced that is what I said, but another press officer present suggests I missed out the words 'believed to be' and simply said he was 'not one of the suspects'. I would later be accused of believing he was definitely not one of them, but of failing to tell the commissioner so. Since that was not in fact true, I could not have said it either to the press or to the commissioner. It now seems so foolish that comprehensive notes of that conference were not taken or a recording made. It feels like a schoolboy error – that they keep a record now at these meetings is a direct result of what happened then.

By 17.07 the press were going berserk. The CRA briefing was over, and outside Scotland Yard the BBC went live with breaking news that, 'The man shot dead at the tube station is not thought to be one of the men shown in the CCTV pictures.' The reporter then quoted what the commissioner had said earlier, that the man had been challenged and refused to obey. The press were also reporting that the man had jumped the ticket barrier and was wearing a bulky jacket. We now know this was wrong. That information came from eye witnesses who mistook one of our firearms officers for the man they were chasing: it was they who had jumped the barrier and worn bulky jackets to hide their pistols, not the dead man.

It was to be an evening of meetings. I left the CRA

downstairs and was soon back on the eighth floor for a meeting of the Met's Management Board, which was followed immediately by another to discuss communications. At some point I must have been told they had found a wallet near the man, but my team would not have made any great fuss about that until it was proven relevant – we didn't deal in speculation. Ian Blair chaired both meetings, most of which we spent discussing the aborted bombings of the day before.

The commissioner and I were both at the first meeting, along with Alan Brown, the Gold commander dealing with the response and resourcing of the attacks, Deputy Commissioner Paul Stephenson, two other senior officers, Dick Fedorcio and Caroline Murdock, the commissioner's chief of staff, who took notes. There were two other people at the meeting whom Ian had felt it was prudent to invite. I imagine the purpose of including the Metropolitan Police Authority (MPA) chairman Len Duvall and his chief executive Catherine Crawford was that they shouldn't feel detached from the progress of the investigation. At the time I supported their inclusion, but there was a drawback: the boundary between the operational independence of the Met and the overview role of the MPA was in danger of being blurred. How could the chairman and chief executive remain detached in the future if they were later asked to scrutinize and reach conclusions about the way we had conducted ourselves in that meeting and the decisions we had taken – which, of course, is their job?

As it turned out, this first meeting was at the heart of the scrutiny into the shooting. When the IPCC received complaints from the dead man's family that we had misled them and the public, Len and Catherine were witnesses and had to provide witness statements yet they also had to decide whether we who had been in that meeting should be punished and if so how. The MPA has the power to discipline the police. When the IPCC in effect recommended it should consider disciplining me, Len and Catherine were among those who had to deal with the issue. In hindsight they should never have been at the meeting: we were discussing operational matters. To my mind, it was another example of the politicization of the Met.

Caroline Murdock wrote a version of the meeting from her original notes and I believe it's the fullest and most accurate. In it she says: 'AC Hayman commented that whilst he believed that on the balance of probabilities the man was not one of the four, the MPS [Metropolitan Police Service] needed at that stage to say that he still might be, as they did not yet know that he was not.' We discussed what to put out in a formal press release. I said that while it looked increasingly likely that he wasn't one of the bombers, our focus was on catching them and we didn't want the press to be distracted by the shooting.

Later I would be accused of misleading those at the meeting, by giving the impression that the dead man might have been involved when (the IPCC claimed) I knew he wasn't. Yet I could not have known this because the factual confirmation of his identity did not come until the early hours of 23 July.

In any case, whoever the deceased was, I didn't know that he wasn't involved in terrorism: I couldn't say either way. And that was what I said. My view was supported by Catherine Crawford, who told an independent inquiry that, 'AC Hayman gave the impression it was looking increasingly unlikely that the deceased was one of the four wanted men.' Len Duvall said his 'recollection was that the man was not one of the four sought in relation to the bombing but the connection to terrorism could not be ruled out completely'.

The commissioner took a different stance: he told the IPCC, which later investigated all this, that at the meeting they had the impression 'there was the possibility he was not one of the bombers but he was believed to be involved'. I recall that the meeting had the impression that nothing could be completely ruled out but it was looking as if the dead man was not one of the four wanted bombers. However, until his identity and a fuller picture became clear we couldn't absolutely rule anything out. If Sir Ian took the view that he might be the bomber, why did he not direct that more pro-active action was needed? Also, had I thought the commissioner held that view I would have challenged him and tried to find out why.

To put it another way, at that meeting Sir Ian was still swaying towards the probability that the man who had been shot was involved in terrorism, while I and others were moving to a position that suggested the likelihood was that he was not – though none of us really knew and the discussion was speculative.

At the time of his retirement Sir Ian continued to leave hanging the point that he would have expected to be told if the shot man had been innocent. The IPCC report accused me of misleading the commissioner and the public, and of covering up for several hours on the day that they'd shot the wrong man. I absolutely refute that suggestion.

After the meeting I went straight back to my office to catch up with my top team. Everything was moving so fast and I needed to hear where they were at and to debrief them on the press conference, the CRA and the commissioner's meetings. Midway through our session there was a knock at the door and Dick Fedorcio was standing there. 'Andy, I've got a press release we're going to send out as a result of the meeting we just had.'

I said to him, 'I'm chairing a meeting. Who's seen the release?'

I recall he named two people. Now I might have given it a cursory read but I do remember saying that if those two had seen it and were content with it it was fine by me. It was published as follows:

> The man shot at Stockwell is still subject to formal identification and it is not yet clear whether he is one of the four people we are seeking to identify and whose pictures have been released today. It therefore remains extremely important that members of the public continue to assist police in relation to all four pictures. This death, like all deaths related to police operations, is obviously a matter of deep regret. Nevertheless the man who was shot was under police observation because he had emerged from a house that was itself under observation because it was linked to the investigation of yesterday's incidents. He was then followed by surveillance officers to the station. His clothing and behaviour at the station added to their suspicions. While the counter-terrorist investigation will obviously take pre-eminence, the investigations into the circumstances that led to his death are being pursued and will be subject to scrutiny through the IPCC [Independent Police Complaints Commission] in due course.

Later I would take the direct hit for sanctioning that release – and again I would be accused by the IPCC of misleading the public in implying the man was a terrorist when they claim I already knew he wasn't. Not true. My recollection is that I hadn't written it and neither was I the ultimate authority. The (in my view woeful) IPCC report failed to show why my actions more than those of other members of the Management Board, who had either written the release, read it or both, warranted punishment.

By now Scotland Yard was rife with rumour and innuendo. There was a meeting with leading Muslims, who were apparently told that the man shot was not a Muslim and not connected to the bombings. At 6.45 p.m. the commissioner was told by one of his staff that they could not formally identify the dead man visually and needed to wait for DNA samples. She said that to her knowledge he was not a terrorist.

At 7 p.m. the commissioner left the Yard to go, I presume, to his Chelsea flat and did not return until 9.30 the next morning.

Later, results came through on a Halifax Building Society card. The National Terrorist Funding Investigation Unit had established it belonged to Jean Charles de Menezes. It showed his address was not the one where the wanted bomber Hussain Osman lived, but an address nearby. This did not rule out the possibility that he could still have been linked to the bombs but the case against it was building.

At 7.30 p.m. Peter Clarke arrived back from holiday. I filled him in and soon after eight I passed the baton and also left the office. I had only had two hours' sleep the night before and now I had the chance to catch up and allow the teams to get on with their forensic work without interference. I left knowing who the dead man wasn't – Osman – but not knowing who he was. I wasn't going to express as fact matters that had not been verified as such – but I would pay a price for this.

During the night there were developments. I was not kept abreast of them – and neither was the commissioner. He maintains to this day that he did not know until the next morning that the police had shot an innocent man while the view that I knew and did not tell him prevails – to my anger: it was not the case.

There is a big difference between categorically knowing the identity of someone and believing or suspecting it. On 22 July we were under extreme pressure, the situation was critical, and someone in my position cannot resort to speculation or guesswork: we have to work only with facts. All afternoon views had been bouncing round Scotland Yard but whatever the rumours and possibilities we could not have known then that the dead man was not a terrorist. It was not until the early hours of 23 July 2005 when detectives working on his identity officially confirmed, through a work colleague of his and through his family, that he was a young Brazilian called Jean Charles de Menezes.

I had no reason to keep information from the commissioner. Neither was there any reason why I should have been woken during the night when they finally identified Jean Charles de Menezes to pass that message on. I was in charge of the bomb investigations but I was not in operational control of the crime scene at Stockwell station where de Menezes was shot. Assistant Commissioner Alan Brown was Gold commander, head of internal investigations and professional standards, and it was his job. I respected him and left him and his team to it. Alan would maintain control of the scene of the shooting and look for evidence that might help our terrorist investigation, and he had to find the identity of the dead man. He would then hand over to our counter-terrorism investigators so they could check with any evidence linked to terrorism. Only after that, the commissioner had decided, would we hand over to the IPCC, who would investigate the shooting and whether there was any culpability on the part of the police. They would also follow up any other complaints against the police linked to it – which was why I would soon be crossing their path.

My heart goes out to the family who lost their beloved son through the actions of the police that day. But I also believe it was right for my team's focus to remain on catching the bombers. Had we allowed emotion to stifle our efforts, the escaped bombers might have mounted a further wave of attacks and killed even more innocent people. I stand by my judgement.

The next day was a Saturday. I was back at my desk in time for a quick update from my deputies. I was told that during the night Alan Brown had identified the man and handed the scene of the shooting over to our counter-terrorist detectives to look for anything linked to terrorism. That was progressing. I looked up to the TV on the wall in my office as Sky News came live to Scotland Yard as the commissioner was arriving. He told the assembled reporters his force was 'playing out of its socks'. Little did he know just how bad that would sound an hour or so later. He, like the rest of us, was unaware of the bombshell that was about to hit us.

It wasn't until 10 a.m. that we were officially told the horrific news. Alan Brown made the revelation to a meeting of senior officers, myself included, chaired by the commissioner. Our suspicions were proved correct. We had shot an innocent man. He had now been clearly identified as Jean Charles de Menezes, a Brazilian electrician who had no links with terrorism. His tragic fate had been sealed because he lived in the wrong place at the wrong time, his flat in the same block as one of the bombers we were now hunting.

Of course it had crossed our minds we'd shot the wrong man – but when Alan Brown spelt out the harsh reality that morning we were horrified. His words hung in the air. The dead man, Jean Charles de Menezes, was an innocent bystander with no link to terrorism. The room was absolutely silent for what felt like a lifetime, though it was probably only a few seconds. Then I remember thinking, That letter to the IPCC is going to look very foolish. We've got to recover our position as some could interpret from it that we knew it was an innocent person and we were buying time to get our act together before allowing independent investigators in. That wasn't Ian's motivation when he wrote it and I knew that – but we might face an uphill task in convincing others.

My thoughts were also for the dead man's family. His parents were in Brazil and, on top of their terrible grief, they would have to come to terms with the tragic circumstances of his death, which had emanated from a terrorist incident in a country thousands of miles away. For a moment I felt almost overwhelmed. There was so much to do. I needed to put in new resources to deal with the aftermath of the shooting – but without compromising the hunt for the four bombers. We still had to get on with the job we'd started out to do, which was to track and catch them. I thought of the marksman who maybe, in a couple of days' time, I would ask to sit on a rooftop and watch someone I believed to be one of four bombers about to detonate a bomb. How would that marksman feel in the knowledge that a few days earlier one of his colleagues had shot an innocent man?

Nearly two years after the Stockwell shooting I received a letter accusing me of failing to notify the commissioner as soon as I knew that the man we had shot was innocent. In it the IPCC warned that I faced scathing criticism for my role in the aftermath of the shooting. It was about to publish a report alleging that I chose to mislead the public because I told reporters at the CRA briefing that we had shot the wrong man, but failed to tell my boss and other senior officers at a meeting later that evening. They went further, alleging I 'deliberately' withheld the information from the commissioner. The family of the dead man had complained of a cover-up at the Met – and the investigation concluded that I was to blame.

I was shocked and deeply hurt. I felt that what they alleged was grossly unfair. They had spent many hours interviewing me, had read all the different versions of what had happened and clearly had not understood. In my opinion, they had cherry-picked from different accounts of that day, ignoring some by the most upstanding of witnesses and using others that were less reliable.

The IPCC has a panel of expert investigators from all walks of life who scrutinize complaints as transparently as possible in the interest of boosting public confidence in the police. They are either former police officers or investigators from other bodies such as Customs. They also include ex-store detectives. I had been compliant and helpful with them. I now saw I would have to change tactics and defend myself vigorously. No other officer had been punished over the shooting, and I wanted to clear my name. I sent a full rebuttal of the allegations via my lawyer.

You may conclude it was a fuss over minor detail. All I know is that I briefed both the press and the Met's Management Board that the dead man was not believed to be one of the four bombers. I could not have gone further because formal identification didn't happen until the middle of that night. Time and time again I've been over the facts – the chief executive of the MPA, Catherine Crawford, told the IPCC I'd given the impression it was looking increasingly unlikely that the deceased was one of the four wanted men. The chairman of the MPA, Len Duvall, was also at the Management Board meeting and he told the IPCC he recalled being told that the shot man was not one of the four sought in relation to the bombings, 'though a connection with terrorism could not be ruled out'. Even the commissioner told the IPCC he remembered being told, 'There was a possibility he was not one of the bombers but he was believed to be involved.' I believe that shows I did not mislead the meeting as to the status of the dead man. Neither does it conflict with what I told the crime reporters.

The IPCC appears to have ignored my lawyer's letter. They published the allegations and accusations and though, as a professional officer, I accepted the outcome of the report, I did not agree with it. I believe that if the investigation had been really thorough it would have reached a different conclusion. In my view it muddled details and missed out critical words from statements; its authors omitted to speak to key players, like my deputy Peter Clarke.

I didn't get too agitated about the situation because I was confident that a cart and horses could have been driven through the holes in the IPCC's conclusions, and was pretty optimistic that at a disciplinary hearing the overwhelming weight of evidence in my favour would win the day. A hearing would have been chaired by a senior barrister, supported by other senior people who, I feel, would have seen that the IPCC had failed to show motive, my likely gain and, more importantly, the evidence to prove their case.

In the event the MPA decided not to support the IPCC's recommendations. The IPCC adjusted their position and recommended I receive 'management advice' from the chairman of the MPA and from the commissioner. To this day I have received none. I still wonder why the IPCC spent something like an hour in a live press conference severely criticizing my actions and concluding that I should face disciplinary charges, then never followed through to make sure I got the words of wisdom they had called for. All I know is that when the IPCC report was published several newspapers claimed I had been made a scapegoat, and colleagues within the Met let me know they shared that view.

The IPCC carried out two investigations into Stockwell. The first went into the events surrounding the shooting. It has been well documented: an innocent man lost his life, and his family and the wider community needed that to be investigated. The report was critical of individual officers involved in the shooting, but the Crown Prosecution Service did not find enough evidence to charge anyone over it. The second IPCC investigation related to my actions.

The outcome of the investigations cannot have brought consolation to Jean Charles de Menezes' family. I can only say there was no cover-up by the Met over his tragic death – if there had been it would have been unearthed because we have rarely faced such intense scrutiny. There have been six inquiries altogether into the incident – two by the IPCC, one by the MPA and another by the Met. Then the Health and Safety Executive brought a case against the Met and found it guilty of putting the public at risk over the shootings; it was fined £175,000 and had to pay £385,000 in legal costs. The sixth investigation was the inquest into Jean Charles's death, which returned an open verdict. Each investigation had a different focus and tested different issues, and I believe that now all bases have been covered.

Jean Charles's death has brought big changes in the way we operate. There is a new, tighter chain of command; there is a new model for handling crises; note-taking at meetings and briefings is now routine. CRA briefings are minuted, internal briefings, including those to the firearms teams, are recorded, and there is a different protocol for working with the IPCC.

But the harsh truth is that there is little alternative to the shoot-to-kill policy. Faced with a potential terrorist you believe is about to detonate a bomb and kill many innocent people, what else can you do? In the de Menezes case it led to tragedy but in another situation it may be a life-saver.

After the 7 July attacks, police were responding to reports of suspected suicide bombers at a rate of four or five a day. On one occasion we reacted to reports of a cyclist behaving suspiciously in Parliament Square. Undercover officers and armed police were deployed and had the Kratos shoot-to-kill rules available to them as a tactical option. They watched the man and quickly decided he was not a threat. He was wholly unaware of how close he came to being shot.

We ask our armed police and commanders to make split-second decisions, and on the day that Jean Charles lost his life, no officer had gone to work to kill an innocent man. Circumstances led to the mistake, not the strategy. This is a plan without a get-out clause. We have to support officers who volunteer to conduct such a difficult job. If they blink when faced with a life-and-death situation, mass casualty and death may result. The terrorist will look to exploit any weakness or loss of confidence by the police.

So, many significant shifts in policy and new directives have emerged from the mistakes of Stockwell. But one issue that remains unresolved is the conundrum faced by law-enforcement agencies: how do you balance the operational requirement to collect evidence and secure public safety against the risks it presents? In Stockwell the police operation aimed to protect the public from four suicide bombers on the loose and to collect evidence that could be marshalled against them for their attempted attacks on 21 July. The inherent risks in pursuing that aim were accounted for but, sadly, the mistaken shooting was not avoided.

There's an interesting contrast between that outcome and other operations. Take, for example, the arrests of the two 21/7 bombers in their flat in West London: it was achieved safely and attracted much praise. The operation involved several hundred police officers, the majority of whom were armed. Had there been no one in the flat or, worse, we knocked on the door to the wrong flat (it does happen), I guess the praise would have quickly reverted to criticism.

7. The Great and the Good

EVEN IN THOSE DIFFICULT DAYS FROM 7 TO 21 JULY 2005 AND afterwards, there had been highlights: the bravery and dignity of the injured and the bereaved, the heroism of the public in the aftermath of the bombs, the resilience and determination of both police officers and colleagues from the security agencies. Throughout this period we also had tremendous help and support from the Royal Family, who made a number of interventions, both private and public.

Part of my job in overseeing anti-terrorist operations was to ensure the safety of VIPs, diplomats and royalty. The Queen and her family are iconic targets and we had to keep them safe. But they also play a vital role in countering terrorism. From doing my job I learnt that the Royal Household were often several steps ahead of anyone else. They had a good instinct on whether and when to become involved. They're particularly good at three things: reassuring the public that no one has been forgotten; underlining the view that what the terrorists do is wrong and an infringement of our society; and encouraging the security and emergency services. All this undermines the terrorist. We regarded the Royal Family as a supportive partner in our response to the bomb attacks.

On the protection side, a multi-agency committee is charged with establishing the degree and nature of protection for royalty. The Royal and VIP Executive Committee (RAVEC) is chaired by a part-time senior civil servant at the Home Office. The Queen's private secretary sits on the committee as Her Majesty's representative. My head of Royal and Diplomatic Protection, Commander Peter Loughborough, represented the Met. He is also the Earl of Rosslyn and, as far as I know, the only serving policeman who's a peer.

When the bombings happened he immediately reviewed all royal, diplomatic and VIP security and gave me his risk assessment. He was also contacted by Buckingham Palace who, I assumed, told him the Queen wanted to play her part in the response to the attacks. He was told she was deeply concerned and wanted to convey messages of reassurance and caring to the injured and bereaved. I had met the Queen privately when I was chief constable of Norfolk and I was not surprised she wanted to do this. I had absolute faith in Peter's ability to act on her request and to do what was needed. He negotiated with RAVEC and they decided that the benefits of a series of royal visits outweighed any security risks.

On 8 July, just over twenty-four hours after the attacks, the Queen made a rallying call for public unity. She condemned the terrorists and boosted the morale of the emergency responders. Like most, I had watched on television similar messages after tragedies. I probably dismissed them as routine – the right thing to do. Now, having seen their effect first-hand, I understand their positive impact. The Queen visited survivors of the explosions at the Royal

London Hospital in Whitechapel, and said, 'Those who perpetrate these brutal acts against innocent people should know that they will not change our way of life.'

It was highly unusual for the monarch to comment so soon after an incident but the Queen felt she should do so. Meanwhile the Prince of Wales and the Duchess of Cornwell visited the injured at St Mary's Hospital in Paddington.

Although Royal Protection was delegated to a special unit in my department I took a special interest in the security of the Queen, especially with the new heightened risk. That's because when I was chief constable of Norfolk we were responsible for her security when she visited her home at Sandringham. On my first day in the top job in Norfolk at the beginning of January 2003, I was a bit shocked to receive a phone call from the Royal Household inviting my wife and me to Sandringham for lunch with the Queen. It was apparently a regular event that on the third Sunday in January the chief constable and his wife went to church with the Queen, had sherry at the vicarage and then lunch at Sandringham House. I remember going home and telling Jane, 'You'll never guess what – we're going to lunch with the Queen!' We both thought it would be good fun and a real privilege. We assumed there'd be lots of people and we'd be lucky to speak to her. The only guidance I was given was to make sure we addressed her as 'Your Majesty' first and thereafter as 'ma'am' (to rhyme with 'ham', not 'arm').

We turned up for the service, which was taken by the Archbishop of Canterbury, went on to the vicarage, and then we arrived at Sandringham. Out came a footman and a lady-in-waiting. The latter took Jane to the ladies' room and I went into a hall where I walked over to the blazing fire and looked around. It was a room grand in architecture but relaxed in style. The Sunday papers were piled on a table and there were several half-done jigsaws. I thought, Mmm– there ain't a lot of people here. I'd imagined it would be a big event and we'd be able to get lost in it. A minute ago I was worried about getting the pronunciation of 'ma'am' right. Now I was wondering what on earth I was going to talk to the Queen about all through lunch. Then in she came with the Duke of Edinburgh, followed soon after by Jane, and the conversation started. It was very easy – I can't go into detail because protocol doesn't allow it – but before I knew it we were ushered through to the dining room. To my astonishment, there were only twelve of us, including the Archbishop. I sat to the right of the Queen at the oval table. Opposite was the Duke of Edinburgh with Jane next to him. On my right was a house guest of the Queen.

I sat down and turned to Her Majesty, only to find her chatting nineteen to the dozen to the person on the other side. Had I offended her? I'd thought the pre-lunch conversation was fine. I felt a nudge from the guest on the other side, who explained, 'It's two courses to the left and two courses to the right. You'll have conversation when the Queen moves off the main course – you get sweet, cheese and coffee. You don't talk across the table.'

Eventually the sweet course came up and at this point the Queen turned to me. We started to talk about crime and victims of crime, and how important it was that you focused on who had done it, rather than becoming preoccupied with the victims. I was really struck by the fact she understood so much – and then I remembered she, too, had been a victim of crime.

In July 1982, at 7.15 one morning, a thirty-one-year-old father of four, Michael Fagan, broke into Buckingham Palace and made his way unchallenged into the Queen's bedroom. She woke up and found herself alone with a barefooted man dressed in jeans and a dirty T-shirt. There was outrage at the time because he could have been a terrorist or an assassin. Calmly she kept him talking for ten minutes, discussing the coincidence that they both had four children. When he asked for a cigarette she coolly picked up the phone and called the Palace switchboard – but her restrained manner did not bring an urgent reaction to what would have been a very odd request from Her Majesty, especially at that time in the morning. She had to call a second time before she got a response. The incident ended calmly with Fagan's arrest. It was a stark reminder that the Queen faced many types of threat, from terrorists, organized criminals and unstable or unpredictable people acting alone.

From that time I have had a soft spot for the Royal Family and sometimes think the press has been less than fair to them. The conversation I had with Her Majesty at Sandringham came back to me when, as head of Specialist Operations, I became the Met lead for her protection. I must make sure, I thought, that I never let something like that happen on my watch. I was very aware that on my predecessor's watch, a comedian, Aaron Barshak, dressed as Osama bin Laden in a pink ballgown, had talked his way past police at Prince William's twenty-first birthday party at Windsor Castle. He had mixed with guests and members of the Royal Family before jumping on stage while Prince William made a speech.

When it came to the Prince of Wales's marriage to the Duchess of Cornwall I was taking no chances. I was insistent that we put Barshak under surveillance in case he decided to be silly. I thought there was a fair chance he might try to embarrass everyone again as it was such a high-profile royal event. Lo and behold, we followed him covertly to the *Sun* newspaper offices, where he appeared to be carrying a dummy bomb. It gave me the excuse to arrest him and hold him in a cell for the two days the wedding was on. Now, when the terrorist risk is real, we cannot be distracted by pranksters from providing adequate security.

My views on our Royal Family, and the role its members could take in the wider fight to undermine terrorism, became more firmly entrenched several weeks after the 7 July bomb attacks. Much of the publicity had died down when Prince Andrew, the Duke of York, contacted us discreetly and said he wanted to make a private visit to Scotland Yard to meet those involved in the investigation. When I met him, I sensed that while he knew it was right for the victims and bereaved to meet the Queen, he felt that with his military background he could give the emergency and security services support and encouragement. He had been through conflict himself in the Falklands War and, as a former naval officer, understood that even the professionals could benefit from a pat on the back. It was strictly a private visit – although news of it leaked out because the camera crews camped permanently outside the rotating New Scotland Yard sign spotted him.

I was waiting for him in our reception area and was momentarily taken aback when his Jaguar drove up and he stepped out from behind the steering-wheel. From the minute he arrived he gave the impression he really wanted to be there. He wasn't in any hurry, keen to speak to and meet as many people as he could. I led him straight to the first lift, which we'd jammed open in anticipation of his arrival. We went immediately to Peter Clarke's office. On the way up the Duke's private secretary ran through the itinerary, suggesting a few changes. I pointed out we had people working on the inquiry across London, though the hard core were at the Yard.

Once we arrived at Peter's room on the thirteenth floor

there were no formalities: it was like a meeting of old friends – Peter knew the Duke because he used to be head of Royal Protection. Chief Superintendent Tim White, one of our senior counter-terrorism officers, was also in the room along with Commander John McDowall. The Duke accepted a mug of tea and we briefed him. He had no interest in polite chit-chat but asked focused and searching questions. He knew when to joke and when to be sombre and serious. He offered sympathy for the dreadful circumstances of the bombing, asked about operational strains and wanted to know if we were able to function adequately and had access to everything we needed.

He also made it clear he didn't want to spend too long talking to the bosses: he wanted to walk the floors – and I have to say he must have worn down his shoe leather. He visited every nook and cranny of the Yard. For two hours he was on his feet. He saw the CCTV analysts who'd spent the best part of a month viewing footage. He spoke to the detectives now undertaking the biggest murder investigation ever seen in the UK, and the forensics teams who'd spent so long searching the tunnels. We had established the largest major-incident room I'd seen in my entire career – it spanned two floors, each with a corridor going round the entire circumference of the building with large open-plan offices off each side of it. He walked from pod to pod, chatting to every single person he could see, introducing anecdotes from his own experience that resonated with people operating under strain.

'I guess you've had the same problems here as in the pitch of battle,' he told one group. 'You pull a lever and press a button and it doesn't work.' He said the classic problem he'd found himself up against, especially in the Falklands, was communications failure. 'When comms go down,' he commented, drawing an analogy with what happened underground after the attacks, 'it becomes a very lonely place'. His contribution buoyed everyone. He left as he'd arrived – driving himself rather than leaving that to his protection team. His visit was the talk of the floors for days – a much-needed morale boost to the team as they worked meticulously through the evidence to piece together the true story behind the July bomb attacks.

As we progressed through the summer of 2005, and the raw shock of the attacks subsided, we were all struggling to find the best ways to hunt and stop the terrorists. This was new territory for everyone: police, government, MPs, lawyers and so on. The political debates in particular were very time-consuming, taking place when most of us were still doing the day job. The one person who really seemed to understand this was the prime minister, who in those early days kept the politics away from us as much as possible.

My dealings with Tony Blair were professional and focused – it was a formal and mutually respectful relationship. First, my team and I had to protect him. Early in 2005 I studied the reaction to an earlier threat against him. It had happened in 2002 at the time of the Queen's golden-jubilee celebrations. Intelligence suggested there was a significant plot to target Tony Blair and his wife Cherie during the ceremonies. The Blairs predictably insisted on taking part as planned so Sir David Veness and the then commissioner Lord Stevens worked out a plan in response to the threat, placing a shield of undercover armed officers around them. In his memoirs Lord Stevens said the fact that nothing untoward happened was 'a tribute to our intelligence-gathering and to the precautions we took'. Three years later I studied the operation so that if the need arose I could respond in a similarly appropriate way.

As well as providing protection I also had to work very closely with the prime minister on policing strategies. When I had been a chief inspector many years earlier, and he was shadow home secretary, he had grasped that sweeping plans to reform the police could not work because they were private-sector ideas being imposed on a public-sector organization that wasn't ready for them. He saw that while changes were needed they had to be feasible within the police structures that then existed.

I first found myself working to him directly when he became prime minister and we were developing a new anti-drugs strategy. It was in the late 1990s and I was chair of the Association of Chief Police Officers' drugs committee and advised him on aspects of his plans. I was surprised how adventurous, even controversial, he was, investing heavily in drugs treatment programmes aimed at reducing the demand for illicit drugs by getting people off a habit. This idea had not been fully tested in practice and was therefore a leap of faith, but it had the potential to improve the health of the nation, reducing drugs-related crime and trafficking. It was a risk but Tony Blair's desire to plan for the long term seemed unique, given how many politicians look for quick fixes. Did it work? Probably not as well as we'd hoped: there were never enough rehab places and other events took priority. When I came to work with the prime minister on anti-terrorist legislation, I felt the trust we'd built up during the drugs work set us in good stead.

Now that he was prime minister and I was in charge of the UK police counter-terrorism strategies, we'd meet by the fireplace in his office at the House of Commons over a fine china cup of tea, in the Cabinet Office at Number 10 or at COBRA. He seemed very conscious that it had been on his watch that the first suicide bombers had arrived on the streets of the UK. He never discussed why terrorists were focusing on Britain – it would not have been appropriate, and my job was to concentrate on the investigations, and on preventing future attacks. He was a strong leader, and serious in his approach, never raised his voice or said a cross word, though he could voice irritation. At times he was witty and amusing.

The prime minister, of course, had a sharp eye on the politics of the day, which his forceful, uncompromising statement on 5 August, a month after the 7 July bomb attacks showed: 'Let no one be in any doubt, the rules of the game are changing,' he said, then announced a catalogue of measures aimed at undermining the terrorists and making the country more secure. It was a message to the terrorists that they would be targeted and hunted down – there would be no tolerance. At the same time the prime minister was alerting the public to the potentially controversial fact that our civil liberties would have to be dented in the search for the perpetrators of the atrocities and those who helped them, and in the push to stop further attacks.

After this we met more frequently: I worked directly to him, seeing through those parts of his plans which related to policing, the new anti-terrorist laws, community initiatives, police and intelligence structures aimed at countering terrorism. He pushed to ensure things got done and saw that we had the budget to deal with the heightened terrorist threat. He supported our operational independence. We had to go to him when we were considering decisions that would have political or economic repercussions – putting six thousand extra police on the streets, for example, or closing the Underground – but he also placed faith in us, confident of the way we handled things. He was a man who let people have their head – he delegated – and would set us all off in a strategic direction.

I made it my personal responsibility to handle his security after he stood down as prime minister and as an MP. More than ever now, in these days of the Al Qaeda threat, his role in the world's response to it, the Iraq war, his continued high profile and work as an envoy in the Middle East, Tony Blair requires 24/7 protection. He is no longer prime minister, but the threat to him hasn't disappeared.

In my role as assistant commissioner in charge of Specialist Operations I also had to deal with three home secretaries. My often daily dealings were no-nonsense, straightforward and personable. Charles Clarke handled the July 2005 bombing, while Dr John Reid was in the post by the time we were confronted with a series of even more complex, sophisticated and potentially lethal plots in 2006 and 2007. Both men held the reins during what I believe was one of the most difficult periods we have ever faced when it comes to terrorism. Dr Reid didn't suffer fools gladly – if people weren't pulling their weight he let them know it, though I think his bark was worse than his bite. I felt I knew where I stood with him: he said what he wanted and asked us to get on with it.

I also spent a few months supporting Jacqui Smith when she was grappling with the terrorist threat to the UK. Her style as home secretary was completely different from that of her predecessors – probably less formal and less hands-on. She inherited the early thinking to split the Home Office, with Jack Straw assuming the lead for the justice system. I'm not convinced that was the right move: we now have two departments dealing with one process. The Home Office deals with preventing and trying to detect crime, but once a crime is committed and the courts and punishment systems kick in the Justice Department takes over. There's a danger that the two departments won't communicate with each other and become detached and, of course, the new system relies on the two ministers getting on.

It's undeniable that the job of home secretary is massive but one person needs to take an overview of all the issues covered by both departments because they are so closely intertwined. Now both departments compete against each other for budgets and profile rather than always working together.

Counter-terrorism is, politically, highly charged but I found that behind-the-scenes discussions and briefings did not usually recognize party boundaries. The Privy Council is an ancient committee made up of senior MPs and other leading figures that advises the Queen and the prime minister and helps regulate a large number of institutions in the UK and the Commonwealth. It has provided rules under which people like me can brief politicians. These ensure that material from briefings can't be used for political gain or passed on. The rules allow opposition parties to be briefed as long as government or operational secrets are not compromised, and without them discussions on sensitive terrorist operations would be deprived of input from well-informed people. If we were restricted to briefing only government ministers, who make the key decisions, we would be limited to just one sounding board on terrorist issues with political dimensions (which is most of them). Under Privy Council rules, I regularly briefed David Cameron as leader of the opposition. I never strayed from the facts, laced with my analysis on how events in the UK were unfolding. I stopped short of briefing him on imminent interdictions, which would have undermined the roles of the home secretary, the prime minister and, ultimately, the government and cabinet, who had to make important and often quick decisions.

Of course, the biggest advantage of this was that we could

get cross-party support for terrorist operations. I had worked on similar principles when I was chief constable in Norfolk. On a quarterly basis I met the leaders and party representatives on the county council, each party separately, making sure they received the same material. This gave me the opportunity to elicit their views, which might help to inform policy development and perhaps bring to light any concerns. I could then either address these privately or, if they had made a point I had missed, could change my original plans.

David Cameron is good at putting you at ease – the atmosphere was always relaxed and conducive to a free exchange of views. We met in his parliamentary office – and I had the impression that, rather than going through the motions, he had a genuine interest in the various things we discussed: his interventions reflected it. He was strikingly concerned about what it was like for those doing the job on a day-to-day basis – he wanted to ensure that policy did not get in the way of practical policing, that it should help, not hinder.

As well as dealing with royalty, VIPs and politicians, there was a third element in the protection work: diplomats. And, as with royalty, many diplomats had and, indeed, still have a role to play in hunting terrorists. It's no secret that the intelligence agencies often use the British embassies as a refuge, working alongside the Special Branch police officers we put in all the big embassies, and when there is an act of terrorism in a foreign country we frequently send out people to offer help and advice, and to glean information. In the immediate aftermath of the hotel shootings in Mumbai, in India, at the end of 2008, when Western tourists were targeted and killed, members of the Counter-Terrorism Command went to India and were supported by British officers already in the region.

I was very aware of the responsibility involved in protecting diplomats and of the importance of understanding and keeping contact with the embassies, which can play such a vital role in hunting terrorists. In May 2005, I went to reconnoitre the hotel in Malta where Commonwealth heads of state would meet with the Queen later that year. I saw this as a good opportunity to get to know that embassy and the workings of embassies generally.

There was another pressing reason for my visit: with the terrorist threat uppermost in my mind I wanted to convince the Maltese that the British protection officers who'd be on duty during the meeting should be armed. This was difficult as they were reluctant to permit people from other countries to carry weapons. At the embassy, I met the 'head of station' – in effect, my equivalent in MI6. I wanted him onside to persuade the Maltese government that Tony Blair and the Queen needed armed protection. We worked hard, and I attended a series of top-level meetings with ministers and officials, but eventually the deal was done. In November 2005, the Queen and the prime minister went to Malta, and I am pleased to report that, in part thanks to our meticulous preparations, the meeting went without any major hitch on the security front.

While I was in Malta I found time to get to know the ambassador – a vital contact: two years later we would work closely together again when he was posted to Tripoli to oversee the bringing to justice of the killers of PC Yvonne Fletcher, who'd been shot during a protest outside the Libyan embassy in St James's Square, London, in 1984.

All the diplomats from abroad living in London receive protection to varying degrees. In the main these people go about their daily business with no personal protection. The Diplomatic Protection Group, which uses red-liveried patrol cars, offers armed mobile patrols and, in some instances, static sentry posts. It is the largest armed unit in the UK. Trevor Lock is probably the best known police constable to have worked for this division. In 1980 he was guarding the Iranian embassy in London when six gunmen stormed it, taking him and twenty-five others hostage. He acted as go-between to the hostage-takers and the police outside, and tackled the lead gunman when soldiers from the SAS stormed the embassy to free them. PC Lock was awarded the George Cross for his bravery.

I had more personal contact with the Israeli and the American ambassadors than with most others because of the particular threat against them. In particular, I struck up a close friendship with the Israeli ambassador, Zvi Heifetz, which enabled difficult political issues that affected the Jewish community to be addressed promptly.

That will have given you some idea of the wider dimensions we had to take into account when hunting terrorists: it wasn't just about responding to attacks but keeping the fabric of our society and its vulnerable targets safe – and at every turn trying to undermine those who supported terrorism. It was important to maintain a wide brief and an open mind – because the next brand of terrorism I was to come across was as bizarre and unlikely as anything that had come before.

8. On Superpowers and Spies: the Litvinenko Murder and a Second Assassination Attempt

STORIES OF SUPERPOWERS AND SPIES DON'T COME MUCH MORE bizarre than the real-life drama that would preoccupy me over the winter of 2006/7. Alexander Litvinenko was a Russian dissident living in London when he was poisoned and died a slow and agonizing death under the glare of the world's press. This was no ordinary criminal murder but one of international significance, and as such it fell to anti-terrorist officers to investigate and ensure that the perpetrators did not strike again.

The terrorist threat to the stability of the UK comes mainly from Al Qaeda-linked groups – but also from other sources, including residual groups from the Cold War stand-off between the former Soviet Union and the West that had dominated the second half of the twentieth century. What no one knew at the time of this murder was that while the diplomats were wrangling over whether the Russian state was behind that killing, I was mulling over a briefing I had given President Vladimir Putin just over a year earlier in which we had discussed some of the UK's most sensitive intelligence issues post-7 July, as if he were a close ally. What an enigmatic man he proved to be.

It had taken place during the first week of October 2005, three months after the 7/7 bomb attacks, when we were still working like crazy on that and the 21/7 investigation. Suzanna Becks, my deputy, alerted me: 'Andy, Downing Street meeting Wednesday – you and Eliza, COBRA, top-secret briefing with the Russians.'

I was in overall command of security plans for a visit that week by President Vladimir Putin – now the Russian prime minister – which included a full-scale summit in London of European Union leaders. Talks on the thorny issue of Russia's ongoing conflict with neighbouring Chechnya were likely. Only the week before, Amnesty International had accused Russian forces of 'gross human-rights violations' in Chechnya, and we had to be prepared for protests and demonstrations.

On top of this, President Putin was considered to be at high risk of assassination: he would bring his own body-guards to protect him alongside our armed officers. The other visiting leaders were regarded as potential terrorist targets, too, and had to be protected.

I phoned a civil servant I'd been dealing with at Downing Street about this to find out more about the meeting. It transpired that during the three-day visit the Russian President wanted a security exchange: he would talk about tactics they used in dealing with Chechen rebels and we would discuss our handling of the July bombings.

I picked up the phone and fixed a meeting with Eliza Manningham-Buller to discuss what we'd talk about when we met Putin. Later that day I went across to MI5 head-quarters, an old 1930s-style office block overlooking the Thames.

The reception area is bland, as it is in most government institutions. The security guys knew me and ushered me through to Eliza's austere, wood-panelled office. She was punctilious about order and tidiness and I knew her staff would have plumped up the cushions in the seating area before I went in – it was one of her foibles. As ever, the papers on her desk were neatly stacked, the room minimalist and functional.

We worked out the line for our forthcoming briefing. She would handle intelligence – what we knew about the bombers, their international links, those pulling the strings. I would give an operational briefing, describing the forensic way in which we had pieced together what had happened on those two devastating days in July. We worked out how her input and mine would complement each other.

I took my brief very seriously. I decided it would be useful for President Putin to see the mock-up of one of the 7/7 bombs we had made. It was reconstructed exactly like the original bombs, albeit without explosive. On Wednesday, 5 October 2005, I put it into a rucksack like the ones the bombers had used and hoisted it on to my back. Such was the sensitivity of the issues we'd be discussing that Tony Blair had decided the meeting with Putin should be held in the room where we normally met for the emergency COBRA sessions. It was one of the few times a foreign leader had been allowed into this underground cellar in the bowels of Whitehall: I read that as a sign of the prime minister's commitment to a close partnership and even friendship with the Russians. I felt privileged to be part of it.

Eliza and I were first to arrive at the meeting. I had brought my rucksack, and I sat there, the dummy bomb beside me on the floor, slightly nervous, going over what I would say. The prime minister swept in with President Putin – I was surprised to see how short he was – and a team of advisers and translators. Putin was immaculately dressed and courteous, though he wore a steely expression that he would drop only once during the meeting. We had been given five to seven minutes each to talk, before taking questions from him. Tony Blair opened with his view on the security situation, then Eliza and I had our say, with me explaining the rucksack and the bomb, before the conversation opened up. It was not free-flowing because we were talking through interpreters.

The Russians were impassive, not unfriendly, more un-giving – dispassionate. Putin was dead-pan as he asked a series of questions. Thirty or forty minutes into the meeting he began to speak – and now I discovered what really wound him up. He talked about the horrific siege at the school in Beslan in the North Caucasus region a year earlier. Chechen rebels had held hundreds of children and teachers hostage for three days, keeping them half naked in appalling con-ditions without food or water. They had wired up the hall they held them in with explosives. When Russian troops stormed the building, the rebels had shot the children randomly as they tried to run away; 396 people – mainly children – died, and 783 were injured.

As Putin talked, his demeanour changed. He never lost his composure, but his face showed expression and emotion and his vocabulary became more colourful as he relived the events of that awful day. His fury and disgust with the rebels was visible – it was the only time I saw his austere outer mask slip. This world leader had another side, which the public rarely saw, and it proved that we can all be touched by terrorism.

Later, Tony Blair and President Putin put out a joint statement pledging to increase bi-lateral efforts to reduce terrorism, resolving 'to continue to strengthen our partnership, in particular by increasing practical co-operation between our security agencies'.

It was a good meeting. At least, that was what I thought then. Fourteen months later I looked back on it with scepticism and bewilderment, as relations between Russian and British diplomats, politicians and the secret services deteriorated to such an extent that it seemed we could almost have been heading back to an old-fashioned Cold War-style stand-off that has not to this day been fully resolved.

The bizarre and torturously slow murder of the Russian dissident Alexander Litvinenko was at the heart of the freeze. The saga shows that fact can sometimes be stranger and more surreal than fiction. If I'd written it as a novel it would have been a fantastic read – except no one would have been able to suspend disbelief. Not least because the story didn't end with Litvinenko: we were to come across what appeared to be another audacious assassination plot later.

Alexander Litvinenko was a former KGB spy, who spent his career fighting terrorism and crime but broke cover in 1998, accusing his bosses of ordering him to assassinate a billionaire Russian businessman. He fled to the UK, where he was granted political asylum. Here he rubbed shoulders with some of the fiercest critics of Russia and of the then President, Vladimir Putin.

The other key character in this story is Andrei Lugovoi, a Russian MP, who had once been a KGB bodyguard and went on to become a wealthy businessman in Russia. He placed himself firmly in the Putin camp.

Lugovoi claims he travelled to London several times to meet Alexander Litvinenko and discuss joint business opportunities in the security world. On 1 November 2006 the pair met in the bar at the Millennium Hotel in Mayfair. The next day Litvinenko became ill. No one really knew what was wrong with him. Eventually he was rushed into hospital. There was no reason to bring in counter-terrorism officers or to join up the dots, to read too much into the fact his real connections were in Russia. He was ill. That was all.

When the medical assessment became more complex, implying that Litvinenko might have been poisoned by a radioactive chemical, and it became clear he was going to die, we were called in. The stakes were potentially very high. At Scotland Yard we called a meeting to decide whether or not the investigation should go to the Murder Unit in the Specialist Crimes Directorate or come to the Counter-Terrorism Command of Specialist Operations – my department. In the end the case's political, diplomatic and potentially terrorist dimensions tipped it our way.

Bear in mind we were still investigating the July 2005 attacks and a host of other more complex terrorist plots, but now we had an investigation that appeared simply off the wall. Assassinations, yes, but radioactive poisonings? Towards the less likely end of the scale – but it supported my firm belief that a detective should never rule any possibility in or out without evidence. We were back on the crazy tread-mill of meetings and discoveries on an international level at an astonishing pace.

Take 23 November 2006. I was woken at 6 a.m. by a call on my mobile from one of our overnight investigators that Litvinenko was dying. A meeting of COBRA had been called for 8.00 a.m. to be attended by ministers, security agencies and other involved parties. I would be there to discuss the implications for the investigation. I headed straight for the office and a 6.30 a.m. meeting with Peter Clarke. Suzanna Becks agreed to take on my scheduled meetings, while Peter would take care of the everyday running of the Litvinenko investigation. He outlined his ideas for command

and control, allocating officers to specific tasks with a clear chain of command. We arranged a series of meetings through the morning so that everyone involved was up and running. Though we wouldn't go public with it yet, as far as we were concerned this was no longer a poisoning inquiry: it was an international murder investigation – doctors were telling us the poisoned man had only hours to live.

With COBRA set up, I anticipated a fast-moving, high-level and demanding investigation with frequent interventions from ministers. I would need to work at speed. I followed what had, over the previous eighteen months, become a well-worn procedure: I put together a team of five people who were happy to be available 24/7 through the duration of the investigation. By 7.15 a.m. they were in my office.

'This guy was unwell,' I began. 'He goes to Outpatients at Barnet General Hospital where he's made to vomit, but it doesn't stop. He's eventually admitted and transferred to a special unit at University College Hospital. Doctors suspect leukaemia but the patient claims he's been poisoned. Now the guy's dying and it's no longer a passing illness.

'When we took over the inquiry the samples of poison found in Litvinenko had been sent for specialist testing. The scientists think it's polonium-210, a highly dangerous, very unusual radioactive material. Where can you get it? In the UK? In Russia? Can you absorb it through the skin by touching or only through ingestion?' I tasked an officer with finding out. I assumed the Department of Health would help.

I raced downstairs with Peter Clarke and we jumped into the car – our driver was already turning on the engine. We made the short journey down and round Parliament Square, crammed with rush-hour buses, and up Whitehall to the Cabinet Office on the left just after Downing Street.

We went in together. The meeting was chaired by a senior civil servant, who wanted information for the home secretary, John Reid. MI5 and Health Service officials were also present. Peter did the police briefing: there were three main crime scenes where radioactive traces had been found – the Millennium Hotel, where Litvinenko and Lugovoi had met on 1 November, the Itsu Sushi Bar, which Litvinenko had also visited that day, and his home in North London. Traces of the radioactive substance had also been found in the vehicle that had taken him to hospital.

The problem of his body was raised. It would be in a toxic condition, too hazardous for a post-mortem to be carried out. No one could say how much polonium he'd taken, or whether there was an antidote. It was agreed we would carry on with the investigation while the Department of Health and the Health Protection Agency looked into the health issues.

We discussed what, if anything, we should make public but failed to reach a firm conclusion. We had to consider in particular everyone who had come into contact with Litvinenko, including the police who'd guarded his hospital bed, the hospital staff and the public who'd been in the areas he'd visited when he was poisoned and just afterwards.

Back at Scotland Yard we decided it was important to commit to a press strategy. At 11 a.m. I phoned the home secretary's office and we all then agreed that John Reid would take the overall lead, with the health secretary to cover the health issues.

At one o'clock the home secretary called another COBRA meeting. By now we had pulled our teams out of the scenes of crime: we had no idea if they would be contaminated and how dangerous that would be. Instead we sent in radiological experts from the Atomic Weapons Establishment. We reported all this to COBRA and went on to discuss the uncertainties about what we were dealing with: could the substance penetrate clothing or skin or must it be ingested? Were we certain it was polonium-210, as was being suggested privately, and if so, in what strength or quantity? There was real frustration. No one could say how it was made or where it had come from. If it had been imported, then how? Had there been a lapse in airport security or could it be legally brought into the country?

The home secretary asked the government's chief scientific officer to establish how much we knew and what advice should be given to the public. The Foreign and Commonwealth Office was asked to make contact with the Russian authorities to request their fullest co-operation. I remember pointing out that we had to define who the victims were: it was important to deal with them gently but we should take care in what we said to them – they might be something other than a victim. That meeting lasted two hours and at 3 p.m. we adjourned. John Reid called another COBRA meeting for 7 p.m. In the meantime Department of Health officials would hold a press conference to put out messages of reassurance without being specific about what we'd found.

I was hardly back in the office when my secure phone rang. It was the home secretary, and he sounded pretty annoyed. The Department of Health had held a press conference immediately after COBRA and he felt that what they had said had not been consistent with what we had agreed at COBRA. The meeting had been somewhat tense because the health officials had had little reliable information. I had a flash-back to the 7 July bomb attacks when I had been embarrassed at a COBRA meeting because I had been expected to give information and had none. I had some sympathy with the health officials – but rather than say they didn't know, they fudged a bit, which is not good for breeding confidence in people. Dr Reid felt the press conference had gone too far in implying there might be a risk at the scenes. We agreed we'd deal with the problem at the next COBRA meeting. But at 4.20 p.m. he phoned me again and asked me to nip round to see him.

This time my driver took me to the brand new steel and glass Home Office building in Marsham Street, Westminster. As I was ushered in, the home secretary pointed to the flat-screen television in his office. Where, he wanted to know, had Sky got their latest breaking news from? They were saying police had confirmed that radiation had been found at the Millennium Hotel and in the Itsu Sushi Bar. We certainly hadn't gone public with that and neither had John Reid. He was concerned that the story was starting to slip away from us and if we didn't get a grip on it we could have widespread panic. It went back to the earlier press conference: the wording used might have implied radiation had been found so Sky had put two and two together and had then managed to firm it up. I have no idea how they did it – perhaps from people working at the crime scenes, whether police or employees of the businesses, or even members of the public. In any event such high-profile police activity always drew attention and media speculation.

The home secretary and I agreed there was only one thing the police could do: go public and be specific. So, against our better judgement, but with the blessing of the home secretary, we were forced by circumstance to issue a press statement. It confirmed that radiation had been found. I still have the two pink Post-its on which it was hastily scribbled: 'We can confirm that traces of polonium-210 have been found at the Itsu Sushi restaurant in Piccadilly, the

Millennium Hotel near Grosvenor Square, and at Mr Litvinenko's home in Muswell Hill. The sushi bar and parts of the hotel are closed whilst an examination continues.' Little did we know that months would pass before some rooms could be reopened.

I knew the home secretary was now putting pressure on the Department of Health to bring out statements on safety and risk issues. By 7 p.m. we were back at COBRA. It was not an easy meeting. John Reid appeared pretty cross. Actions from the last COBRA meeting had not gone to plan, information had been shared with the public that we felt should not have been, and there was still a lack of clarity, which was complicating the situation. We had been pushed by the press into going public instead of directing inform-ation in a measured and considered way. He didn't blame anyone but I could tell he expected better.

That evening Alexander Litvinenko died. Over the following days we had briefings, COBRA meetings, confrontations over interpretation, and I was again at loggerheads with the health secretary, Patricia Hewitt. It wasn't that we didn't get on – we did – but events set us opposite each other on how to proceed. I was frustrated that our officers couldn't follow through lines of inquiry as we wanted to because we lacked information on what we were handling. We didn't know if it was safe for our forensics teams to go into the affected locations so they didn't at first. We didn't know if it was safe for our detectives to speak to Mr Litvinenko's wife without being contaminated. And at first I had no advice on what I could tell the hard-working officers who had sat day and night by his bedside: were they contaminated and, if so, had they contaminated their families? What about the nurses and members of the public?

At the height of the misinformation I remember being told that all those who'd been anywhere Litvinenko had been were likely to have serious health consequences in the future. Twenty-four hours later that judgement was reversed when the health authorities changed their view. At that point I decided not to pass on any information to anyone unless I'd had it confirmed in writing or it had come from an authoritative source. And it wasn't just me. People who thought they could be contaminated were advised to call NHS Direct, which was receiving hundreds of calls. By the end of the week thousands of people who might have been affected were being tested. If I'd been contaminated would I have been happy to be told to call NHS Direct? I don't think so.

On 24 November, a friend of Litvinenko stood outside University College Hospital and read aloud what he said was a letter Litvinenko had written on his deathbed, claiming he was the victim of an international conspiracy. In it, Litvinenko apparently accused the Russians of involvement in his death and said his killer was 'barbaric and ruthless'. In Moscow President Putin said there was still no 'definitive proof' that Litvinenko's death had been violent. It was true that we were still calling it 'unexplained', but it was not a line Putin would be able to sustain for long. We were all well aware of the diplomatic implications for relations between Britain and Russia.

Meanwhile, the home secretary said publicly in the House of Commons that Britain had told the Russian authorities we expected 'all necessary co-operation with the investigation'.

The following day, as the list of contaminated addresses grew, the prime minister stepped into the fray in a bid to reassure. He pledged that there would be no 'diplomatic or political barrier' standing in the way of this police investigation.

Now as our case was hardening, the press was pointing the finger at Lugovoi. Back we went to COBRA to discuss what we should do. The Health Protection Agency revealed that at the two hospitals where the dying Litvinenko was treated, four thousand people had been tested and 160 were thought to be mildly contaminated. However, scientific test results were coming through and the HPA and the Department of Health told us where people were contaminated the amounts would be so small that health problems, either now or in the future, were unlikely.

By 4 December 2006, five weeks after Litvinenko had been poisoned and two weeks after he'd died, we were still searching a huge number of places in London. The Russian connection had become very strong. I wanted to send counter-terrorism officers to Moscow to forward our investigation. There was much diplomatic wrangling. Nine of our officers were briefed by MI5 and MI6, put on standby and warned never to let their guard down once on Russian soil. Finally they were allowed by the Russian authorities to fly to Moscow.

While our men were struggling in Russia, Alexander Litvinenko was buried at London's Highgate cemetery on 7 December – a security nightmare in which British police mingled with private bodyguards as some of the most controversial Russian dissidents in London turned out for it. There were fifty mourners, led by Litvinenko's wife. The pallbearers included a Russian dissident and also Akhmed Zakayev, the Chechen resistance leader who had earlier won a court battle against extradition from the UK. It wasn't an event to mend bridges between us and the Russians – and relations appeared to be souring by the minute.

Litvinenko's wife was becoming more vociferous in her view that the Russian state was implicated in her husband's death – something the President and the Russian authorities have always vehemently denied – though she did say publicly that it was obvious President Putin hadn't poisoned him personally.

Back in Moscow the authorities were talking of sending their police to the UK to investigate. Then there was a breakthrough: our officers there finally got to interview Lugovoi – with Russian officials sitting in. He though has always maintained his innocence, not least in interviews with the BBC and in the newspapers. He claimed he'd been framed and was a scapegoat, that he was a victim because he, too, was contaminated, that Litvinenko had been a British spy and had tried to recruit him to spy on Putin and the Russian authorities. He even suggested the British authorities were behind the poisoning.

Over the weeks that followed there were claims and counter-claims – was Litvinenko killed because he was a dissident who was just too vociferous in the way he and others in London had undermined the Russians? Had he got hold of incriminating information on a powerful Kremlin figure, or been dealing in arms and oil, and made new enemies?

As the rumours and conspiracy theories grew, so did the number of people in the UK tested for radiation. It ran into thousands, though the number of people who actually tested positive once lengthy tests had run their course was eventually put at thirteen – well below the 160 originally thought to be contaminated – with the long-term risk to their health apparently small.

On 31 January 2007 we were confident we had enough evidence to bring our prime suspect to court. We handed our file to the Crown Prosecution Service (CPS) so that their lawyers could work out whether there was a chance of a successful prosecution. I was cock-a-hoop. I'd been outraged that someone had used such a dangerous means of assassination in London, carrying around a noxious substance without regard for anyone else, then administering it in a public place. I was proud that we had managed to produce strong evidence, despite the health, media and diplomatic complexities. And we'd put our case together in a very short time.

For months CPS lawyers studied the case. On 22 May 2007, Sir Ken McDonald, the director of Public Prosecutions, announced publicly that Andrei Lugovoi should face trial: 'On 23 November 2006, Mr Litvinenko died in a London hospital of acute radiation injury,' he began. 'He was found to have ingested a lethal dose of polonium-210, a highly radioactive material. During his difficult, fatal illness and following his death, the Metropolitan Police Service in London conducted a careful investigation into how this had happened.

'Among the people of interest to police in this inquiry was a Russian citizen named Andrei Lugovoi.

'In late January 2007 the police sent a file of evidence to the Crown Prosecution Service so that we could make a decision about whether criminal charges should be brought against anyone who might have been involved in these events.

'Prosecutors from CPS Counter-Terrorism Division have carefully considered the material contained in that police file. They have also asked the police to carry out further inquiries, which are now complete. And, finally, they have consulted with me.

'I have today concluded that the evidence sent to us by the police is sufficient to charge Andrei Lugovoi with the murder of Mr Litvinenko by deliberate poisoning. I have further concluded that a prosecution of this case would clearly be in the public interest.

'In those circumstances, I have instructed CPS lawyers to take immediate steps to seek the early extradition of Andrei Lugovoi from Russia to the United Kingdom, so that he may be charged with murder – and be brought swiftly before a court in London to be prosecuted for this extraordinarily grave crime.'

Once the CPS had shown us the green light, our next objective was to get Lugovoi into the country. This was where my ignorance in Russian relations showed: I remember saying to someone from MI6, 'We've got the best hand here – there will be an occasion when Lugovoi wants or needs to come to the UK and the team and I will be putting our best thoughts together to try and entice him. The moment he steps on UK soil we'll nab him.'

The person I was speaking to had spent years on the Russian desk. He looked over his glasses and said to me, 'I admire your enthusiasm Andy, but you've got no chance of ever speaking with Lugovoi again in the UK.' How right he was. Russia refused to extradite him. Later in the year diplomatic relations deteriorated further when the UK expelled four Russian diplomats from their London embassy. Then, in what was viewed by most as a tit-for-tat move, Russia expelled four British diplomats from Moscow. Relations have never broken down fully, but the episode has clearly put a distance between our two countries. Meanwhile Lugovoi is now a Russian MP, living freely in Russia, often seen in Moscow but always moving with a bevy of bodyguards. He is still our prime suspect.

Amazingly, there was another case where an assassin was operating here in the UK. We've never named him. But this story gives useful insight into the political and diplomatic complexities of cases like this.

By good intelligence work we discovered a plot against another man here in the UK. Our job now was to thwart it. We devised a scheme, putting our best 'assets' on standby to follow the assassin covertly. He was not a UK national, and the target could potentially have been high profile. Because of this we had no choice but to inform our political masters of the operation, in case it brought problems.

In the corridors of Whitehall it caused uproar. We argued that our plan was the least risky course to follow. We wanted to follow the assassin covertly to corroborate and gather new intelligence about him and any others working with him, about any plots they were involved in, and about their contacts. But the politicians and diplomats went bonkers at the idea.

They favoured a different solution. They were concerned that if the country from which this individual came discovered one of their citizens was being followed it could damage the UK's relations with that country. A series of meetings was held, there was much to-ing and fro-ing between departments and, to our annoyance and disbelief, the police plan was rejected.

We were running out of time and the stakes were high. The civil servants and politicians didn't want to take risks. Downing Street decided to set up a meeting to find a solution. Peter Clarke came with me, and a number of officials from Downing Street and the Foreign and Commonwealth Office were there too. The meeting was chaired by the prime minister's adviser on foreign affairs Sir Nigel Sheinwald, who is now our ambassador in Washington.

To my astonishment, diplomats at that meeting suggested we should intervene early before we could even corroborate the intelligence we'd received. I felt this was a ridiculous idea and told the meeting so, using some pretty graphic language: it would be barking mad, crazy, I said, to show one's hand when we were not in a strong position and could potentially intensify the risk to the target. Peter and I argued strongly and we won. Then unbeknown to the assassin we began to make complex preparations for our covert operation to follow those we believed to be involved.

But the political argument still wasn't over. Some ministers were very persistent and did not give up. I understood that the foreign secretary, Margaret Beckett, was not happy. She had supported us in previous cases but now she favoured a different solution to the one we were planning. I believe she had a conversation with the home secretary, who decided to call another meeting. John Reid wanted to go through the issues again with us. He decided we should meet discreetly in his room at the House of Commons.

'This is very difficult,' he said. 'I understand you need to take the lead operationally, but I need a greater input and more control strategically and from a political point of view.' He favoured early intervention – stopping the plot before anything could happen.

Once again I could see the argument going the other way. I knew my men and women on the street, preparing to carry out the covert surveillance, would feel agrieved if, despite their efforts, the man was let off the leash. I suggested to John Reid that he should refer the matter to Tony Blair. Then whatever was decided he'd have covered his own back. He agreed and briefed the prime minister. Downing Street studied our plans again and then, to our massive relief, Blair stuck by the decision his adviser, Sir Nigel, had made. The covert operation was back on.

We employed a significant degree of resources around the

assassin to ensure we knew what he was doing, trying to identify any threat and ascertain whether he was carrying out reconnaissance or actually planning to carry out the murder. Through this we obtained further intelligence that the assassin had discussed plans to meet an individual we suspected he wanted to kill. He appeared to be frequenting the target's usual haunts.

But the assassin couldn't find his target and became increasingly frustrated with this failure. We were dealing with a professional hit man here: all the time he seemed to be using what he thought were effective counter-surveillance measures – although ours were better!

The resources we employed were successful. We were able to build a portfolio of information on a number of different areas during the operation.

Eventually the assassin went to Heathrow airport. He had failed to find his intended target. He had failed to acquire a gun, and planned to go home. We couldn't tell if he and his accomplices planned to return and try again but we decided to take no risks. We arrested them at the airport, and took them to Paddington Green police station, where for two days our anti-terrorist detectives questioned them. Then we handed them over to Immigration, who seized their visas and deported them.

We had amassed new intelligence and I believe we saved the target's life, and in so doing sent a strong message to any would-be assassin that we'd be on to them. The mission was a success.

At the time I felt elated on two fronts. First, we had not compromised public safety at the cost of collecting intelligence, and our success had vindicated the prime minister's support for our plans. Second, the operational decisions dovetailed neatly with the political imperatives.

Some may disagree, arguing that the politicians *had* interfered with our plans. I don't share this view. We were allowed to sit as operational experts unhindered by the politicians, and formulate plans we believed right for the circumstances. The scale of the operation required political cover so we presented our ideas to the politicians for endorsement. This differs from the COBRA process: there, politicians in effect become entwined in the operational planning. We meet and they sometimes start interfering rather than letting us get on with the job.

I believe as a result of this incident any would-be assassin will think twice before trying to operate in the UK again. It worries me though, that this assassin is still at large.

This whole, sorry affair was a strong reminder that though our main focus was on Al Qaeda-sponsored terrorism; there were many other threats to the security of the UK too.

9. How We Hunt Terrorists, Part 1: Surveillance, Tactics and Technology – the Tricks of the Trade

YOU MAY THINK THAT, THANKS TO FILMS AND TV SPY DRAMAS like *Spooks*, you know everything about hunting terrorists. Believe me, you don't. It's not about small armed teams of spies or cops in life-and-death confrontations with terrorists. It's about sophisticated technology most people have no idea even exists. It's about long, patient hours watching people. It's about years spent infiltrating groups in the hope you might pick up one tiny snippet that indicates you've come across a terrorist.

A lot of it I can't tell you about – we don't want the terrorists to know how we get their phone numbers or what our methods are. We don't want them to know how far away we can be and still pick up what they're saying on sophisticated microphones, or how we can pick out a particular voice in a crowd. By the time you read this book it will have been vetted by MI5, among others, to make doubly sure I haven't inadvertently let slip trade secrets. One thing is for sure: despite the concerns of civil-liberties groups, the surveillance society of CCTV cameras, listening devices and databases recording our email and phone activity, our criminal and car records, and anything else we care to think of, is paying off big-time when it comes to catching criminals and terrorists.

Surveillance is the key. When the best spies and the most sophisticated technologies meet, the results can be amazing. I have no doubt that surveillance operations we have mounted in recent years have helped save many lives. Recent court cases have proved that we can bug, film and covertly record as never before. We have vehicles equipped with advanced technology to help us monitor the movements of targets. And we have skilled officers who can facilitate eavesdropping inside a property, and who can film and follow suspects day after day, quietly, patiently, without arousing suspicion. We could have all the kit in the world, but without the skills of those men and women, and of the people at base watching and listening to every second of surveillance tape as it comes in, it would often be of little value.

There are two types of surveillance: lifestyle intelligence-gathering, which is long-term, and evidential intelligence-gathering, which can be very short-term. If information comes in about someone suggesting they may be up to no good we need to find out what they're up to. We try to understand more about that person: we watch how they lead their lives, studying their routine, work, home, social life, finding out which pub or gym they use, who their friends and associates are. The purpose is to build a picture of them. Sometimes this makes clear that the suspect is not involved in any criminal activity, in which case we challenge the original intelligence. Sometimes, though, it strengthens the intelligence and will inform future surveillance operations.

Often there is no time for lifestyle surveillance and we have to mount a surveillance operation blind; the only purpose will be to prevent an atrocity, or catch a terrorist, and gather evidence, as in the surveillance we carried out on the flats in Stockwell, which ended in the mistaken shooting of Jean Charles de Menezes.

Most surveillance operations use foot, static and mobile surveillance techniques. 'Static' means fixed observation points: if a particular location is of interest, police and MI5 officers find a discreet vantage-point from which cameras and personal binoculars can be trained on the premises. The surveillance team will record comings and goings to establish lifestyle patterns and contacts. They won't often want to knock on the door posing as an innocuous caller to establish if anyone is in; rather, they'll want to reduce the chances of arousing suspicion, especially if they're in 'bandit country' – an area in which the community is exceptionally hostile to law enforcers.

Technology can do a lot of the work: fixing a camera to a wall means you don't have to stand there and use your eyes – with links you can view from miles away for as long as the camera is on site. When I was a uniformed officer on patrol in Essex, there was a particular spot in Leigh-on-Sea, in Castle Drive, near the railway station where commuters parked their cars. In those days it was isolated, used as a lovers' lane but also notorious as a honey-pot for car thieves: they could access vehicles without being seen. At its worst, two or three cars a day were being stolen and, as it was so quiet, it was near on impossible for static surveillance – you'd have stood out like a sore thumb. Instead we managed to hide a camera in the undergrowth. It beamed its picture to the police station via a link on the station roof two miles away. We didn't have to risk a human observation point and it freed up officers to do other things – we could have one person keeping an eye on the footage in the warmth and security of our offices. It turned out to be a great idea as the thefts stopped and the convictions of car thieves followed, as a direct result of the monitoring. The road became a no-go area for the criminals.

Despite the TV image, surveillance work is not glamorous. Even if you're lucky enough to be in a van rather than out in the cold, you can't run the engine – any criminal would be suspicious of a vehicle parked night and day outside a house with the ignition on. And even with modern technology human functions may be problematic. What if you need to go to the loo? We have moved away from peeing in crisp bags or empty Coke bottles; now we use purpose-designed army-supply bags. We rarely have mixed-sex teams in a van.

A surveillance operation can sound pretty exciting, and there are moments when you do feel the thrill of the chase, but in reality the hours you spend sitting alone, in a car or house with no activity, far outnumber those when you're on the *Spooks*-style run for the suspects. Surveillance officers are always getting minor injuries after being cramped in a car for hours, then suddenly having to move fast – like an athlete who hasn't done warm-up exercises, they pull a muscle or damage a cartilage. That doesn't mean they're not fit; they have to keep in shape because they don't know how long they'll be on the go. They use far more energy than their unwitting suspect.

Once a surveillance team is on the move and actually following someone, a minimum number of people is needed: if you go below that number it could make the surveillance unsafe or risk compromising the operation with the suspect realizing they're being followed. They have to be disciplined and work as a team. Imagine on a Sunday morning the under-ten football team being coached by one of the fathers: before kick-off he reminds the members who they should each mark on the other side, and how to pass the ball as a team – only to discover that all his players, bar the goalkeeper, chase the ball rather than keeping to their agreed formation. Disaster. It's no different in surveillance:

you don't want all the team around the suspect at any one time as you don't know where he or she is likely to go. You need to keep officers in reserve to cover any eventuality.

The more sophisticated suspects use counter-surveillance manoeuvres. It's a skilled surveillance officer who can react naturally to this – unlike a colleague of mine who, during a training exercise, was following a target in a shopping centre and ended up running up a down escalator against a flow of pedestrians and hopelessly not reaching the top – bit of a giveway, that.

Not all surveillance operations are successful. After July 2005 the plots we came across were increasingly sophisticated. The terrorists were using more complex tactics and that meant we had to do the same in hunting them. It was suspected that Al Qaeda-inspired terrorists wanted to develop bombs with radiological or biological elements, although we weren't convinced that they yet had the capability to do so. That was uppermost in my mind when we tackled the next incident. It happened a little less than a year after things had gone so badly wrong with the mistaken shooting of Jean Charles de Menezes at Stockwell and, to my horror, took us down a similar route.

It was May 2006. We had intelligence suggesting that the components of a chemical device were being passed from terrorist safe-house to terrorist safe-house and had ended up at an address in Forest Gate in Newham, East London. It is an area with a large Muslim population and we didn't relish the thought of weighing in to find it.

Working with MI5, we did everything we possibly could to prove or disprove the intelligence we had and exhausted all lines of inquiry. We didn't know how reliable it was. We were left with a dilemma: did we walk away and risk leaving it hanging or go into the house to see if the bomb was there? Would anyone have forgiven us if we'd walked away and a device was then detonated, killing more people? Of course not. But we also knew that going into a house on intelligence that might prove unreliable could be problematic. Whichever way we moved, there were likely to be significant consequences.

I sat down with my deputy, Peter Clarke, and we had one of the longest conversations I can remember ever having, as we thrashed out what our tactics should be, considering every possibility and the repercussions of the different actions we could take. In the end, our overwhelming preference was to go into the house and find out for ourselves whether what we'd heard was true.

Our intelligence suggested that the device had a dirty-bomb element, possibly an infectious bacterium or a lethal chemical, and those passing it round had been trying to get a detonator. We didn't know whether or not they had achieved that so in our planning we had to assume the bomb was viable. We couldn't risk a polite knock on the door, which might trigger panic and fright, and push those inside to detonate their device if it was primed. No, this would have to be a size-twelve boot kicking the door in. Yet we needed to combine the element of surprise with belt-and-braces measures for public safety: the house was in a built-up urban area and this was a textbook health-and-safety hazard for people in neighbouring homes as well as for the police and the suspects.

On the police side, we had reached the threshold of risk that dictated this should be an armed operation. Our firearms team demanded chemical, biological, radiological and nuclear (CBRN) protective clothing. They'd trained for this eventuality but there's a big difference between training and reality.

It was decided the raid would take place in the early hours of Friday and would be conducted before sunrise at about 3 a.m. for the element of surprise – which would be tough to maintain: the operation planners told us we would need to deploy 250 officers in the interests of keeping the public safe. With eight to a Transit van, the convoy would be highly conspicuous. I remember saying to Peter, 'Thirty plus Transit vans descending on two or three East London terraced streets? Won't that appear to locals like heavy-handedness?' Peter and I challenged long and hard the need for so many officers. We were told that we were going into a densely populated area and must have enough officers on standby to carry out a fast evacuation if the need arose. Again, our officers worried about the Madrid scenario: if they moved in, would the terrorists detonate a bomb? We had to put public safety first. We agreed to reduce the numbers as soon as the initial raid was over.

Given the nature of the operation and the likelihood of a long day ahead, Peter and I went to bed, leaving the operational commander, Deputy Assistant Commissioner Alf Hitchcock, in charge. Before I left the office I reviewed the plan line by line and personally certified it with my signature.

Now came problem number one. There were logistical delays, not least because the firearms team had to kit up in their CBRN suits. It was well after 3 a.m. by the time they were *en route* to Forest Gate. They arrived two hours late – it was 2 June and sunrise was creeping across the skies. Problem number two: it was a Friday but no one had taken into account the obvious implications of being late on this particular day of the week. We were raiding a Muslim home and you could almost have guaranteed that the occupants would be up early for Friday prayers. Little did our teams realize the element of surprise was slipping away.

The forward rendezvous point was Upton Park football ground – a stone's throw from the target address. There, those going into the house wired themselves up with microphones so they could communicate with us and we could hear their movements and comments. Then, quietly, they moved in to surround the target address. This brought a further delay as firearms officers in their CBRN suits had to make their way secretly across the boundaries of fourteen homes, climbing over fences to get to the back of the house.

We did not know what we would find. We knew that two young men – our suspects and thus our targets – were probably inside and, from surveillance, we knew their families lived there too. And we worried, of course, that there might be dangerous and possibly unstable explosives. Also, people lived in houses close by – presumably innocent members of the public. We had a lot to think about.

One set of officers kicked down the front door, and made way for a team from the firearms unit. Usually they would pour in but their CBRN suits restricted their movement. More like the Michelin man than Superman, they waddled in as speedily as they could. They were shocked to find the house wasn't one but two buildings: it had been knocked through to the one next door and was twice the size they had expected. And the building work looked unstable. They were immediately worried – but the operation had started: they couldn't pull back now.

Those we were after were awake and up, ready to pray. Not surprisingly, they thought they were being attacked by criminals and tried to defend themselves, their family and property. The officers heard the frightened voices of men and women upstairs. One youngish man came rushing down, another just behind him. There was a scuffle on the stairs. A firearms officer struggling with his weapon in his unfamiliar outfit pulled the trigger and a bullet was discharged, hitting one of the residents.

Back in the operation's control room in Scotland Yard – the one that had been used on the day of the Stockwell shooting – a monitoring officer shouted, 'Guv, they've shot someone!' to that night's Gold commander, Detective Superintendent Dick Gething.

His heart plummeted. He knew the grief this would bring, whoever had been shot and whatever the circumstances. It could be very bad news for those involved and for us.

I was asleep when Peter Clarke rang. When I picked up the phone, he said, 'Andy, are you awake? Because if you're not you soon will be.'

Tragically, someone had been shot – and I knew that decisions made in quick time would be pored over in very slow time. The Independent Police Complaints Commission (IPCC) would investigate more than thoroughly: we had to be accountable.

Alf Hitchcock, who'd been running the operation on the ground, also phoned. This time the victim had survived with a flesh wound – and we had learnt hard lessons after Stockwell that I immediately applied. We went into lock-down. I arranged a fast, professional handover of primacy at the scene to the IPCC – there would be no letters to senior officials in Whitehall. It's not something I wanted to do but if we did it properly and with good grace, I thought, we could still ensure that we gathered the evidence vital to our anti-terrorist operation. We and the IPCC ran two parallel investigations at the house in Forest Gate with two completely different objectives: to investigate a police shooting and an apparent terrorist plot.

Things went from bad to worse. With the building unstable, we had to shore it up and evacuate neighbours before we could begin our search.

I was already back in the office watching events unfold via television news coverage. There was a flurry of activity, building equipment going in, armed officers outside and in, police manning cordons to keep press and public back, forensics teams emerging with bags of potential evidence. One of my team tapped me on the shoulder. 'Andy, they're wearing the CBRN suits inside out.' It was a moment of comedy in the midst of all the stress.

In East London we arrested two brothers, and over the next two days we pulled apart the house and garden, searching every inch inside and out. But we found no device. In time we released the men without charge.

Two weeks later they held an emotional press conference. They described how they had felt terrorized – they had feared they were going to die and demanded an apology. I had no choice but to comply. Shortly afterwards, choosing my words carefully and with advice from our lawyers and our press office, I announced, 'I am aware that in mounting this operation we have caused disruption and inconvenience to many residents in Newham and, more importantly, to those that reside [at the address we raided]. I apologize for the hurt we may have caused. While we have not found evidence of what we were looking for at the house, the intelligence received did raise serious concerns for public safety. On that basis we had no choice but to mount a robust operation, which required a fast armed response.'

I have to say that, in the same circumstances, I would do the same again to protect the public. The incident shows just how tough the dilemmas we face can be – and how dangerous and unpopular the work of the Counter-Terrorist

Command is. But it is the unsung heroes who work covertly and cannot be publicly recognized who bear the brunt of this and I salute them.

And although those we arrested were found to be innocent of any crime, I believe our investigative methods are necessary and have helped numerous times to disrupt genuine plans by others. Preventing attacks and crimes before they happen may not bring great publicity, but the plots we stop are our biggest successes.

All is not always lost if a surveillance operation appears to be compromised. When you're eavesdropping on a team who are also under human surveillance and you hear the words 'I think we're being followed', you pull back – and you'd be amazed to discover how often the suspects revert to their previous behaviour.

There isn't a big distinction between the expertise of MI5 and our skills, and on typical operations we work together in integrated teams – as we did when we were hunting the 21 July bombers. There's always an agreed command structure. If we're using human and technical surveillance we have listening stations and monitoring rooms where we log everything that's happening, whether on cameras or via the microphones of those carrying out the surveillance. The control room in Scotland Yard has a bank of screens for each camera, and computers for the sound, with people logging and others communicating with those on the ground, then passing messages to the senior officers in command of the operation.

In a critical matter such as 'Do we abort?' the control room takes advice from the ground. Sometimes, though, the senior officer at base, detached from the unfolding events, can make a more considered decision. I was once running a low-level surveillance operation and decided things were getting out of hand: our surveillance team were taking unnecessary risks – the danger to them didn't merit the advantage of getting the suspected criminals. I pulled the operation.

On a normal no-hitches, tight operation, with a slick team, the boss back at base doesn't rule the roost, but is heavily reliant on whoever has eyeball of the target. They're wired up with hidden radios so they can talk to each other and to you. They will continue a one-sided conversation when they're on the move, discreetly giving their location, movements and views, taking orders or giving instruction.

Then there are the agents who enable us to eavesdrop inside a property. I don't know the intricate details of how they do it without alerting the people who live or work there. It's easy enough for anyone to get wireless Internet connection and Bluetooth technology, but in the law-enforcement agencies we have access to even more advanced technology for secretly listening to suspicious conversations in the interests of stacking up evidence. Of course, we have to have a warrant from the Home Office or a senior police officer granting permission. And to get authority for eaves-dropping we have to demonstrate that conventional methods, such as human surveillance, wouldn't work, and that the use of technical intervention is proportionate and necessary when balanced against the crimes we suspect are in the planning. If either test fails, the warrant will not be authorized. Human surveillance is, by its nature, more resource-intensive and has higher risks of compromise but the use of technology, especially when it involves breaking into a privately owned vehicle or building, has to be justified.

Some suspects have discovered bugs in their homes – but technical devices are compromised or found far less frequently than human surveillance teams.

*

And there is nothing like long-term surveillance to bring results.

We had our suspicions about a group of people who would meet in a street in East London and needed to establish whether or not they were a terrorist cell. Our surveillance operated a covert camera to get excellent shots of the group meeting. The slightest loss of nerve, even a blink of an eyelid towards the group, would not only have exposed the surveillance team but might also have blown the entire operation.

From then on, for months we put the suspects under surveillance and followed them. We logged everything they bought; we filmed and listened to them and used all sorts of other intrusive techniques to get a wide view of what they were up to. MI5 and Counter-Terrorism Command had been granted permission to do this through warrants from senior police officers and from government. And this was why.

M15 had been watching young Muslims who had been travelling to obscure parts of Pakistan and Afghanistan for years. They had studied those who were associates of people belonging to terrorist cells that had already been uncovered: in 2004 a group had been planning a conventional fertilizer bomb on a club or shopping centre. Some who knew them had no links whatsoever with terrorism – but others did.

The intelligence agencies also investigated young British Muslims who had gone to obscure parts of the Pakistan–Afghanistan border at the same time as the 7 and 21 July bombers, or who'd been in the region at times when intelligence suggests groups of the Al Qaeda leadership had gathered to recruit and train young militants.

Against this background the agencies became concerned about one particular group who had been to Pakistan.

Friends and acquaintances of these men noticed they were particularly angry at the continuing deaths of innocent Muslims in Iraq and Afghanistan, and signs in them of behavioural change. We put them under surveillance.

One of the men visited Pakistan, and on his return journey investigators opened his baggage, took a look and resealed it. We found evidence in his case that could be used to detonate and make bombs. Now we were really worried. With MI5, we set up one of the UK's largest ever surveillance operations.

One of the men we were watching appeared to take on the role of quartermaster, buying items like clamps, drills, syringes, glue and latex gloves – things he couldn't possibly need in quantity in everyday life and which could potentially be used to make explosives. Our undercover officers saw him throw away empty hydrogen-peroxide bottles.

We were on the trail as the cell bought a flat in cash. Was this to be the bomb factory? We upped the ante – eavesdropping on the property. Now we listened to all their plans. We watched them make and test peroxide explosives. We filmed their methodology, constantly assessing whether public safety was at risk if we continued the surveillance. We watched them construct devices. Our scientists tried to copy what they were doing, and concluded that if a detonator was attached, the devices were viable as bombs.

MI5 overheard them discussing numbers – were they referring to the number of targets the group planned to attack? Another time we heard them make numerous calls to chemicals companies.

They applied for new passports and junked their old ones to hide visits to Pakistan – which they clearly knew fitted the profile of the modern terrorist.

By now we were convinced they were planning an attack

– but we wanted to let the operation run so that we could collect as much evidence as possible to prosecute them rather than simply disrupting their plans.

At this point John McDowall, deputy head of Counter-Terrorist Command and the senior investigating officer in charge of this particular operation, rushed rather breathlessly into my office. Peter Clarke, his boss, was not around and he had something important enough to tell me in person.

He told me the surveillance information suggested the men were planning an attack bigger than the attacks in the USA on 11 September, 2001 right here in the UK. Imagine the effect if they succeeded – the horrendous loss of life.

Then I took a mental step back. We were on top of this. I felt confident that we would not allow the plot to come to fruition. The only caveat I had was that we didn't know if other terrorist cells were running parallel to this one: what if this was the second and the first was close to fulfilling its plans? It was an unnerving thought, but we had no evidence to suggest this was part of a wider conspiracy. I knew that at John's level there was communication daily, sometimes hourly with MI5. We spoke and decided to let it run. Once again we pushed the surveillance button, upping it to an even higher level to ensure nothing was missed. At this point the police were chairing the Gold command meetings because we had moved on from pure intelligence-gathering and were now, with our surveillance tapes, gathering firm evidence we hoped to put before a court once we had arrested and prosecuted the cell – as we wanted to.

We had another flat in London under surveillance too. To our incredulity we heard several of the suspects record what appeared to be suicide videos full of anti-Western rhetoric. We knew from past experience this didn't mean the attack was imminent – but it might be close. We still felt we had the tactical advantage: we were keeping tabs on the men but there was more to be done in gathering evidence which might stand up in court.

The stakes were high. We couldn't tell where the planned detonation would occur. An error on anyone's part now might mean at best loss of evidence but at worst catastrophic loss of life.

We had briefed our counterparts in America on the alleged plot. At the highest level they were looking for reassurance that this was not going to slip through our fingers. I was briefing the home secretary on progress, he was briefing the prime minister, Tony Blair, and *he* was briefing the US President, George Bush.

The operation had been going on for weeks. We knew where the men were, and where they lived. We knew everything about their lifestyles, their movements, their acquaintances, friends and families. We had them bugged and they were followed 24/7. We had contingency plans in place if we suddenly needed to arrest them.

None of my senior team had had a holiday for a year, so some weeks earlier we had decided to take a leaf out of Eliza Manningham-Buller's book. Immediately after the 7 July attacks she'd sent staff home in anticipation of the long haul – she wanted some rested and ready for when others became exhausted. I knew we would be working ridiculous hours once we moved in to make arrests so we fixed our summer breaks. John went away first, followed by Peter, and on Peter's return I left for La Manga in Spain with my wife, family and some friends. I knew it was unlikely that I'd get the full two weeks. Peter and I had half speculated that, given the pace of the operation, by the time I left we were probably seven or eight days away from the arrests.

I went equipped with a secure satellite phone, having arranged with Peter that I would speak to him every evening at 8 p.m. A couple of days into the holiday, things were on a stable footing. I was about to order dinner and decided to make the agreed 8 p.m. call just ahead of that. Peter reiterated that I probably had another three or four days before I would need to come back ahead of the arrest phase. We hung up. I sat down to my paella. Less than an hour later, the cork hardly out of the wine bottle, he was back on the phone. Things had changed.

The Americans it appeared felt it was getting dangerous and that we should bring the operation to a close. We didn't want to do that. We believed we could gain more evidence and thus a better chance of securing convictions if we let things run a little longer. Our US counterparts were especially worried about a man we suspected – but couldn't prove – could be pulling the strings in Pakistan and might even be a vital link between the men we were following in the UK and Al Qaeda. The Pakistani authorities arrested him.

It happened as I settled down to my dinner in Spain. We were caught unawares and colleagues in the UK were forced to take action into which we would normally have put considerable time and planning. We had no choice but to move in on the cell. If, as we suspected, the man was linked, his detention might scare them and push them into accelerating their planned attack: we had to get to the men in the UK before they found out he was in custody. We couldn't risk letting this run on now, Peter said, and I agreed. We'd gathered evidence we felt incriminated them. We strongly felt that an attack was imminent – and just as we could close our side of the operation early, so could they.

I felt frustrated that I wasn't in the UK. I hadn't really

wanted to leave for my holiday but had known it was the right thing to do. All I wanted now was to get back to be part of the team. I had a very small window in which I could return before things went crazy: once news of the suspected plot was published I knew international security measures would be tightened.

My plan B was to fly home in a UK military aircraft but that would be expensive. Instead my backroom team pulled out the stops. At 9 p.m. they were set the task of getting me to the UK, and within half an hour they had booked me on to a scheduled flight leaving Alicante at midnight. I should be home before the public knew anything about the plot.

I rushed back to the apartment and packed a few essentials – I was not calm as I was anxious to get a cab and make the hour-long journey to the airport in good time for the flight. I ran outside and flagged down a passing cab. In it, I gathered my thoughts, systematically checking what I would do when I arrived in the UK. Then I did the usual travel check: money, passport. To my horror I discovered that in my panic to get packed I had taken my six-year-old daughter's passport rather than my own. Time was tight but I had to make the half-hour round trip back to the apartment. I felt sick – and incredibly silly. Fortunately I caught the plane – just.

Meanwhile the home secretary, John Reid, had been pulled out of a football match: he had been watching Chelsea play at Stamford Bridge in West London. Peter briefed him on the plans to begin the arrests.

I landed at Gatwick airport and was met by Sussex Police Special Branch, who drove me to my waiting car and driver. I changed from my polo shirt and shorts into a suit, and on a blue-light run we raced through the night to New Scotland Yard, Peter and the team.

I was stunned by the progress they had already made. The task was to spontaneously locate and arrest more than a dozen people – an incredibly tall order because we didn't have the luxury of choosing when to do it: early morning, while they were still asleep would have been normal. I think the police service often operates at its best in these types of circumstances: contrast this operation with the one in Forest Gate, where we had spent hours poring over risk assessments and health and safety guidelines and still got it wrong. This time there was no fuss, no drama and no time for studying health and safety rules, just fast, old-fashioned police work.

At 5 a.m. Peter Clarke and I drove across Parliament Square to a COBRA meeting chaired by the home secretary. On the way Peter told me that when John Reid heard we were going to pull the surveillance operation, he had said he felt it was near on impossible for us to achieve the arrests. Now, some eight hours later, I took a back seat, immensely proud as Peter, in his understated manner, informed the meeting that nearly every one of the suspected key players was already under arrest.

In a way this was not the end but the beginning of the investigation. We believed we'd stopped an appalling plot, but we also knew that this could cause chaos for the public. We were in familiar territory: we increased security causing immense public inconvenience but, because the men might face trial, the law prevented us publishing much detail about what they were accused of.

As is often the case at times like this, as the arrests were made, the threat assessment for the UK was once again raised to Critical, implying an attack might be imminent. Intelligence assessed that unknown cells, either in the UK or abroad, might try to undermine the arrests by carrying out an attack.

The Critical signal sent a warning to private and public organizations, to ports and airports, power stations and so on that they should adopt their most stringent security precautions. At Scotland Yard we implemented the Rainbow List to protect the public. We also went to great lengths to keep mainstream Muslim communities in the loop. Those we arrested were Muslim, but held extreme views and espoused violence in a way that the majority of Muslims abhorred.

It crossed my mind, as that long night turned into day, what crazy times these were. The police and security agencies had dealt with the fatal terrorist attacks of 7 July 2005, the fatal shooting by police of Jean Charles de Menezes, the failed bombs of 21 July 2005, and now this. Any one of those events would have challenged the command resilience of the Met.

I drew back significantly from private briefings to the press: I felt that it would be totally irresponsible to give any hint as to why these extra security measures had been introduced and relied on the trust and confidence the media, I believed, now placed in me. I kept what I told them fairly general, and asked for their co-operation, assuring them that when the time was right I would give them a blow-by-blow account. Other Whitehall departments took a different view: someone was clearly briefing the details – probably because, as I had felt after the 7 July attacks, they wanted speculation kept to the minimum. Without crossing the line of inappropriate disclosures, they were giving as much information as possible so that the reporting was responsible and not scaremongering.

The arrests meant we had to instigate thorough searches of homes, offices and all the other places used by the suspects. Also, we had to start analysing their phone and computer records. As soon as the arrests started we made arrangements for lawyers specializing in terrorism to camp alongside our officers in Scotland Yard. We were downloading evidential material in real time – that is logging, filing and prioritizing everything that we found on computers seized during the searches, everything that the suspects said in interviews, everything we discovered about who they'd called or emailed. The lawyers had a wall chart with each defendant's name on it: when key elements of evidence were relevant they would be written up under an individual's name. They wanted to be absolutely clear when they felt a defendant could be charged and there was a viable chance of a successful prosecution.

The moment from arrest to charging is always a race against time – and never more so than in this case. We were up against it. The scale of the evidence we were bringing in was vast. Almost everything belonging to, or that had crossed the paths of, the suspects had to be analysed and logged. By law, we are expected to have the key elements of our case and the main evidence gathered by the time the suspect is charged; clearly we can't always do this and often continue investigating after that. If anything played into the debate of extending the length of time we could hold a suspect between arrest and charge, this did. In the past month the limit had been raised from fourteen to twenty-eight days – but we had supported the government's moves for a longer period of detention. The home secretary was acutely aware of the importance of this case to that debate and keen to discover if it would show the need for powers to hold suspects longer before they must be charged. It was another example of how politics and policing were becoming closely intertwined.

The political argument was the last thing on our minds – we had a job with a time limit and had to make the most of what we'd got. I also had to deal with the internal police politics. One of the scenes we had identified shortly before the arrests was a house close to a large recreation area where people walked dogs. We'd seen the group going there and lying face down to communicate, and suspected the place was being used not just for meetings but for something more sinister. We had no proof but thought they might have a hide there.

That search was a logistical nightmare. We decided that, come what may, we would search the entire area of heath thoroughly. It was huge, hilly, with a mix of dense woodland and open spaces with many foot- and bridle-paths – a popular spot with people and with deer, badgers and other wild animals. Some areas back on to residential areas and others are popular meeting places for lovers. We were digging up every single piece of turf, combing under every bush and through all the undergrowth. Nothing would be left untouched. If we had ended the surveillance operation weeks earlier we would not have found that house and we certainly would not have searched that common ground.

For the surveillance officers who'd followed the suspects day and night for many months before, the arrests of the suspects were the pay-off they were looking for: it would now be the job of lawyers to use what they had found to see if they had enough to prosecute the men.

10. How We Hunt Terrorists, Part 2: the Brave and the Bizarre

OUR SURVEILLANCE OFFICERS ARE BRAVE, BUT OTHER MEN AND women working for us have, arguably, an even tougher job. I cannot emphasize strongly enough the steely nerve of our undercover officers, or agents, as they're known in MI5. These people nurture and befriend a criminal or terrorist, leading a double life, so that eventually they can be exposed and brought to justice.

Take the South Mimms case. Our tactics were conventional. We needed to track a suspect. Intelligence suggested he was trying to purchase firepower, including a ground-to-air missile-launcher. Several years previously we had discovered what we believed were early plans to use such weapons around the perimeter fence at Heathrow airport. It looked to us as if someone had flattened the ground in preparation to bring them in. All airports now have dedicated patrols that randomly check places on the perimeters from which planes could be shot down.

In the frenetic days after the July bombings in 2005 we heard that one Kazi Rahman was looking to buy arms. He had links with terrorists but until then it had been thought that he wasn't personally involved. An undercover MI5 officer, using the name Salim, befriended him, and offered to introduce him to an arms dealer. That dealer was an undercover police officer known as Mohamed. For months the three were wheeling and dealing as Rahman upped the stakes, ordering more and offering more cash. His wish list included a Man Portable Air Defence System (MANPADS), a shoulder-launched surface-to-air missile.

Undercover officers are chameleons, a breed unto themselves. I'm amazed at how close they get to their quarry. On one particular operation I recall an undercover officer being asked by a major criminal if he'd be his best man – how the hell can a police officer infiltrating a criminal gang get *that* close to the top man? It must be an innate skill, not one you can acquire on a Home Office training course. The undercover officers used in drugs work are impressive, but for a different reason. Because we're asking them to infiltrate drugs-users and dealers, they have to be young, which means they're less experienced and therefore more open to the dangers of undercover work.

The annual V concert at Chelmsford is held over two days and the pop fans camp overnight. When I was in charge, we ran a massive undercover drugs operation. Officers were looking for dealers and therefore posing as buyers; they averaged less than five years' service but they operated as if they had fifty years under their belts. Any undercover officer has to be tough and cool to infiltrate and become a trusted friend within the criminal and terrorist underworld. The job is to gather intelligence and turn that into evidence, which they give anonymously in court. Little can beat an undercover cop describing to a court and jury the inside story of criminal activity.

As 2005 wore on we reached the point in the arms-dealing case where we had to force a sting: the cover would have to be blown for the simple reason that our 'arms dealer' could not produce the arms. We decided on South Mimms as a rendezvous, a common meeting point for criminals and cops. It's at the junction of the M25 and the A1 heading north. The service station there is busy day and night.

With any sting, the operation must not overstep the mark. The agents can't encourage or entice the criminal or they'll be accused in court of setting them up. The actions and words of the criminal or terrorist must be spontaneous. Our MI5 agent and the undercover police officer were wired up. Plainclothes officers, some of whom were armed, provided backup nearby, watching and waiting, ready to move in.

It was like a movie set: at the centre there was a van, ostensibly with the missile-launcher and other guns inside, while the rest of the car park was overrun with undercover cops, some in cars and vans with cameras, others on motorbikes in case the target ran. Round the corner the Silver commander was in radio contact with Gold at base. Finally the terrorist appeared, weaving through families, coach parties and other travellers, and walked up to the van. As he did, his undercover 'associates' turned on him and the backup cops moved in.

Rahman was jailed for possessing guns, silencers and ammunition for the purposes of terrorism. Had he got his missile and carried out his threat to shoot down a plane, hundreds of innocent people would have died. His trial judge said that what he had been trying to buy was 'dreadful and dangerous'. He added: 'I have no doubt what was intended was the deaths of large numbers of citizens.' This type of sting often concludes with a guilty plea in the courts – a sign of the overwhelming strength of the evidence.

Plots like these were not thwarted solely by undercover work. The work of the human spies was complemented by state-of-the-art bugs, microphones, and the amazing Internet technology that underlies nearly every modern-day investigation. Take the mobile phone. Even as a police officer I'd smile at what I and others are prepared to say when we're using one – 'I can't talk about this or that', then going on to do so, sometimes making the most indiscreet revelations on the train or in the office. We just forget ourselves. Mind you, so does the criminal.

When a terrorist or other criminal uses a mobile, though, they're telling us much more than the content of their conversation. We can pinpoint the area from where they made the call and work out who they called. We used this technique to track one of the 21/7 bombers to Rome. We can check all telephone records, mobile and fixed-line, to build a retrospective picture of a terrorist's activities. Which brings us back to the argument for extending the time we can hold suspects before we have to charge them: the longer we have, the more closely we can examine bank accounts and Internet, computer and mobile usage before the suspect has to be charged or released.

In the early days the authorities were cautious about revealing eavesdropping and bugging methods in court. They were worried that if the criminal learnt how they had been bugged the tactical edge for the investigation would be lost. I totally support that view. However, I was delighted when Sir Ken McDonald, the director of Public Prosecutions, and Eliza Manningham-Buller, at MI5, agreed that some surveillance evidence could be made public because the greater need was to achieve convictions. The constraints they placed on what could be released were pragmatic and did not disclose anything above what the average member of the public would expect from spies. After all, many a celebrity has been bugged by tabloid newspapers in scandal scams so people know that pinhole cameras can be concealed in tiepins, that most furniture can be used to conceal listening devices and that mobile-phone conversations and text messages can be monitored. Despite that knowledge, though, criminals need the mobile phone and can't resist speaking to each other in public places where they can be overheard.

Even with my limited experience of doing surveillance work I have sat in a bar just feet away from a house burglar talking to his criminal handler, describing the loot he had stolen the night before and was trying to sell on. This enabled us to follow those two individuals for the next couple of days and catch them red-handed.

In my role as the UK police lead for countering terrorism at New Scotland Yard, I advised the government on the benefits of keeping telephone, email and Internet data for at least twelve months. I cited cases where such details had been critical in bringing terrorists to justice. After the 7 July attacks, the then home secretary Charles Clarke sent me to Berlin to do the groundwork on introducing new European Union rules to this effect. I had no idea, of course, that several years later the powers that were introduced as a result would also be used to target fly-tippers, tax and housing-benefit dodgers and trading-standards swindlers. They were certainly not intended for that. This is where I believe civil-liberties campaigners have a very good point. I am all for using these things to catch those who threaten our society but I don't approve of 'mission creep', which means they're used for other, lesser, things.

The mobile phone was the key to almost everything in one recent case. It was exploited by the terrorists and by us. The attack happened on 29 June 2007. There was no intelligence to go on so we had to identify those responsible quickly as they were terrorists on the run. We and MI5 pulled together all our capabilities.

It was a Friday night in the West End of London. Thousands of people were out and about, enjoying a night on the town. The area was full of noisy revellers, young people queuing to get into popular nightclubs, couples enjoying late-night meals as the theatres and cinemas ended their evening performances, celebrities and the super-rich at their favourite haunts. Central London was buzzing, as it is every Friday night. And, also as every Friday night, the emergency services were out in force too, police and ambulance staff dealing with the inevitable incidents, accidents and crimes that come with large gatherings of people.

In the middle of all this a sinister and potentially devastating terrorist plot was unfolding, carried out by doctors – the very people you and I would expect to be helping society, rather than planning mass murder. They drove up to one of the most popular and well-known clubs in Haymarket in which five hundred plus people were dancing and drinking the night away. They left one car outside Tiger, Tiger, the other by the nearby late-night bus stop. The vehicles were Mercedes saloons, innocuous enough in central London at that time of night – they might have been minicabs, or have belonged to members of the public.

They were packed with a lethal cocktail of gas canisters, petrol and nails. If set alight, they would create massive fireballs and explosions that would send the steel nails flying through the air at terrible speed. There can only have been one aim: to cause maximum injury to many innocent people. The terrorists also left a mobile phone rigged to the bombs in each car: the plan was that when they rang the first mobile from another phone it would trigger the explosion – a ploy often used by the IRA. As people ran away from it they might be caught in the second detonation – a cowardly, outrageous act by people who should have been curing, not killing people.

The terrorists, thank goodness, had been careless and the mobile detonators failed to work. We know from their phone records that the bombers repeatedly called the mobiles in the cars to no avail. A passing ambulance crew detected vapours and reported the first car. By the time we realized there was another, through CCTV and eye-witness reports, it had been removed because it was illegally parked and taken to an underground car park.

This meant that there were two mobile phones – one in each car – with details that quickly identified the bombers and the new phones they were using – they recorded the numbers of the phones that had been dialling in as the bombers tried to detonate the devices. Instead of leaving a bomb wreck the culprits left vital clues for us. They fled north, with us in hot pursuit.

We now finally traced the details of who they were, using the phone and car details. To our shock one was an NHS doctor who, American intelligence sources suggested, used to belong to an Al Qaeda-inspired cell in Iraq before coming to the UK. MI5 had fleetingly come across him before, mixing with people of extremist views, though not with anyone known to be involved in terrorism. This was another case that would push us to realize many more on the fringes of extremist activity should be followed up.

By 5 a.m. we had found their bomb factory in Scotland. But they were not there. By lunchtime on the Saturday we had reliable intelligence they were in Scotland though, near Glasgow. But it was like looking for a needle in a haystack. We didn't know the car, we didn't know where they were heading. As we followed them from London, we knew we were still about half an hour behind them.

I was sitting in my office, taking calls, ensuring resources were available, keeping forces whose areas we were travelling through up to date. We didn't know if the men were suicidal but we had to get to them before they attacked again. In the background the television was showing Saturday-afternoon sport: it was around three o'clock, and to this day I remember the feeling of helplessness as the Sky newsflash came through and we saw the story unfold before our eyes. The second I saw it, before I'd had word from anyone else, I knew we were too late. Once again the terrorists had got through on my watch. The manhunt was over: the bombers had driven their fuel-packed jeep up on to the pavement and straight into the doors of the passenger terminal at Glasgow airport.

Initially we didn't know if there were injuries or deaths, though we soon saw the heroism of the public, which, it transpired, would save the day. The driver was seriously injured and would later die, but his passenger was wrestled to the ground by passers-by, then arrested.

So, I was in my office. Peter Clarke and John McDowall were still upstairs in theirs. Once we knew it had been a suicide attack and that the bombers had survived, there were two imperatives. First I had to deal with the fact that we were operating in a different judicial territory: I needed to be sure we recognized and observed Scottish law; second, I was detached from the crime scene and, with my national responsibilities for terrorism, I had to exert some control over that. There would probably be disagreement between ourselves and the Scottish authorities as to who would be in charge. I was confident the chief constable of the Strathclyde Police, Sir Willie Ray, would have no qualms whatsoever in handing me jurisdiction over the terrorist investigation, but I was less confident that the Scottish Parliament would allow it. Yet again the vulnerability of UK policing to political structures was exposed.

Over the next week a disproportionate amount of effort was directed towards convincing the Scottish first minister and his attorney general that it was right to hand the case to London. I think Peter Clarke swung it. I sent him immediately to Scotland in a military helicopter to take charge on the ground. His influence and negotiating skills secured the agreements we needed, though not before some amazing playground antics from some of the politicians. I remember one particular video conference call conducted in COBRA where we and government ministers in London were communicating with Scottish ministers. The Scots were determined they were equipped not only to deal with the investigation but also to try any suspects in their courts. No one was prepared to give way.

We had been so lucky in not having had mass casualties at Glasgow airport: the attack had taken place on the first day of the Scottish summer holiday and there were four thousand people at the airport. If the vehicle had got through the doors there would have been massive loss of life – yet here we were having an ugly debate over who had primacy, heels dug in. And there was nothing to say there wouldn't be more attacks, perhaps as retaliation. Intelligence analysts had raised the threat level from Severe to Critical for the next few days.

The police took a different view from the politicians: officers from both forces were co-operating brilliantly on the ground, sharing offices and getting on with the job. Both the Met and Strathclyde Police knew it was sensible to give the lead to London where we could make connections with other cells and cases and draw on our considerable experience in hunting terrorists. It took some days but, eventually, logic prevailed and the case came to us.

I know I keep banging on about the frustration of politics but this example, along with many others I have mentioned, is surely starting to make a strong case for detaching politics from policing. At times I think some politicians can't help themselves. The lure of getting in the spotlight or having hissy fits over who is most important simply gets in the way. And, quite frankly, it's despicable.

The Haymarket–Glasgow case highlights the importance and the difficulties of using legal powers as a tool in fighting terrorism. The day after the Glasgow attack I realized just what an ass the law had become. I was summoned by the new prime minister, Gordon Brown, to Downing Street – he'd only been in power a few days.

'Is the whole of the country pulling together to prevent further attacks?' he asked me. It was a terrible moment. I'd had a good rapport with Tony Blair but I hadn't yet built a relationship with the new incumbent at Number 10. I looked him in the eye, fingers crossed behind my back, and reassured him we were on top of the job.

I was taking a punt. If it went wrong I would have to return and tell him the powers his government had given us to fight terrorism had been balked at by some chief constables who weren't using them and who, in my view, were making our job of tracking terrorists harder.

Let me explain. Section 44 of the Terrorism Act, 2000, gives police and the home secretary powers to define any area in the country, over any period of time, when we can stop and search any vehicle or person, and seize articles of a kind which could be used for terrorism – even if there are no grounds for suspicion.

Our intelligence told us that terrorists did not stay at home: they travelled to terrorist camps to train, or to potential targets, or to meet other members of their particular cell. The 7 July bombers had gone to training camps in Wales, for example. And yet we had the crazy situation where some chief constables chose to invoke Section 44 and some did not. Take Cumbria: we knew terrorists were travelling there to train and bond but its chief constable didn't use Section 44. Neither did Bedfordshire Police, even though we knew Luton was a hotbed of extremism. Terrorists were able to travel across counties knowing that in some places the chances of being stopped and searched or questioned were nil. In the wake of the Haymarket and Glasgow bombs, we were trying to create a hostile environment in case other terrorists were planning to attack. Part of our wider tactic was to make it more difficult for them to move around, especially if they were carrying bombs.

So, on that Sunday morning, as the world woke up to the developments in Glasgow, I had called an emergency meeting of the Association of Chief Police Officers (ACPO) Advisory Group. Senior officers from across the country were gathering in London and I was banking on persuading everyone to invoke the powers of Section 44 – hence my little white lie to the prime minister that they were already working together to do all they could to hunt down those behind the latest attacks.

I drove from Downing Street to the Yard. The streets were quiet, just a handful of tourists around, armed police patrolling the bastions of power around Whitehall, street cleaners and me. The journey took about a minute in the car. Inside, New Scotland Yard was buzzing.

There were about fifty senior officers in the room when I walked in. I was immensely grateful to the then deputy commissioner, Sir Paul Stephenson, for attending the meeting to support the operation. His presence meant that the discussion had real significance.

I explained to the meeting why I wanted them to invoke Section 44 nationwide. I explained it would be initially for the month of July and that the Home Office approved the plan. Many chief constables gave me a hard time. They did not want it to be used in their area because they believed it might upset sensitive communities and create too much controversy. I thought this was political correctness gone bonkers – and wondered if, in some cases, they just didn't want the hassle they'd get from civil-liberties groups. We were fighting terrorists hell-bent on murdering innocent civilians anywhere in the UK – as Glasgow had proved – and the government had given us powers to make it more difficult for them to move around, yet those on our own side didn't want to use them. Sir Paul piled in with strong support, and by the end I thought we had convinced most. Some had to get further clearance in their areas but in the main, throughout July 2007, Section 44 was in place over huge tranches of the country. That morning I was able to return to the prime minister and say with more certainty, and relief, that our colleagues in other forces were on board.

Isn't this a fascinating way of working? It's rather twee and typically British, yet it has the potential for disaster. The contrast with the Serious and Organized Crime Agency (SOCA) is telling. Its director general simply circulates in the UK a tactic he feels appropriate. Yet in terrorism, which is at least equally serious, no one can do that.

Other legal powers have proved invaluable in hunting terrorists. In the early days after the 11 September attacks in the USA, we were concerned that key suspects were allowed to operate freely because we hadn't strong enough evidence to bring them to court. We were given powers to detain them without trial, as long as a judge who specialized in terrorism was convinced of the need for us to do so in a secret hearing involving, among others, MI5. When this was challenged in the courts it was deemed unlawful and we were given the power to put these suspects under control orders instead. Only a handful of suspects are held in this way – we far prefer to bring them to trial. But I believe that the power to do this has enabled us at the very least to disrupt and thus prevent some plots.

Although I advised government on what we needed, I was still detached, of course, from the process of law-making – that was the job of lawyers and politicians. It was assumed, correctly in the main, that we'd take what weapons we could – and if that meant stronger legal powers to fight terrorism, that was all to the good.

I was now getting my head around a much newer threat: the increasing power of the Internet. Over the years the use of fingerprints and DNA to achieve convictions has been overwhelming. When a terrorist leaves his physical finger-prints at the scene of crime it's clearly incriminating and puts the onus on him or her to explain why they're there – a fantastic tactical edge for the police. Now, there are modern equivalents too: the cyberspace fingerprint and the financial fingerprint. We've shifted significant resources away from conventional detectives to financial investigators and com-puter hackers. You'll have seen how, when we arrest terrorist suspects, detectives remove literally tons of computers, hard drives, documents including bank statements, credit cards, phone sim cards, mobile phones, etc. Each of these items can reveal the equivalent of a fingerprint for the investigator. A mobile sim card contains all phone and text-messaging traffic – we've often found new leads and suspects through sim-card analysis. It doesn't tell us what was said, but it pro-vides us with a point of contact to interrogate.

Computer hard drives do the same: they'll show email

traffic and Internet usage – not what was written but patterns of contact. When we want to establish what was said or written we have to bug or eavesdrop and that means obtaining a warrant from the home secretary.

As for financial analysis, every time someone uses a credit card or hole-in-the-wall cash dispenser, writes a cheque or transfers money, they reveal lots of information that helps the investigator build a picture of them. Sixty pounds withdrawn from a cashpoint will give a location, a specific time at which the suspect was there – which makes getting hold of the relevant CCTV footage from local cameras much easier and, bingo, we have an up-to-date photograph. If he's on the run and has shaved or dyed his hair, we'll know. We've often trapped fugitives by following their cash withdrawals.

Petrol stops also give us masses of information – a time and place, CCTV pictures of the car they're driving and others they're travelling with. Automatic Number Plate Recognition (ANPR) also has a role to play here.

As we exploit the new technologies, though, so do the terrorists. In October 2005 the arrest of two terrorists planning an attack in Bosnia led us to a man with whom they were in Internet contact in London. Younes Tsouli was king of the Internet terrorists and he was helping the pair prepare their attack from his modest room in Shepherds Bush. He conspired through cyberspace, under the name of 'Terrorist 007', with people he never met face to face, promising he would eventually meet them 'in a better place' – i.e. in heaven. He would browse the Internet searching for home videos made by US troops in Iraq, then pass them on to terrorists who would study them for details about the inside of US bases there so that their attacks could be more lethal. Al Qaeda leaders in Iraq used him to build websites and he became the main distributor of their evil videos.

It was only after his arrest and our IT experts had un-ravelled the secrets on his computer that we realized just how significant he was. Information on his computer led to terrorist arrests all over the world, including the UK. Tsouli and his two co-conspirators were jailed in 2007 for incitement to commit murder through the Internet. He's now serving sixteen years in Belmarsh high-security prison in South-east London.

The cyberspace plot presented a new challenge to us all. Imagine men who had never met but who had a common desire to commit mass murder of innocent victims for the purpose of terrorism. They have minimal knowledge and expertise on how to mount attacks. They have little idea of how to organize themselves and belong to no real terrorist association, yet all those prerequisites are achieved over time through the Internet. It's like paedophile-grooming: the paedophile looks to befriend and influence a potential victim. The cyber-terrorist does the same. In this particular case the men involved had never met physically: their contact was through email.

Their case showed just how far Al Qaeda's propaganda has spread via the Internet.

Our surveillance society means we are all watched and monitored as never before. Some may not like it – civil libertarians from all persuasions continue to argue it's gone too far. I believe it's a necessary part of life, a vital weapon in our armoury if we are successfully to hunt and prosecute terrorists.

11. The Nature and Character of the Modern Terrorist

WHEN I FIRST BECAME HEAD OF SPECIALIST OPERATIONS, THE conventional wisdom was that none of the terrorist plots we came across were linked. For more than a year I continued to believe this. It was wrong. In truth, we simply didn't have evidence to link the plots. Had we assumed links without firm evidence, though, we might have been drawn down misleading avenues, wasting time when we needed to follow up what evidence we had.

We now know that many, if not most, of the major plots of the last five years are linked to varying degrees – and many go right back to the fertilizer plot of 2004, which we codenamed Operation Crevice. For months we followed a group from Crawley in Sussex as they planned a devastating series of attacks at the vast Bluewater shopping centre, to the east of London, and other crowded places. They stockpiled huge quantities of fertilizer – a classic ingredient for making bombs – and kept it in a storage depot in West London. The people who worked there tipped us off: they thought it a very odd thing to be storing when most people use the space for things like furniture, books and documents. The plotters were jailed. But before their arrest MI5 had secretly filmed and recorded them, and inevitably others they associated with were filmed too: friends and family, people they socialized and worked with. At the time neither MI5 nor the police followed these people up, first because they did not appear to be in on the plot, and second, because they had to prioritize when it came to putting people under surveillance; those on the periphery of the fertilizer plot were not deemed an immediate danger to the public. We didn't even know most of their names.

We certainly do now. The 7 July suicide bombers Mohammad Sidique Khan and Shehzad Tanweer were covertly filmed and recorded by MI5 associating with the fertilizer plotters – but they weren't identified or followed up until after the 7 July attacks because there were more dangerous people to track. I know to some this may appear to have been a terrible error but, as I said in Chapter 3, the 7 July investigation, when you are covering named suspects with surveillance it's not unusual for unknown associates to enter the fray. It would be impossible just on the basis of a new face appearing to divert resources towards its owner without working out whether it's worth it. You would lose focus and fall between two stools. That said, a basic investigation will be mounted to try to identify that person. And if that draws a blank you put it aside to return to when you have time.

Mohammad Sidique Khan, the leader of the 7 July cell, trained at an Al Qaeda camp on the Pakistan border in 2003 with the leader of the fertilizer plot.

And remember the police sting at South Mimms when Kazi Rahman had been trying to buy weapons including a missile-launcher? It transpired that he was a friend of several fertilizer plotters and trained in the same camps as they did in Pakistan.

Dhiren Barot did too. He was jailed for life in 2006 for plotting to blow up office blocks in the UK and America. He was trying to make a dirty bomb. Indian and Hindu by birth, he converted to Islam at the age of twenty and, in the mid-1990s, travelled to Pakistan, where he turned to terrorism. He became a high-ranking member of Al Qaeda and helped the 11 September terrorists before turning his sights on the UK. In 2004 he trained in the tribal regions of Pakistan with Mohammed Babar and other fertilizer plotters.

The links to the fertilizer plot continue to come to light. What was more, many of those involved in the plots I've mentioned worshipped with or were influenced by extreme radical preachers, like Abu Hamza and Mohamed Al Bakri.

Hamza set himself up as the imam of Finsbury Park mosque in North London until it was raided in 2003. Here, under the cover of the mosque, he provided shelter and encouragement, guidance and grooming for young terrorists, including Richard Reid, the shoe bomber, Zacharias Moussaoui, convicted of the 9/11 attacks in New York in 2001, and Kamel Bourgass, jailed for the fatal stabbing of PC Stephen Oake in Manchester in 2003. Hamza, who lost his hands and an eye in Afghanistan many years ago, has now been jailed for inciting murder. He also faces extradition to America, where the authorities want to try him on global conspiracy charges.

Similarly, in 1996 Bakri founded the extremist group Al Mujaharoun, which is now banned in the UK. He described the 9/11 hijackers as 'the magnificent nineteen' and the 7/7 bombers as the 'fantastic four'. In August 2005 he fled the UK to self-imposed exile in Lebanon, where he remains.

Many of these terrorists supported extreme Kashmiri groups, their first links with terrorism in Pakistan, which led them to Al Qaeda – this was how Al Qaeda member Dhiren

Barot was radicalized. It's politically difficult to shine too strong a light on any single aspect but I think the Kashmiri links that exist between the terrorist plotters and attackers in the UK are difficult to avoid – although in the early days we did not appreciate the potential significance of the link.

The web spreads wider: where we found no evidence of links before, we see them now. In the winter of 2004/5, the leaders of the 7 July attacks, Mohammad Sidique Khan and Shehzad Tanweer, and the 21 July cell leader Muktar Said Ibrahim, were in Pakistan at the same time. Did they plan an ongoing series of attacks on the UK? Mohammed Hamid, convicted of organizing terrorist training camps in the UK, taught the 21 July bombers. With hindsight, we know that MI5 had come across the Glasgow airport bomber Bilal Abdullah, a former NHS doctor now in jail for life, but, as with the 7 July ringleader, he was not considered a significant threat.

The current director general of MI5, Jonathan Evans, acknowledges their understanding that the threat is still growing. He said in a speech in 2007: 'The deeper we investigate, the more we know about the networks. And the more we know, the greater the likelihood that, when an attack or attempted attack does occur, my service will have some information on at least one of the perpetrators.'

I share his view. I remember back in 2005 and 2006 briefing journalists that Al Qaeda was a loose affiliation of like-minded groups who shared the same ideals but had no firm leadership or control – or, indeed, access to Osama bin Laden in hiding. That was what we and the intelligence agencies believed then. But as we uncovered more plots and made more arrests we have changed our view. We now firmly believe that Al Qaeda has a central leadership who pull the strings. European intelligence chiefs believe it has spiritual leaders – Abu Qatada, for example, who was once described as the spiritual head of Al Qaeda in Europe. After 9/11, when German police raided the Hamburg flat of some of the hijackers, they seized tapes of outrageously radical sermons by Abu Qatada in which he was stirring up hatred against the West. At his hearing in a special terrorism court in London, the judge described him as a 'truly dangerous individual'. He's in Belmarsh jail, along with Abu Hamza, Tsouli and other terrorists. Abu Qatada is nearing the end of a long-running legal attempt to avoid deportation to Jordan, where he came from and where he's been convicted of terrorist offences *in absentia*.

Al Qaeda also has a military structure based around Osama bin Laden and Ayman Al Zawahiri (who appeared on the suicide video of the 7 July leader, Mohammad Sidique Khan, on other Al Qaeda videos and is the chief strategist) and around its foot soldiers hiding in the mountains and caves of Afghanistan. We believe there is another layer of 'masterminds' and businessmen who oversee the campaigns in the UK and other countries. We have an idea who they are but they distance themselves from the attacks and it's difficult to find firm evidence against them. But when there are arrests and the cells are forcibly disbanded, their plans disrupted by us, another cell emerges, no doubt brought on by a mastermind somewhere abroad. It's just like the computer game Space Invaders in which you eliminate one cell only for another to appear – two weeks after the 7 July attacks, the 21 July plotters appeared.

All in all a much clearer picture of the modern international terrorist is emerging. Seventy-five per cent of the plots against the UK originate in Pakistan. The cell structure is similar to that used by the IRA. They have a cell leader, or 'emir', who brings together a group of like-minded friends and militants from Al Qaeda terrorist training camps. He answers to a mastermind and to the Al Qaeda leadership on the Pakistan–Afghanistan border. He is also the strategist for the cell. In the case of the 7 July attacks, which cost just a few thousand pounds to mount, the cell leader financed them. Working with him is a quartermaster who organizes the buying and collects supplies – guns, ammunition, explosives, fake passports, etc. Then there is a bomb-maker, and finally the foot soldiers. Let me explain in more detail.

This paramilitary approach suited the IRA: it gave it a hierarchy that some aspired to move up. It was also evident in the Maze prison, and we are keen to ensure it doesn't take a hold with Islamic militants held at Belmarsh in East London. It is a major concern for the prison authorities that Friday prayers have become the focal point for potential radical preaching in what should be a safe and secure establishment. There have been incidents when prison guards have been attacked by groups of Islamic inmates who, in my mind, are trying to turn the tables as to who is in charge. Although prisoners are moved between jails, the problem persists. It seems to me that there are striking similarities between those who have been sent to prison for minor crime and come out prepared to commit major crime through indoctrination by serious criminals, and Islamic prisoners in jail for minor crime who leave having been harshly radicalized. The dilemma for the authorities is how to avoid intruding on worship by mainstream Muslims in jail, while preventing extremist prisoners exploiting religious gatherings for terrorism.

The IRA was directed at senior level covertly in Belfast or the Republic of Ireland; Al Qaeda is directed covertly by bin Laden, Al Zawahiri and their lieutenants abroad. The IRA had technical expertise in how to prime and deploy bombs;

potential suicide bombers also receive instruction from Al Qaeda specialists in the terrorist training camps. The IRA leadership had people who obtained supplies and funds for cells that needed it; Al Qaeda groups in the UK purchase their own equipment, but nevertheless answer to the mastermind abroad – a Mr Motivator who seems to have visibility across all the individual cells that are operating, giving them encouragement. It's a sinister ingredient of the Al Qaeda philosophy, which differentiates them from the IRA: Al Qaeda asks young individuals to commit their lives to the 'cause'.

I believe that a strategic plan has been drawn up outside the UK for a stream of attacks here. Why else would there have been a series of year on year attacks since 9/11 when this country has never previously hosted such evil international terrorism? I know where my money lies.

Some Al Qaeda plotters have used bomb recipes like those of the IRA – the fertilizer plotters, for example, and the Haymarket–Glasgow bombers. But here the divergence between the two organizations shows again. The IRA tended to go for timing devices or remote detonation while Al Qaeda prefers vehicle or person-borne self-detonation devices. The IRA targeted crowded places and iconic sites – Harrods, shopping centres, the BBC are good examples – places that would attract the most publicity and inflict potentially a high death toll. But, unlike Al Qaeda, they issued warnings – not for any moral or decent reason but to try to shift responsibility from themselves to the authorities. It was a shallow, weak argument: if we failed to evacuate effectively after the warning the blood was transferred to our hands. The Al Qaeda terrorist doesn't bother with that argument. He targets exactly the same types of places but attempts simply to achieve the highest death toll possible.

Attacks not just in the UK but elsewhere show just how far they'll go.

Look how often a single suicide bomber has mounted a vehicle-borne bomb attack – on a hotel, for example. In 2004, at Sharm el Sheikh, a popular tourist resort in Egypt, three bombs went off within minutes of each other. The most devastating was a suicide car bomb at the Ghazala Gardens Hotel. Nearly a hundred people, many of them tourists, were killed. There were similar bomb attacks against Westerners in Bali in 2005.

Al Qaeda, or Al Qaeda-linked terrorists, use other methods, too, which show just how ruthless and determined they are to kill. I have seen military footage of typical vehicle-borne attacks in Iraq. In one example a military checkpoint was the target; a uniformed US trooper, stopping vehicles, peered into a car to talk to the driver and you could see his terror as he realized he was about to become the sole victim of an attack. Seconds later the suicide bomber detonated the car bomb, instantly killing himself and the trooper. In this way, Al Qaeda was making a statement: 'This is how confident we are. This is how close we can get to your soldiers. Even your checkpoints aren't safe from us.' You can imagine the impact it would have had on the platoon.

I used to brief my protection teams using CCTV footage of another technique favoured by Al Qaeda. The target was a VIP driving in a protected convoy. The bomber was following the convoy, waiting for an opportunity to infiltrate the protected chain of cars. You may wonder why protection vehicles travel literally bumper to bumper within the convoy. It's to stop any would-be suicide bomber driving into a gap between the protection officers and the principal. Sadly, on that occasion, the protection team allowed a gap to open. Within seconds the bomber had exploited the opportunity, accelerating and overtaking the rear protection vehicle. In place between the protection vehicles and the VIP's car, the terrorist attacked, detonating his car bomb on the move, killing the VIP and the protection officers in the car behind him. They are ruthless and, since they are geared up to die too, they are fearless, a lethal enemy now operating within the UK. That is why we are building huge concrete walls around key buildings, and rebuilding main roads so that there is a bigger gap between the road and the building itself, which helps to keep vehicles at a distance.

In November 2008 ten co-ordinated attacks in Mumbai, in India, killed more than 170 people, many Westerners among them, illustrating how ingenious and creative the terrorist can be. While we are devising tactics to thwart what we think is their bombing strategy, they are plotting new ways to work: 9/11, 7/7, 21/7 and the multiple shootings at tourist spots in Mumbai graphically illustrate the range of options they are prepared to deploy, and we must assume they have not exhausted their creativity.

I encouraged senior police officers to plan for the unthinkable. 'Try and put yourself in the mind of the terrorist,' I'd say. 'Push the boundaries of what could happen because that's what the terrorist will do.' The events in Mumbai have certainly raised the bar. I found it was a tough call between disclosing details of the types of attacks we were preparing for and avoiding scaremongering. The Haymarket–Glasgow plot carried out by doctors, against a busy nightclub and an airport terminal, resembled one of the scenarios my former team had anticipated, yet before those strikes I would have found it difficult to warn the public that such an attack was possible.

MI5 warns that we are in for the long haul and must expect a generation of this before we can be sure we have finally routed the terrorists. And we must think laterally about who they are: instead of flying directly to Pakistan, then travelling on into Afghanistan, they'll go via different countries to avoid suspicion. Al Qaeda has structure, but some attacks are carried out by autonomous regional groups that espouse similar, sinister ideals: to attack Western people and economies, and to promote the idea of Islamic states. Intelligence analysts, looking at all the information from across the world, believe Osama bin Laden is still alive and in hiding but is less hands-on, more of a symbolic figurehead.

So, what's the overall assessment now of the threat to the UK? There are five levels relating to the threat from international terrorists – mainly those linked to Al Qaeda – which inform decisions about the security needed to protect our national infrastructure: Low means an attack is unlikely; Moderate means an attack is possible but not likely; Substantial means an attack is a strong possibility; Severe means an attack is highly likely; Critical means an attack is expected imminently. Government and businesses will adapt their security plans according to the official threat level, putting extra measures in place when it is highest.

The Joint Terrorism Analysis Centre (JTAC) sets the threat level. The last time it dropped as low as Substantial was shortly before the 7 July bomb attacks; it went up to Critical after 7 July, 21 July and the Haymarket–Glasgow attacks for example. Most of the time it remains on Severe.

It's MI5's job to keep on top of the intelligence. It currently has at least two thousand suspects under surveillance – obviously with police help at times. Early in 2009 the director general, Jonathan Evans, gave a rare glimpse into his assessment of the threats: 'There have been eighty-six successful convictions since January 2007 of whom approaching half pleaded guilty, which has had a chilling effect on the enthusiasm of the networks. They're keeping their heads down.' But, he added ominously, there was a 'capability war' going on between the terrorists and MI5. He confirmed Al Qaeda suspects have learnt to avoid speaking to each other in or near buildings, possibly because they're getting information on surveillance from court cases where methods have been disclosed.

As well as potential bombers there are significant numbers of supporters. Jonathan believes that, 'They are doing things like fundraising, helping people to travel to Afghanistan, Pakistan and Somalia. Sometimes they provide equipment, support and propaganda.' But he doesn't think Al Qaeda has a 'semi-autonomous structured hierarchy' in the UK. All the signs still point to masterminds abroad: 'The strategic intent of the Al Qaeda core, in Pakistan, is to mount attacks in the UK, and their model is to use British nationals or residents to deliver the attacks.'

The threat from international terrorist groups is sophisticated, complex and more serious than ever. There are obvious potential targets where security is paramount – not least the forthcoming 2012 Olympic Games in London. And on top of this we still have to contend with post-Cold War complications – the Litvinenko case showed that – and agitation from Irish republican dissidents, which the murders of two soldiers and a police officer in March 2009 in Northern Ireland proved. And, of course, we still have to deal with lone terrorists who are not linked to any group. There are future threats, too: our children will have to deal with the threat of cyber and nuclear attack. The 2012 Olympic Games could probably withstand a bomb attack, but a widespread computer or electricity failure could have an extremely destructive effect. Fortunately, people are working on how to prevent and respond in the event of such attack.

But the intelligence agencies and the police remain focused on hunting Al Qaeda-inspired terrorists. To do this effectively, we need to understand what makes a young man or, in some cases, woman, turn to the group's ideologies. What drives them to the point that they're willing to die in murdering numerous innocent people? There's little doubt in the UK that the wars in Iraq and Afghanistan, the fruits of British foreign policy, have had influence, and Israeli attacks on Gaza have given British extremists more ideological ammunition.

MI5 has concluded there is 'no single path' to violent extremism: economic, social and personal circumstances, as well as foreign policy, play their part. Jonathan Evans is scathing about the way terrorist organizations use the Internet to recruit young British Muslims: 'It's a form of child abuse, trying to exploit young people over the Internet.' Al Qaeda has become expert at propaganda, using dramatic images of people suffering in Iraq, Afghanistan and Gaza, to try to radicalize them.

Take Hammaad Munshi, Britain's youngest convicted terrorist, locked up for two years at the end of 2008 for 'making a record of information likely to be useful in terrorism'. This is a shocking tale of a teenager's fascination with extremist material, which was exploited by an older man for terrorist purposes. Munshi was studying for his GCSEs when he was recruited over the Internet by Aabid Khan, a cyber-terrorist who groomed young Muslims and encouraged them to go to military camps in Pakistan. Munshi was traced through his Internet exchanges with Khan. They discussed how to sneak metal through airport security, and he downloaded details on how to make grenades and lethal chemicals; he was discovered with a collection of Al Qaeda propaganda videos and documents.

His mentor, Khan, and another conspirator were jailed for twelve and ten years respectively for possessing articles for the purpose of terrorism. Munshi himself appeared to be forming a cell targeting the Royal Family and the London Underground.

Like the doctors involved in the Haymarket and Glasgow attacks, Munshi came from a respected Muslim family and was educated, unlike others who had been brought up in relative poverty, which had compounded their antagonism towards Western society and values.

The Internet is not the only route to radicalization. We latched on to one group of terrorists running outdoor training camps and put them under surveillance in Operation Overramp. What we discovered was mind-boggling. Young men, and sometimes women, were being sent to camps, which appeared to have legitimate status, like Boys' Brigade, Girl Guides or Christian summer camps. They'd go initially for a weekend or a week. On the face of it, the camps were a collection of comical, rowdy Muslim men sleeping rough in the hills of Cumbria or the New Forest, using sticks as guns – hardly the stuff of trained terrorists. But our investigations in the weeks after the July bombings delivered a shock: the camps were run by Mohammed Hamid, a veteran of Pakistani military camps who called himself Osama bin London, and Attilia Ahmet, an associate of the jailed extremist preacher Abu Hamza. Hamid had taken two of the 21/7 bombers on a paintballing trip only three weeks earlier. All the bombers had spent camping weekends in the Lake District. And Hamid had called or texted them at least 173 times in the months before the attacks. These were not soft-touch camps but a cover for terrorism.

We were not going to be caught out again by not

following people up. Police and MI5 acquired the necessary warrants, and were able to eavesdrop on a property that Hamid used. They heard him denounce the West to his recruits in the name of Islam. He described the murder of fifty-two innocent people by the 7 July bombers as 'not even breakfast for me'. He predicted there would be six or seven atrocities in the UK before the Olympics. Later, one of our undercover officers infiltrated the group. At one of the camps someone asked him for money to pay for a one-way airline ticket to send a suicide bomber to Somalia. In my view Hamid was a despicable man, in his late forties, grooming others far younger than him to be terrorists.

In 2006, through new legislation passed by Parliament, the police gained the powers to arrest those attending terrorist training camps. In the autumn of 2006 Hamid and his followers gathered in a halal Chinese restaurant in South London and that's when we arrested them. I have analysed surveillance material from operations including Overramp, and come up with five phases in a person becoming radicalized. It's a personal view, no more than that. Phases one to four take place either at home, in Pakistan, or at more subdued camps. In phase one they'd be taught about Islam. Once they have a basic understanding, the elder's teaching shifts in emphasis and they move into phase two: here the elder starts to question the Western view, and plants the seeds of discontent, portraying Muslims as beleaguered, and Islam as neither valued nor respected by Westerners. The war in Iraq is mentioned, and the students are encouraged to see for themselves by surfing the Internet. They now have an understanding of Islam, with a perception that they're on their own and that the West doesn't like them. Bilal Abdullah, one of the Glasgow bombers, demonstrated this sense of isolation from and anger towards the West. He was an Iraqi who'd lived in Baghdad as it went through two wars. He saw his friends killed and built up a hatred for the West that motivated him to come back to the UK where, even though he was a doctor, he started committing acts of terrorism.

So, phase one teaches Islam. Phase two develops a sense of isolation from the West. In phase three the person on the road to radicalization is taught that he must fight back. Now his instructors try to legitimize acts of terrorism. Once he is through to phase four he has usually passed the barrier of no return. It is now that he will go to a camp. Now he and his potential co-conspirators, like-minded *jihad*ists who wish to fight a 'holy war', will attend the outdoor-sports camps in the UK, sleeping rough in his underpants with no bedding to toughen him up. He is taught, with the others, how to handle weapons and make bombs. All this is as much about building trust among them in the face of danger. It has a paramilitary feel – another similarity with the IRA.

Phase five sees the group deployed on a mission – one of the cell will be put in touch with a mastermind, the contacts often set up through the leader at the camps, or via him and contacts in Pakistan. It is for this reason I supported new laws giving us the power to arrest suspects and charge them with 'acts preparatory to terrorism' and 'attending training camps for the purposes of terrorism'. Before those laws were introduced we had no powers to intervene in the early stages before the cell started preparing for a specific act of terrorism. We had to wait until the training was almost finished at the very earliest. Obviously if we can move upstream, and have a legal basis for earlier intervention, we may get to potential terrorists before they are fully radicalized, which might make it easier to then wean them off violence.

In the wake of international terrorist attacks across the world, the word 'radicalization' has taken on a whole new meaning. In some quarters it has become taboo, replaced with 'violent extremist'. As for which word best describes what, I prefer to speak as I see.

From my contact with Muslims, I have found, and I stress this, that the vast majority are appalled that some of their number have resorted to terrorism. It is very difficult for them to reconcile their faith in Islam with mass killing. A further aspect of their dilemma is that many find it hard to share information with the police and the authorities. Even though the 7/7 and 21/7 plotters attended mosques and lived in their communities, but behaved strangely and out of character, no one reported them to the police. It may have been that the communities genuinely didn't suspect terrorism but I believe some ignored any hint of it.

Surely someone buying large quantities of hydrogen peroxide, or, more telling, their skin and hair lightening due to prolonged contact with lethal chemicals would have raised questions in people's minds. If they didn't want to talk directly to the police, they could have contacted Crime-stoppers or Neighbourhood Watch. It is now commonplace for people to ring Crimestoppers to report suspicious activity, be it drugs-dealing or other crimes. The public have truly become the eyes and ears of the police. I read my weekly Neighbourhood Watch bulletin, which offers crime updates to help me prevent crime where I live. These initiatives are part of our everyday life and should be directly transferable to terrorism. But intelligence, or information, from the public about terrorism is negligible. In the trade we call what we're looking for 'community intelligence'. Crimestoppers and Neighbourhood Watch are so successful because there is a high level of trust and co-operation between the public and those to whom they give information. That lack of trust and co-operation among some Muslims is at the heart of why community intelligence on terrorism is almost non-existent.

This unwillingness to work with the police presents only one dimension of the challenge facing us all in defeating terrorism in the UK. The others involve potential future terrorists, and the non-Muslim community.

Many commentators have tried to determine what radicalization is and how it happens. Presumably once that is known preventive strategies can be formed. For me the first question is straightforward, but the second is trickier. A radicalized person has strayed from the mainstream view and converted to more extreme opinions, where their interpretation of and values associated with Islam are at odds with the moderate view. The trigger for making this switch may be quite complex and may involve issues personal to the individual. The concept that Muslims across the world are feeling isolated, oppressed and beleaguered because of certain actions by the Western world – in particular the conflicts in Iraq and Afghanistan – seems to be a common thread.

The government strategy to tackle this is included within their counter-terrorism plan, the long-term strategy known as Contest, with its four principal strands: Prevent, Pursue, Protect and Prepare. While I agree with the themes, there's a danger that each agency will tend to concentrate on the one they feel fits most neatly into their area of work, rather than take a cross-cutting approach, which I think would be more effective. I've already explained how the police are involved in the Pursue strand, by disrupting terrorists and their operations, through intelligence- and evidence-gathering and bringing them to justice.

'Prevent' is concerned with tackling the radicalization of individuals, both in the UK and elsewhere. The government's plan is to tackle the issues that lead someone to become

radicalized, such as disadvantage, inequality and discrimin-
ation. It aims to deter those who facilitate terrorism and
encourage others to become terrorists by creating an
environment in which it's difficult for them to operate. Also,
it aims to engage in the battle of ideas by challenging
ideologies that extremists believe justify violence. The
government talks about winning the hearts and minds of
British Muslims; it wants to ensure mainstream Muslims feel
able to challenge the extremists and to persuade those wavering to dispute the extremist view.

It is important to identify the grievances that some in the
Muslim community feel so that sustainable solutions can be
found. This means putting money and time into community
projects – and engaging the support of non-Muslims – which
will pay dividends long term, though in the short term that
may not be obvious. More integration is required across all
communities, regardless of race or religion.

Finally, how do we stop someone becoming a violent
extremist in the first place? We need to address the reasons
that drive young Muslims, men in particular, to radicalization. We need to challenge their extreme views, create new
role models.

We also need to change the way mainstream Muslims view
the police. Many see us as a punitive body – and the last
thing they'll do is ask us for help if they know their loved one
is being radicalized. A few years ago the police and other
authorities were seen by drug-dependent users as the gatekeepers to jail, not to treatment. In the past if you had a drug
problem you wouldn't expect a sympathetic ear from the
police: you'd be straight into court. Over time, though, we
have repositioned ourselves to show we can provide a safe
haven that will lead to treatment against addiction.

Now apply that to the terrorist agenda. Wouldn't it be

fantastic if we could rely on the families and partners of people like the 7 July bombers to contact us if they saw their loved ones on the road to radicalism or, indeed, if potential bombers themselves came forward believing they needed help? Wouldn't it be great to stop the attack before it happened and help them back into the mainstream community? As with drugs and other offences, there could be a twin-track approach, with preventive work alongside punishment. Of course, as with drug-dependent users, it's not straight-forward. I always used to chuckle when people described the panacea for drugs-related offending as treatment, in the belief that if you took away dependency you'd stop the addict committing crime. In reality a drug-dependent user is likely to go in and out of treatment. There'll be setbacks and the whole process could last years rather than months. It would be the same with people who are radicalized. Should you punish or help, follow the strict letter of the law or apply some compassion and leniency in the hope you can wean the suspect off terrorism? I know if I were a victim I would find it very difficult to support this idea. But it has been done – as part of the Irish peace process, for example.

So far I have charted the major plots against this country since 7 July 2005. What I find striking is the way in which the plots have become more ingenious and imaginative, and the profile of the terrorist is not constrained to one par-ticular background or persona. The majority of convicted terrorists since 7/7 have been born in the UK. They've been either unemployed or working in lower-income jobs and in the main they've committed suicide attacks. But Bilal Abdullah and his accomplice, who attacked the Haymarket and Glasgow airport, defy that profile. They were doctors by day and terrorists by night, originating from outside the UK. Their background and their initial use of non-suicide car bombs contrast with the preferred methodology of other terrorists who have attacked us.

There are also 'lone bombers', where the divergence goes further. These terrorists operate without connection to any other group – perhaps the most difficult to detect until they actually attack. David Copeland was the first 'loner' I came across. Known as the Nail Bomber because he put nails into his devices to cause maximum injury, he attacked innocent people in Brixton, injuring fifty people, and the East End of London, injuring thirteen. But his worst attack was on the Admiral Duncan pub in Soho in London's West End. Three people died, four needed amputations, twenty-six suffered serious burns, and another fifty-three were injured less seriously. For thirteen days in 1999 he terrorized London with his racist and anti-gay attacks. Copeland belonged to the British National Party and a small neo-Nazi organization, the National Socialist Movement.

His most recent equivalent is probably Nicky Reilly. In 2009 he was jailed for eighteen years after admitting attempted murder and preparing an act of terrorism. He had walked into a busy family restaurant, Giraffe, in Exeter with the express intention of detonating a bomb. It was a viable nail-bomb device, which he tried to assemble in the restaurant's toilets. The device exploded there, thank goodness, leaving him injured, but allowing everyone in the restaurant to escape.

Reilly had learning difficulties. As early as June 2003 he told doctors he was interested in terrorism, but he maintained throughout his trial that he had not been brainwashed or indoctrinated. Instead he claimed he was doing what God wanted. He wrote: 'Everywhere Muslims are suffering at the hands of Britain, Israel and America . . . you torture and destroy Muslim lives by taking a father or a son or a brother, even you torture Muslim women.'

His case shows we cannot rely only on profiles. There is no given description of the terrorist. And as we hunt them, none of the security or law-enforcement agencies can risk discounting lines of investigation because a person doesn't *look* suspicious. Before the arrival of the Glasgow bombers, Reilly and Copeland would have fallen short of the profiles known at that time. The basic principles for investigation are to maintain an open mind, never to close down any line of inquiry unless the evidence discounts a theory, and follow the evidence to prove or disprove. In this way you avoid making assumptions or applying stereotypical views.

By releasing the CCTV photographic stills of the 7/7 bombers walking in line, casually dressed and carrying rucksacks, we showed that the terrorist can look like any young men who are travelling. The Haymarket bombers were smartly dressed in suits as they travelled from Glasgow to London, stopping off at motorway service stations. It is believed the terrorist who attacked the Taj Mahal Hotel in Mumbai mingled as an employee. Potential witnesses to these events would not have batted an eyelid at meeting any of these men. No one was perturbed or suspicious.

This tells us that for the public to be our eyes and ears they need more details of the terror threat facing the UK. It will enable them to form accurate images and impressions that will equip them to be more suspicious and alert. MI5 have gone some way towards this by publishing the number of terror cells being monitored, but I fear a lot of people dismiss that as statistics. It doesn't help when people underestimate the seriousness of the threat: it is not diminishing. The attacks that have succeeded and the attacks we've stopped prove that. We must respond.

12. COBRA with No Bite

THE CURRENT STRUCTURES FOR HUNTING TERRORISTS DON'T work. My experience at the heart of counter-terrorist operations has convinced me of this. I want to end this book by suggesting something pretty radical for a police officer. I think that the COBRA system, in which all the experts rush to a 'crisis meeting' instead of getting on and dealing with the situation, is nonsensical. I think the current police structures which allow operational independence for every chief constable with no one in overall command of all counter-terrorism issues nationally are a recipe for disaster. It's time for change.

That I can criticize current structures doesn't mean I think we failed – far from it: what I've written shows we've made a huge difference. But I feel we achieved what we did *in spite of* the structural and operational confines we had to work within. The professionalism of the police and MI5 stopped unwieldy and outdated ways tipping the balance from success to failure.

My three and a half years from 2005 to 2008 as head of Specialist Operations were incredible. It's been a privilege to serve through such testing and tough times. I was lucky to have a strong team – we worked extremely hard but there wasn't a day went by without us having some fun too. There is nothing better than to finish a long day on a light note in the local pub.

Despite that, the job has left me questioning the arrangements for dealing with critical incidents and I have found them wanting. You may wonder why, if I feel so strongly, I didn't tackle it when I was there. To a certain extent I did: I earned a reputation within the force of saying things as they were – but I was also aware that if I was too outspoken or overstepped the mark I could find myself isolated. I don't believe I went that far.

Dealing with policing was like walking a tightrope, yet criticizing government and political structures was even more difficult. You're expected to toe the line and to advise – and that's quite proper: we are public servants working alongside ministers and civil servants. I have now found that outside and free of the uniform I can influence and stimulate debate more easily.

My motivation for suggesting change must be absolutely clear. It's not a case of leaving the job and suddenly everything appears obvious. I don't want to be overly critical of a profession that has served me well – I don't see myself as a poacher turned gamekeeper. I want to offer a reflective account of my experience specifically in regard to counter-terrorism, which I hope will raise awareness of the issues I believe need tackling. You can judge whether or not I'm right. I hope that as I've pointed out the difficulties of juggling the complexities and intrigues of Whitehall with fast-moving live terrorist investigations, I can now offer possible solutions.

Let's start with COBRA. There's a bomb attack and all hell breaks loose. Everyone scrambles – emergency responders, police, intelligence agencies, government departments – and rushes around trying to deal with it. Within an hour we're pulled off the job and summoned to the COBRA rooms in Whitehall. Of course, a meeting like COBRA should be called to co-ordinate the response, and the role of senior people is to detach themselves from the detail and plan ahead. But my experience takes us beyond that point.

The first time I attended COBRA I was in awe – I was sitting alongside the highest in the land. There were more knights there than at King Arthur's Round Table – it was like a *Who's Who* of the great and the good in Whitehall. But the bubble soon burst. As time went on I sat at those meetings with some people I knew but a lot of others I'd never set eyes on. It was like being asked to play in a football cup final with team mates I had rarely trained with and who, in some cases, were playing in positions with which they were unfamiliar.

I had attended regular training exercises on terrorist scenarios throughout the year, but as I sat in COBRA I was intrigued that attendance at those practice runs had been patchy when I compared them with meetings following a real event – then the big stars always showed. At the time of the Haymarket and Glasgow bombs, for example, some of the key players had never even entered the COBRA room before, let alone chaired or participated in one of its meetings. I would not have been surprised to find key participants wandering around the corridors of the Cabinet Office like lost sheep, trying to find out where to go. I'm not talking about when, by a twist of Fate, someone finds themselves dealing with a crisis on their first day in a job and, anyway, that's rare. I'm talking about those who've been in a job for a while: surely they should familiarize themselves with COBRA as soon as they are in the role. It's essential preparation.

I completely understand the need to get the politics right as governments could fall if they failed to deal with a terrorist crisis adequately. However, my experience taught me that the politics tended to dominate much of the thinking and decision-making when we should have been setting it aside to focus on the operational response to the crisis. It may sound harsh, but I think some colleagues felt it more important to make a decision to put them in a good light than one that was truly for the good of the nation. What we actually needed was to see a blend of political considerations and sound operational judgement. If that mix isn't right, you risk stock-market crash, the threat of a public inquiry, and loss of confidence in the ability of the authorities to govern internationally and domestically.

Sometimes the meetings worked – I've mentioned a handful of those that did – but more often they didn't. People would jockey for position in front of influential ministers, squabbling for the highest place at the table. I have been there when COBRA appeared to be little more than a stage for those looking to impress – or a forum where government can be seen to be doing something. I've wondered at times if it's just a photo-opportunity for elected members to be seen walking into the meeting and thus 'in control'. I can think of several occasions when a COBRA meeting was called and the circumstances simply didn't justify it – for example, over bad weather that hadn't yet materialized. Either this was showboating, or those calling the meeting didn't understand what the crisis committee was for.

Meanwhile junior colleagues are out on the front line – some of them risking their lives or facing terrible traumas – waiting for guidance. If only they knew! I would at times question if we, the law-enforcers, the emergency responders, the intelligence officers and the investigators, were taken seriously enough. One Whitehall official had the nerve to tell me after a particularly uncomfortable COBRA meeting: 'Mr Hayman, you must remember we are coming to the party with the brains, the cops are simply operational.'

Well, I disagree. It's time to stop the point-scoring and form a committee in which real experience is the criterion for membership – rather than that you happen to be the elected politician or his or her civil servants. Let's not try to outdo each other. Let's work together, efficiently and fast. We need something radically different. Leave the politicians and their cronies to get on with general policy-making: when it comes to life-and-death decisions we need a body separate from government – yes, unelected – with the real expertise and knowledge needed to deal with the crisis. We would be better off without the interference of politically motivated people who may be driven by a more personal and thus irrelevant or at worst damaging agenda.

Politicians taking such a strong lead in times of crisis come to the table with a strong public mandate. But the higher up the tree they climb, the more power and influence they exert, the more important the briefs they're given and the committees they sit on. Finally they become ministers and some of them end up sitting on COBRA. Some have seen their decision-making platform widen significantly since their election as a Member of Parliament, but their public mandate remains the same. Put simply, they were elected as a representative of their political party in a given area of the country. The electorate did not vote them in for their skills, knowledge and expertise in hunting terrorists, dealing with floods or stopping the spread of foot-and-mouth disease in animals. And yet that's what they're dealing with. I have seen instances in which a politician has the ultimate sanction on what happens, even if they defy the best experience and operational advice in the room.

Of course, it can be argued that their decision-making is blessed with the advice of officials and the professionals. But I've been in the hot seat when the cabinet has been reshuffled in quick succession, and a minister has changed his or her portfolio two or three times in a year. One day, for example, they might be dealing with the spread of the superbug MRSA in hospitals, the next the number of troops in Iraq or Afghanistan.

A letter to *The Times* on 1 October 2008, from Robey Jenkin of Strensall, in North Yorkshire, entitled 'The Cabinet Ministers' Right of Redress', outlined the same point: he noted that when a minister is appointed to a department there is no job advert or selection process. The employer – the prime minister – routinely appoints ministers based on personal relationships and 'loyalty' rather than any obvious previous experience relevant to the specific brief. The writer suggests that if the proper principles of selection, i.e. skills for the job, are applied to the enrolment of the cabinet, we might get a better quality of politician.

In truth, the real business is often done before or after the COBRA meetings or in bilateral sessions between the professionals. It's a routine we established after the events of July 2005, when it became common practice to hold a pre-COBRA meeting ahead of the main session. The intelligence chiefs, senior Home Office and cabinet officials and the police discuss issues they didn't want to raise at the main meeting for fear they'd be leaked, or to keep the number in the loop of sensitive material to a minimum. As I said earlier, I got fed up with the leaks and encouraged these smaller groups. The alternative would have been to say nothing in the main meeting, which would have been counterproductive. Other senior colleagues attending the main COBRA meetings must sometimes have been irritated to know that an arguably more powerful meeting had preceded theirs. There's no doubt we ran the risk of coming to different conclusions, especially if new information was presented at the main COBRA, and it wasn't an ideal set-up, but it was necessary.

I have to admit that, for operational swiftness, the Association of Chief Police Officers (ACPO) and I, under the protection of the principle of operational independence, sometimes took decisions without referring to COBRA. There were times when we knew it would cause an unnecessary delay if we took everything to the meeting. I felt justified in this action. The delays that would have resulted if we had allowed COBRA time to crawl over operational matters, which we believed were beyond its remit, would have caused problems. These were not the actions of a loose cannon: ACPO and I were getting a grip.

We have at times inadvertently touched on a model that might work better. Important and, in my view, largely operational decisions have rested on meetings I have had with the home secretary, John Reid, which were then escalated to the prime minister. We in effect took the process outside COBRA – and, perhaps more by luck than judgement but with much effort, we found we had devised a process that worked, and allowed operational considerations to dominate.

Compare what we did then with the COBRA process. In both cases we got together before the ministerial meeting with ideas and proposals. But the meetings that the law-enforcement and intelligence agencies had ahead of COBRA were unofficial: they would not have been accepted as part of the COBRA process, so we often went into COBRA giving the impression we were meeting for the first time. It's not that COBRA didn't allow preparation but there was no formality or routine to it. It was up to individuals whether they prepared – it was very *ad hoc*. Yet in reality the operational scrum-downs I had with others ahead of the formal meetings formed the basis of all the discussions with ministers that followed.

I believe we should formalize pre-COBRA meetings. This would ensure that the right group of experts come together, thrash out the operational imperatives, reach agreement and then present specific operational plans to politicians and others at the main meeting. COBRA would still be chaired by a minister or the prime minister, or a senior Whitehall official, but the meeting would become specifically ministerial, dealing not with operational planning but with the political repercussions. It would *not* be an operational meeting. There'd be no blurring between politics and operational issues. Politicians would have an opportunity to cast their political lens across the operations options, which would already have been agreed. This approach has the added benefit of showing that everyone involved understands the difference between constructing operational plans and making political decisions. A minister needs to be in the most informed position to make the best decision and the operational forum would develop that information for him or her. And, of course, there are decisions they must take – do they or do they not close the transport system? – but it's surely better to have all the expert opinion sorted and focused in advance, than a free-for-all in which operational chiefs and politicians vie to get in their pennyworth of opinion.

I remember wasting precious time during one COBRA meeting because we had to explain to a minister why we couldn't take up their idea of carrying out a forensic examination (gathering untouched evidence) at the same time as doing the clear-up operation (cleaning and clearing the site ready to reopen it to the public). Interesting concept!

All in all, I believe we need two sets of meetings – the operational and the ministerial – and we need a very clear definition about what we should expect from COBRA. This would make the meetings shorter, more focused and probably less frequent.

There is something I find even more shocking about COBRA and it's to do with transparency. I have never been able to understand why there is no evidence of any full minutes being taken or that the committee is constitutionally accountable to anyone independent of it. I, as someone who attended COBRA meetings, have never received a copy of any minutes. I can only assume they don't exist, but if they do, how is their accuracy checked and agreed? Yet this is one of the most powerful and important committees in the UK. Can you imagine that a meeting of your local school governors' association, or any government department, would be allowed to go undocumented, no minutes circulated and approved? Maybe it's feared that a request for those minutes to be published under the Freedom of Information Act could compromise decision-making. But any such anxiety is unfounded as this type of information would not be released. I cannot think of any plausible reason why comprehensive, accurate minutes are not taken and kept as a record of government.

It is important that we know who said what, how a discussion was concluded and, more crucially, who was tasked with an action. Imagine if someone at the meeting was given a responsibility, failed to fulfil it, and the consequence was either loss of life or some other critical incident. A scandal would result if no one could recall accurately who had been given the job and why. I know that others who've attended COBRA are also concerned at the lack of visible minutes. I suspect that Cabinet Office civil servants write up loose notes of proceedings *after* each meeting – but that wouldn't reproduce the meeting exactly as it happened.

There is an interesting contrast to be drawn here. After the de Menezes shooting, it was recommended that the activities in a police operations control room must be tape-recorded. Why shouldn't the same standard be applied to COBRA? I don't believe COBRA can hide behind the confidentiality clause because the police control room is handling issues that are just as sensitive.

I have outlined the international terrorist threat posed by Al Qaeda, how different and more threatening it is now than Irish terrorism. Yet the police, the security services and the government are still working in COBRA in the same way they did in the days of Irish terrorism. And the governmental structures used to deal with terrorism are used to tackle other national crises such as floods. That would be acceptable if each of these events required similar means of resolution – but they don't. How can the slaughtering of infected cattle and the cleansing of farms require the same management arrangements as the aftermath of mass-casualty bomb attacks or the kidnap of a UK citizen abroad? They are worlds apart.

The most obvious difference is the footprint of the crisis. The flood can be devastating but it probably stretches over two or three police-force areas at most. It will need a substantial emergency response on the front line and a commensurate command structure. However, it bears no comparison to the aftermath of a terrorist attack, with its international interface, stretching across the whole of the

UK. That needs both uniform and investigative responses with a command structure and policing presence that will, in most cases if not all, outstrip those needed for a flood. I have tried to give you some insight into the type of policing response required, ranging from a comprehensive forensic and scientific capability through to large numbers of police officers on cordons or patrol duties. So why are the response structures still grouped under one strategy, which does not differentiate? It's as if, regardless of the features of a threat, there is an across-the-board response.

This point is strengthened when you review changes introduced since the July 2005 attacks. Take the published National Security Strategy (NSS), published in March 2008. The prime minister, Gordon Brown, told Parliament that new threats demand new approaches, and a radically updated and much more co-ordinated response was required because the potential threats we face come from far less predictable sources, both state and non-state. He said that twenty years ago the terrorist threat to Britain was principally from the IRA. Now it comes from loosely affiliated global networks that threaten us and other nations across continents. And the consequences of regional instability and terrorism – with climate change, poverty, mass population movement and even organized crime – reverberate round the globe. He added: 'To address these great insecurities, war, terrorism and now climate change, disease and poverty – threats which redefine national security not just as the protection of the state but as the protection of all people – we need to mobilize all the resources available to us: the hard power of our military, police, security and intelligence services; the persuasive force and reach of diplomacy and cultural connections; the authority of strengthened global institutions, which, with our full support, can deploy both 'hard' and 'soft' power; and not least, because arms and authority will never be enough, the power of ideas, of shared values and hopes that can win over hearts and minds – and can forge new partnerships for progress and tolerance, involving government, the private and voluntary sectors, community and faith organizations, and individuals.'

I was encouraged that he clearly defined the threats to the UK as ranging from terrorism to the consequences of climate change. I thought we were going to get the radical overhaul I had come to believe was needed. But no. I was disappointed and frankly alarmed at the woeful lack of detail and at the delivery mechanisms he put forward in his strategy. The NSS proposes new arrangements for chairing the Joint Intelligence Committee, but its functions remain largely the same. It is part of the Cabinet Office and is responsible for providing ministers and senior officials with co-ordinated interdepartmental intelligence assessments on a range of issues of immediate and long-term importance to national interests, primarily in the fields of security, defence and foreign affairs.

It is made up of senior officials in the Foreign and Commonwealth Office, Ministry of Defence (including the chief of Defence Intelligence), Home Office, Department of Trade and Industry, Department for International Development, Treasury and Cabinet Office, the heads of the three intelligence agencies and the chief of the Assessments Staff. Other departments attend as needed. The chairman of the Joint Intelligence Committee is charged specifically with ensuring that the committee's warning and monitoring role is discharged effectively. Like the agency heads, he has direct access to the prime minister.

The NSS introduced a new National Security Forum, comprising business experts, academics, community organizations, and military and security experts who will advise the newly constituted National Security Committee. I don't think the relationship and remit of each of these groups or how they fit with COBRA is clear enough. There may be a role for them in peacetime, but during the aftermath of an attack or in the middle of an interdiction to stop a terror attack won't they just add to the growing proliferation of forums? Does COBRA still have primacy? Regardless of what should be the case, will each forum compete for centre stage?

I'm afraid I am far from convinced by the NSS and its supporting structures. There is a basic confusion. It appears to be more a list of threats than a strategic intent, and the structural proposals offer a half-baked solution. In my view, it fails to detail a clear sketch of what accountability, function and relationship each group has to and with the others. Add to that my previous concern over the Contest strategy, in which departments tend to deal with only one of the four strands – Prevent, Pursue, Prepare and Protect – and there's not enough cross-cutting work.

In the absence of any other proposals for change we are back at square one. We must assume the status quo – that is, each agency will have its own arrangements to feed into COBRA, which will remain the government's primary forum for managing a crisis – but now with a further tier of added complexities. It seems to me that what should be a relatively straightforward, non-political security agenda has become overly complicated, and the politics has, arguably, seemed at times more dominant than the debate over the safety of our communities. Of course, all these security plans may change as politicians and governments move on – but even in this scenario I see no current commitment to anything radically different.

When Dr John Reid was home secretary he seemed to understand and grasp the issue. He set up the new Office of Security and Counter-Terrorism (OSCT) in the Home Office, and introduced the home secretary's meeting every Thursday morning, attended by the OSCT and the relevant law-enforcement agencies – I represented the Met. It was a good move as it gave him more reassurance that the agenda was being gripped. Sadly, I think the pace of the OSCT has slowed – through no fault of its director general: there just isn't a strong enough political wind for radical change at the moment.

In summary, COBRA slows everything down. It makes it difficult to respond with immediacy to a crisis and it can blur the lines between what's operational and should be left to the police and other emergency responders and experts, and what's political.

Which brings me to the national police structures: if my idea of COBRA becoming a purely ministerial, political organization with an operational tier feeding into it was accepted, the case for the police service to overhaul its configurations becomes more compelling. Invariably, the president of ACPO is on the long list of people who attend COBRA. He's needed in case there's a demand for police back-up or a joint police initiative across the country. In my day the post was held by Chris Fox and later by Ken Jones – both former chief constables. There was an impression in COBRA that if the ACPO president left COBRA having been given a specific job, it would be done, in the same way that if they asked me to ensure we had counter-terrorism officers on standby nationwide it would happen. I remember going to a meeting with John Prescott when he was standing in for Tony Blair in the summer of 2005. He asked me if I could assure him that, nationally, all forces were pulling in the right direction on a counter-terrorism operation. I had to hesitate in my reply.

That's because we don't have a properly constituted national law-enforcement agency to deal with counter-terrorism. Neither I nor any other officer could or can answer for the country as a whole. Forces were finally persuaded to accept my new role as co-ordinator of National Counter-Terrorist Operations with my deputy Peter Clarke – but neither of us was in overall command of them or of the men and women in each police force who worked on these investigations and operations. That rested with each individual chief constable.

I am at a loss as to why the current law-enforcement structure still presides, one in which we rely on collaboration across forty-three police forces in England and Wales (before we even start thinking about Scotland and Northern Ireland – though most of what I say here applies to them too). We do have a new set of regionally based counter-terrorism units, which I helped to set up. But the absence of a truly national counter-terrorism arrangement appears even stranger when you realize we do have such structures to deal with serious crime through the Serious and Organized Crime Agency (SOCA) and border security through the UK Border Agency. The position becomes yet more bizarre when you consider that a significant proportion of the Border Agency's work is intrinsically linked to counter-terrorism.

If we are to enhance our national ability to tackle terrorism, and achieve economies when it comes to large-scale operations, then we have to change. Right now we have IT and communications systems that still don't match up. The expertise and capabilities of surveillance teams as well as firearms and forensics officers vary in different areas. Command and control across forces is overstretched.

A slim-line single configuration would solve these issues.

I used to think loose collaborations between forces were the solution. But that would need strong links and total commitment from each chief constable involved, and commitment from local politicians on Police Authorities and in the devolved countries, Scotland, Wales and Northern Ireland. The attack on Glasgow airport exposed how difficult it can be to achieve the necessary unity. In February 2009 Her Majesty's Inspector of Constabulary reported that a significant number of police forces were inadequately prepared to deal with a national crisis or major crime. His report called for greater co-operation and support. The Met have recently set up a National Counter-Terrorism Co-ordinating Centre. In my view, that doesn't go far enough.

Instead of collaboration what we need is a national Counter-Terrorism Agency for the whole of the United Kingdom. We are in a halfway house at the moment – neither one thing nor the other. That said, I am aware that in recent times when urgent surveillance deployments have been needed the challenge has been met within two hours. This sounds impressive but is still reliant on goodwill, and the command and control arrangements are unsatisfactory. A national agency would resolve both problems.

Opponents will argue that such an approach detaches operational capability from communities, and that localism will be lost. But it mustn't and needn't be. In truth, we're not getting the intelligence we so desperately need from local communities anyway, though government policy to increase the number of community-based police officers is aimed at rectifying this. Every major terror plot that we have disrupted recently had its roots in intelligence that was not generated by local communities. It's a serious indictment of our community work – think of all the bombing plots in which terrorists living in our neighbourhoods were buying bomb-making ingredients from our shops and discarding suspicious materials in our civic rubbish tips. No one reports this activity. If a burglar or drugs-dealer was operating under our noses the Crimestoppers' or Neighbourhood Watch's phones would be red hot.

The formula for success is to have an intelligence and enforcement plan. Local beat officers working closely with Special Branch must cultivate intelligence from which operations can be mounted to enforce the law and stop terrorism.

I am not for one minute arguing that the solution is an overnight fix but a single-agency structure would accommodate the local connection within its national and international footprint. Accountability for delivery against government investment is spelt out and will be held by one body rather than forty-three.

Sadly, the recent government Green Paper on Policing suggests the opposite. It promotes a framework designed to deliver increased collaboration and co-ordination across the forty-three forces over a number of years. If you dig beyond the glossy brochure it includes some projects to share communication and media services or jointly finance departments, but most of what it suggests is straightforward collaboration. Yes, this will achieve economies of scale but it doesn't touch the operational imperative that international terrorism brings. The ambition of the Green Paper and the ambulatory timescale are not convincing – especially with the 2012 Olympic Games just round the corner. Such a massive event for the UK is a significant threat: it's not good enough to be able to say that we've all joined together in providing a shared press-handling facility or that three or four forces share the same payroll arrangements. What I am talking about is a structure that can deliver a comprehensive, sustainable, operational capability on a stable platform, at least eighteen months before the start of the Games.

Even if economics pushes some smaller forces to reject autonomy and merge voluntarily, it would still represent a hybrid arrangement accommodating localism alongside nationally based initiatives. It would not be what I think is needed: a National Counter-Terrorism Agency to deal with a national threat.

There is an unfortunate backdrop to this whole debate. Scars are still visible from the collapse of a move in the last decade to reduce the number of police forces to create a smaller number of larger organizations that could rightly be labelled Strategic Forces. The process of amalgamation was not well thought through, especially in respect of funding and precept equalization, and it was met with blunt fury by some of the forces involved.

A lot of water has passed under the bridge since those amalgamation discussions. I believe the time is ripe to revisit the debate but with an eye to creating a National Counter-Terrorism Agency at the same time. Almost every plot I have detailed pushed the police to operate across geographical policing boundaries and administrative borders, including international borders. And all the intelligence suggests that the types of attack we face will get worse: nuclear, radiological, and against power sources, like the electricity grid; cyber attacks could bring the country to a standstill by infecting computer systems. One police force alone could not manage such an attack.

We can't placate the many contrasting and competing perspectives. Policy-makers should be encouraged to bite the bullet and return to the rationalization plan, putting in place a fewer number of larger forces that will be capable of reacting and sustaining effort across the breadth of policing. At the same time they should at least introduce arrangements similar to SOCA and the UK Border Agency to deal with counter-terrorism. The compromise of greater collaboration at a time when some forces are not viable due to possible bankruptcy or operational strain is not good enough.

So, in my vision, I have a new national counter-terrorism unit, working alongside fewer, larger police forces, with a two-tier emergency-response committee for times of terrorist crisis: the operational committee and the ministerial COBRA committee. This would complement changes my colleagues and I pushed through to modernize the UK's biggest force, the Met in London. Earlier I described how Sir David Veness and the former commissioner Lord Stevens had worked tirelessly on plans to prevent or deal with a terrorist attack. They would be the last to describe that work as their legacy: their modesty would allow them only to conclude this was simply their job.

I would say the same of my contribution to change. When you have led a command unit, or organization, your impact can be measured by the things you introduced that remain for some time after you leave. Sir David's and Lord Stevens's work lives on. It survived the test of time. We used it as a blueprint for our response to terrorist attack, and we added fresh thinking drawn from the actual experience of attack after they had retired. I would like to think that some of my creations will survive too.

I point to the amalgamation of Special Branch (SO12) and the Anti-Terrorist Branch (SO13), which we merged to form the new Counter-Terrorism Command (SO15). I also oversaw the development of regional counter-terrorism units in Leeds, Manchester, Birmingham and, more recently, the Thames Valley corridor.

These two changes are intrinsically linked but represent different challenges. The formation of SO15 brings together such different cultures and backgrounds that many still feel they will never be compatible. I was surprised how resistant several colleagues were to the move, citing every excuse imaginable for not working together. Some were outraged, claiming the merger would bring a loss of identity. Others couldn't get their heads round merging their separate functions under the umbrella of one department. I had a problem with both arguments.

The protection of each department's cap badge, although sincere, could never be a reason for not amalgamating. Could we seriously argue that inefficiencies should be ignored so that the separate groups could maintain an identity? Similarly, the operational hiccups that were revealed during the July bombings exposed frailties that had their roots in a lack of joined-up working. Instead of complementing one another, each command preferred to work in isolation. I accept that some aspects of their jobs demand each command works alone, but when a free flow of intelligence is needed to feed an investigation, it is crazy to have the intelligence-gatherers detached from the investigators, who are hungry for leads and opportunities to pursue them.

I learnt how strong the feeling can become when a former Special Branch inspector was imprisoned for leaking confidential information to a journalist. He pleaded guilty to handing over top-secret and protected documents. When he spoke to those investigating his case, he was apparently vitriolic about the amalgamation, arguing that the long history of Special Branch didn't seem to have counted for anything. He was misguided. None of the history, expertise, knowledge or experience was being trashed – just garnered towards a more integrated and efficient configuration. I don't recall meeting him and I was certainly not on his Christmas card list.

I believe the track record of success since the joining of the commands has already proved the dissenters wrong. Since the amalgamation, for example, I am convinced the police are working much more closely with MI5, whose officers seem keener to share their intelligence much earlier than before. This enables investigations to turn intelligence into evidence more quickly, and allows the investigation to influence the direction of work.

I'd be kidding myself if I thought the amalgamation of the two commands would be a quick win. It wasn't and it will still take time to bed in. I only hope that time is given, and that it isn't abandoned because it was too difficult.

The national building of counter-terrorism units was a lot more straightforward. The bastion of Special Branch was not so evident out of London, and cultures in the four locations were more open-minded and less intransigent than in the Met. Despite my reservations concerning collaboration over fewer numbers of forces, there was no evidence of chief constables in the affected forces trying to frustrate or resist the move. They were as keen as I was and drove the change forward.

Ironically, just before I retired, the Met, which had been well ahead of the game, able to deal with any terrorist incident thrown at it, appeared to have stood still as it dealt with the early difficulties of changing to the new SO15 formation. The rest of the country had moved fast to introduce state-of-the-art facilities and slick working arrangements.

The new regional counter-terrorism units (CTUs) at Leeds, Birmingham, Manchester and Thames Valley, supported by other covert teams elsewhere in the country, are a real testament to what can be achieved when everyone is pulling in the right direction. Equally, the slow progress in London shows the drag factor associated with difficult change programmes.

I hope the infrastructure I put in place with my chief-constable colleagues has added value to the overall mission. Given my earlier comments on national police-force structures, you can probably guess what I would like to see now. I think the new CTUs should morph into the National Counter-Terrorism Agency I outlined earlier in this chapter, with powers and status on a par with SOCA or the UK Border Agency.

And where would all this leave the Police Authorities, the watchdog organizations over individual forces? They serve a useful and constructive role. They provide a breadth of experience while challenging and supporting the running of a police force. I see no need to tinker with their constitution. If we move to bigger provincial forces, then Police Authorities would cover wider areas too. And I would like to see one big national authority, similar to the one linked to SOCA, to act alongside the newly formed National Counter-Terrorism Agency. In fact, we already have a loose version of this because Police Authority members from the forces that have regional CTUs already meet as a group to oversee what each force is doing. Thames Valley, West Midlands, West Yorkshire, the Met and Greater Manchester each have two Police Authority members who take responsibility for counter-terrorism and meet informally every quarter to discuss what's going on.

All this would be even more effective if we could rationalize the new legal powers we've acquired in recent years to fight terrorism. I believe we need fewer but more focused laws. The to-ing and fro-ing that has gone on within the legislative programme started well before 11 September 2001. It's dogged not only the Labour government but also the law-enforcement and intelligence agencies. With all the best intentions in the world, new laws have been introduced with the aim of preventing further attacks and to punish those responsible for attacks, but the track record for delivery is not good. And while the politicians and judges struggled to find laws that worked, the threat increased. First we had foreign terrorists using the UK as a base for targeting places abroad, then they were home-grown British, carrying out their attacks on British soil. The threat was real, and since 2001 it has not declined. If anything, it's increased.

On 12 November 2001, shortly after the attack in New York on the World Trade Center, Parliament passed the Anti-Terrorism, Crime and Security Act, 2001. This targeted the financing of terrorism and gave police the power to access electronic records of individuals suspected of terrorist activity. Other clauses try to plug the gaps found in the Terrorism Act, 2000. But the most controversial aspect of the new legislation was to bring in something resembling internment without trial, as in Northern Ireland at the height of the Troubles in the early 1970s. This time the government was finding it impossible to deport non-British people who were thought to be involved in terrorism but against whom there was not enough evidence to prosecute them. The Act allowed the government to hold people deemed a risk to national security without charge for indefinite periods. These measures were never going to be acceptable to civil libertarians, and although the government opted out of, or 'derogated' from, the European Convention on Human Rights, that was not sufficient to stop immense opposition. As I mentioned earlier, this law was eventually rejected by the courts. Ministers then introduced 'control orders' to deal with the same group of suspects. These were equally controversial and again a pretty toothless tiger. One minister told me privately that using them was like trying to scoop water with a colander.

As we were approaching 7 July 2005, much of the new post-9/11 legislation was in tatters: either the powers weren't working or the anti-terrorist restrictions were being rejected by senior judges. Yet the threat was increasing and we were soon to see the awful reality of this. Immediately after the 7 July attacks, as I described earlier, the prime minister announced his twelve-point plan for further restrictions. These would form the basis of the Terrorism Act, 2005. This was closely followed by the Terrorism Act, 2006.

For the police, it was like being a child in a sweet shop. I was asked an open-ended question as to what legislation the police required. Although tempting, I never abused the trust placed in me to suggest new laws. I just argued for those things I felt were really needed. For example, I strongly recommended and supported powers to stop people preparing, planning and financing terrorism. I was also strongly in favour of extending the time we could detain terror suspects before we had to charge them. The period was raised from fourteen to twenty-eight days, but the government spectacularly failed to get it raised to ninety days, despite our support, and later failed again to get it to forty-two days. There was the furore over stop-and-search, with many Muslims angry because they felt they were targeted disproportionately.

The legislative programme makes sorry reading, compounded by the fact the police don't always use adequately the powers they are given. If you recall, in the wake of the Glasgow bombing I had immense difficulty in trying to persuade chief constables that stop-and-search powers should be used across the country. Some forces chose not to rock the boat with local communities and were reluctant to use it at all, while others did.

Add to this the scepticism over identity cards. The idea never floated my boat. If you look at countries that use them or, indeed, at other forms of identity such as driving licences and passports, there's always someone able to counterfeit them. They're expensive, they're unpopular, and I'm not sure how they're going to stop criminal activity when all the experience in our investigations has shown that terrorists adopt many identities. In one operation in 2004, 860 passports and foreign identity cards were seized in one raid. In that same operation there were more than 2500 forged documents: does that give you any confidence that, even using the most advanced technology, identity cards will truly identify the people carrying them? Furthermore, for ID cards to work, the technology to read and analyse them has to be in place and there are still big question marks over that. How ridiculous it would be to issue ID cards that the authorities can't always read.

The poor record on terrorism laws and initiatives like ID cards have undermined those Muslims looking for opportunities to build trust and confidence with the authorities. Combine this with their grievances over UK foreign policy – the wars in Iraq and Afghanistan, plus the effects of these on civilian Muslims in those countries – and with the negatives of stop-and-search. It felt to me that for every two steps we took forward in winning Muslim hearts and minds we'd take one step back. The dilemma is that in introducing punitive measures commensurate with the threat, the Muslim community feels isolated. Representatives of Muslim communities should be sitting at the legislative table, helping government to form and introduce the measures, acting as pathfinders.

Another controversial area of work is broaching the need for local intelligence from the Muslim community. As far as the police and intelligence agencies are concerned, winning hearts and minds isn't just about stopping people becoming terrorists – it's about persuading people to come forward with intelligence. We can't pretend the terrorists aren't choosing to hide within those communities – they are. Yet the level of intelligence coming from them, as I said before, is dismal. The police just aren't trusted enough – and it's a shame it sometimes seems that it's one of those taboo subjects in Whitehall and it shouldn't be: how will Muslims learn to trust us if we won't air our grievances too? We must be open. If we are spending millions of pounds investing in Muslim communities we need to get more for our return than pleasant coffee mornings in local halls. We want to work closely with those who'll engage – and, of course, many will – and the day will come when they feel comfortable enough to tell us if they're suspicious about someone, just as they'll ring Crimestoppers or their local Neighbourhood Watch if they're worried about non-terrorist crime.

Recently I returned to my seat in St James's Park, the place where in the hectic aftermath of 7 July 2005 I sought refuge, the place where, over time, I formulated many of these ideas. To my astonishment an ex-soldier I used to nod and chat to then, as he watched the squirrels and pigeons, was still there. We acknowledged each other as if we'd met yesterday. And I reflected on where I am now, retired from the police, busy but less hectic in a different world.

I could see Buckingham Palace in the distance, and I remembered my pride when I took my family there to receive the CBE. It was awarded for my work following 7 July 2005, and I took it as an accolade not just for me but for all those colleagues who, like me and with me, lived through events that represented a milestone in our country's history. They, too, have much to be proud of. For me, the CBE recognized my family's sacrifices – the many times I simply wasn't there for them. After the ceremony I took them to the restaurant near Scotland Yard where, night after night in the months after 7/7, I had a bite to eat. I wouldn't bother with a menu – the chef would bring me out a plate of whatever he chose and I was always grateful for it.

I sat in the park and reflected on my decision to retire three years after the July attacks when I'd been in the police for thirty years and had become eligible to do so. My itinerary had been getting to the stage where it was not manageable. My baby daughters were fast heading for their teens and I was missing out. My work rate was becoming unsustainable, and though I was working hard with a great team, achieving what I considered to be good results, the emerging smear campaign over my expenses, though later proven unfounded, risked undermining that. I couldn't be bothered to play the internal politics or cat-and-mouse with those lodging malicious allegations. I decided to move on. In my new world I continue to be a voice. I campaign and I advise and comment, contributing to newspapers and television stations both here and abroad.

I believe that when the current government is long gone, when the current crop of young officers is leading the Met, and the nature of terrorism has moved on, there will be a public inquiry into the events of the 7 July bomb attacks. The issue is not straightforward, but the insistence of ministers that it will never happen is not a runner. After 7 July 2005, we often considered an inquiry. I was party to some of those discussions along with other senior colleagues from the police, and the security and intelligence community.

The rationale of ministers in producing a 'Narrative' of events rather than a full-blown independent public inquiry hinged on the time available to service such an event. They believed there was a danger that effort and resources would be diverted from the more pressing task of dealing with the attacks and solving the crime. At the time I supported the decision but it now seems flaky. I feel uncomfortable that the events and background to 7 July 2005 are only recorded in that brief 'Narrative'.

Incidents of less gravity, albeit serious in their own right, have attracted the status of a public inquiry, such as train crashes, a death in custody, and even other terrorist attacks. How can there not be a full, independent public inquiry into the deaths of fifty-two commuters on London's transport system? Many people have raised eyebrows at me. They suggest the government's reluctance to stage a public inquiry is nothing short of a cover-up. To my knowledge there is nothing to conceal. On the contrary, there is much to share and learn from. Years down the line, with a new government in place and renewed media and public pressure, it will be impossible to resist, even though memories will have faded.

Those who oppose a public inquiry argue that the events of July 2005 have already been mauled in trials, inquests and internal reviews. But you have to remember that each of those took a specific focus. There has been no overview, no pulling together of each strand of review, and because of this no one can be sure if key issues have been missed.

The 7/7 attacks created a new 'normality' for the UK. The threshold of danger was raised. That in itself is a good reason to hold a public inquiry. It would draw a line under the atrocities, create closure for the families and elicit more operational learning. It might even herald the constitutional and structural changes I believe we need to enhance the way we hunt terrorists.

It would also, without doubt, show the professionalism, commitment and sheer guts of police officers, the security and intelligence agencies, the emergency services and politicians. I have tried to chart how so many of their contributions produced life-saving interdictions on major international terror plots against this country. We should be proud of each other and of the way we bounced from one crisis to another and did our job, accommodating each other's quirks, differing cultures and, of course, the imponderable personalities of us all.

Epilogue

IF YOU ARE INVOLVED IN A MURDER INVESTIGATION YOU normally learn very quickly how many victims you have. As a detective sergeant working at Basildon in Essex, I was involved in a murder inquiry when a deranged mother systematically killed her four children. It was in February 1990. Thirty-three-year-old Oi Tai Ngai fed and put her young family to bed. As they slept she strangled her eldest son Alex with a tie. She did the same to three-year-old Edmund using a belt. She strangled twenty-three-month-old Jennifer and, finally, her four-month-old baby, Samuel.

Her husband had been working at a nearby restaurant. He came home to find the horrific scene. He went from room to room, discovering the corpses of his family. His final discovery was his wife, staring blankly as she lay on the bed cuddling her last victim, her baby son. I can't really describe what I felt when I attended the scene – the enormity of the tragedy, the frustration at my inability to ease the pain of the distraught, broken father. This was the massacre of a family by the family.

Yet even that terrible incident did not prepare me for the horror and fear, the sense of uselessness and utter despair that gripped me, stretching not for hours but days after the 7 July attacks, as the death toll rose from six, to ten, twenty-five, fifty, then fifty-two. Knowing that on our watch so many people had lost their lives, the awful upset of distraught families, and yet their strength and dignity. This was a massacre perpetrated on many families. I truly meant the pledge I made the day I met the bereaved families for the first time. If there is anything we can do to prevent a repetition of the 7/7 attacks, then whatever the politics, whatever the rhetoric, we have to do it. I sympathize with the families with all my heart, but I realize I cannot truly empathize. I cannot truly feel the grief and tragedy as they did because I have not experienced what they have. But I believe that if they see the need for a public inquiry then they should have it. We owe it to them, and to those who died.

Index